D1326220

The Politics of the Poor

The East End of London
1885–1914

MARC BRODIE

CLARENDON PRESS · OXFORD

*This book has been printed digitally and produced in a standard specification
in order to ensure its continuing availability*

OXFORD
UNIVERSITY PRESS

Great Clarendon Street, Oxford OX2 6DP

Oxford University Press is a department of the University of Oxford.
It furthers the University's objective of excellence in research, scholarship,
and education by publishing worldwide in

Oxford New York

Auckland   Cape Town   Dar es Salaam   Hong Kong   Karachi
Kuala Lumpur   Madrid   Melbourne   Mexico City   Nairobi
New Delhi   Shanghai   Taipei   Toronto
With offices in
Argentina   Austria   Brazil   Chile   Czech Republic   France   Greece
Guatemala   Hungary   Italy   Japan   South Korea   Poland   Portugal
Singapore   Switzerland   Thailand   Turkey   Ukraine   Vietnam

Oxford is a registered trade mark of Oxford University Press
in the UK and in certain other countries

Published in the United States
by Oxford University Press Inc., New York

Oxford is a registered trade mark of Oxford University Press
in the UK and in certain other countries

Published in the United States
by Oxford University Press Inc., New York

© Marc Brodie 2004

The moral rights of the author have been asserted

Database right Oxford University Press (maker)

Reprinted 2005

ISBN 0-19-927055-4

For

JANETTE, JONATHAN, *and* CALLUM

with love

PREFACE

This book is concerned with the political views of the 'East Enders' in late Victorian and Edwardian London. The residents of East London in this period have been historically characterized as abjectly poor, casually employed, slum-dwellers with a poverty-induced apathy towards political solutions interspersed with occasional, violent, displays of support for populist calls for Protectionism, Imperialism, and, most importantly, opposition to the significant Jewish immigration into London occurring at that time. These factors, in combination, have been thought to have allowed the Conservative Party to politically dominate the East End in this period.

This study demonstrates that many of these images are wrong. Economic conditions in the East End were not as uniformly bleak as often portrayed. Most workers had relatively skilled and regular employment. The workings of the franchise laws also meant that those who possessed the vote in the East End were generally the most prosperous and regularly employed of their occupational group. Conservative electoral victories in the East End were not the result of poverty. Many of the other 'models' used to support the image of 'East End Conservatism' have been based upon incorrect and often superficial assumptions concerning class, race, and religion.

Political attitudes in the East End were determined to a far greater extent by issues concerning the 'personal' in a number of senses. The importance given to individual character in the political judgements of the East End working class was greatly increased by a number of specific local factors. These included the prevalence of particular forms of workplace structure, and the generally somewhat shorter average length of time on the electoral register of voters in the area. Also important was a continuing attachment to the Church of England amongst a number of the more prosperous working class. The 'personal' was also apparent in the central importance of articulate or otherwise influential individuals in shaping the specific political responses of many working-class subgroups.

In the place of many 'myths' about the people of the East End and their politics, this book provides a model that does not seek to explain the politics of the area in full, but strongly suggests the point that we can understand politics, and the formation of political attitudes, in the East End or any other area only through a detailed examination of very specific localized community and workplace structures.

For the financial support they provided in the early stages of this study, which enabled me to purchase important research materials, I wish to thank The Queen's College, the Faculty of Modern History, and the administrators of the Arnold, Bryce, and Read Funds at the University of Oxford.

The help and support of Dr John Davis, in the roles of both supervisor of my original thesis and then as advising editor for this book, has been invaluable to me. I wish to thank him most sincerely for his encouragement, friendship, and good advice over a period of what is now many years.

I also wish to express my gratitude to both Anne Gelling and Kay Rogers, at Oxford University Press for very greatly appreciated efforts, just when they were required, to assist me to expedite the final stages of the production process.

M. B.

Monash University
Australia

CONTENTS

LIST OF TABLES

LIST OF FIGURES

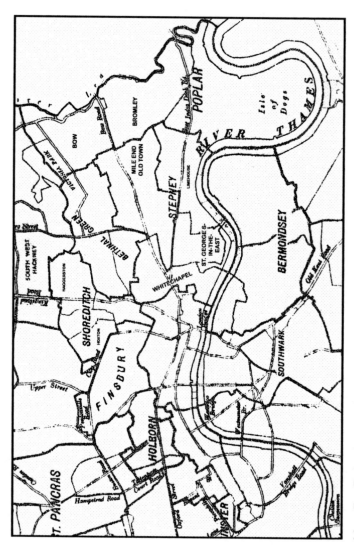

Map: East End and surrounds

Source: Census of England and Wales 1901, P.P. 1902 CXX p. 18.

Introduction

The political and social attitudes of the 'classic' poor of Victorian and Edwardian London have not been subject to any particularly rigorous examination by historians. Yet a support for populist Conservatism, combined with a general apathy concerning political solutions for their fate, have essentially been the attitudes ascribed to this group. Despite significant work which looks in detail at the bases of the political opinions and actions of workers in other parts of England, especially where working-class 'Toryism' appeared to exist,[1] similar analyses have not been applied to the metropolis.

This book has as its focus the East End of London, for a number of reasons. First, the East End has clearly been seen as epitomizing poverty in London in the nineteenth and early twentieth centuries. Christopher Husbands, for example, claims that 'the poverty and social degradation of the old East End need no elaborate documentation'.[2] Also, much of the historical work that does exist regarding the political attitudes of the London working-class poor has been based upon the apparent situation in East London. A concentration upon a restricted geographic area, such as the East End, is also important for this study in other ways. It allows a much more focused and detailed analysis of both the evidence and the particular 'models' that have been used to suggest the apparent Conservatism of the area. It also permits an examination of the importance of very localized and specific social and economic structures in the development of political attitudes and responses. Both of these are key concerns of this study.

The East End is defined here as the area covered by the post-1900 London boroughs of Stepney, Poplar, Bethnal Green, and Shoreditch. This area included, between 1885 and the First World War, eleven parliamentary constituencies.[3] It was extensively described by Charles Booth in

[1] See, as important examples, P. Joyce, *Work, Society and Politics: The Culture of the Factory in Later Victorian England* (1980; repr. Aldershot, 1991); M. Savage, *The Dynamics of Working-Class Politics: The Labour Movement in Preston, 1880–1940* (Cambridge, 1987); and J. Lawrence, 'Popular Politics and the Limitations of Party: Wolverhampton, 1867–1900', in E. Biagini and A. Reid (eds.), *Currents of Radicalism: Popular Radicalism, Organised Labour and Party Politics in Britain, 1850–1914* (Cambridge, 1991).

[2] C. T. Husbands, 'East End Racism 1900–1980: Geographical Continuities in Vigilantist and Extreme Right-wing Political Behaviour', *London Journal*, 8:1 (Summer, 1982), 3.

[3] Bethnal Green North East, Bethnal Green South West, Bow and Bromley, Haggerston, Hoxton, Limehouse, Mile End, Poplar, St George's-in-the-East, Stepney, Whitechapel.

his pioneering social investigation, *Life and Labour of the People in London*.[4] Studied by other contemporary investigators, and later by historians such as Gareth Stedman Jones, the economic and social conditions of East London are apparently well known and accepted. But they are also often misunderstood, as parts of this book will demonstrate. The words of Christopher Husbands are, again, usefully representative of the way in which this area has been historically portrayed. He summarizes its 'degradation' simply by noting that the 'whole of the East End in Charles Booth's maps of . . . inner London in 1889 is liberally covered with black representing streets occupied by residents who were of the "lowest class: vicious, semi-criminal" and dark blue representing "very poor, casual; chronic want"'.[5] Julia Bush similarly uses Booth's work in emphasizing the numbers in the East End who were forced to survive below even 'an ungenerous "poverty line"'.[6]

Booth's published work, and the massive collection of manuscript material he and his assistants left behind, clearly is central to any study engaging with poverty and related issues in London in this period. Indeed, it is a struggle to avoid becoming overly dependent upon Booth's elaborate and pioneering street and population social classification system (the major elements of which are described in Appendix 1 of this book). But, significantly, although Booth's material has been used as a key source by many historians examining London's social and economic history, in relation to East London both his published work and the manuscript data in fact paint a far less uniform picture of poverty in the area than that usually portrayed in historical descriptions.

Some of this can be seen, for example, by comparing the descriptions of the small blocks of streets for which Booth provided individual data on poverty (which was based largely on the information given by London School Board visitors). In the Tower Hamlets division of the East End (i.e. excluding Bethnal Green and Shoreditch), blocks ranged from having 60.2 per cent of residents 'in poverty'—this being in part of the Isle of Dogs—to 10.2 per cent (in an area around Bow Road). Blocks ranged relatively evenly between these extremes, and the overall average for the

---

[4] C. Booth, *Life and Labour of the People in London*, 17 vols. (1902). (Place of publication is London unless otherwise noted.) Useful material on the work of Booth and his assistants can be found in D. Englander and R. O'Day, *Mr Charles Booth's Inquiry: Life and Labour of the People in London Reconsidered* (1993), and also their (as editors) *Retrieved Riches: Social Investigation in Britain 1840–1914* (Aldershot, 1995).
[5] Husbands, 'East End Racism', 3.
[6] J. Bush, *Behind the Lines: East London Labour 1914–1919* (1984), 1.

division was 38.0 per cent 'in poverty', a figure only 7 per cent higher than the average for the whole of London.[7]

Occupations and forms of employment also varied considerably in the East End. In the riverside areas of St George's-in-the-East, Limehouse, and Poplar, dock, gasworks, and similar labouring work was predominant for men. In Bethnal Green, Shoreditch, and most of Mile End and Whitechapel, artisan occupations were much more common, with tailoring and cabinetmaking being the most prevalent. There were also small, strongly middle-class pockets in parts of Mile End and Bow, with significant levels of professional employment.[8]

A large percentage of married women in East London were outworkers for various manufacturing trades—most usually clothing or footwear, matchbox making, brush-, basket-, or sack-making—or they travelled out of the area to do charring or similar work. Unmarried working women were often in factory jobs, such as jam, matches, or confectionery. As James Schmiechen suggests, as well as the vast majority of young, single, working-class women and widows being employed, generally half the married women in working-class areas were occupied in some work.[9] Chapters 1 and 2 examine these important issues of employment and poverty in the East End in much greater detail.[10]

Stedman Jones's work has been of particular importance in providing details and analysis of the types of employment and industries which were of significance in the East End, and, like Booth's study, it is essential for an understanding of these structures. Stedman Jones emphasizes the extent of casual employment, and underemployment, and resultant poverty, amongst workers in the East End throughout the late Victorian and Edwardian period.[11] But in doing so, as Chapter 1 argues, he exaggerates this factor, and this exaggeration has been extremely influential in historical perceptions of East London. A view of overwhelming casualization concentrated amongst

[7] See Booth, *Life*, 1st series, vol. 2, App. 32–3, and vol. 1, p. 36, Table II, and G. Stedman Jones, *Outcast London: A Study in the Relationship Between Classes in Victorian Society* (1976), 132.

[8] See the descriptions of Mile End in Chs. 2 and 3 below.

[9] The true extent of female employment cannot be calculated from the census data, as homework or other forms of employment for married women was often hidden. J. A. Schmiechen, *Sweated Industries and Sweated Labor: The London Clothing Trades, 1860–1914* (1984), 68–9.

[10] See also Jennifer Davis's excellent discussion of this issue in 'Jennings' Buildings and the Royal Borough: The Construction of the Underclass in Mid-Victorian England', in D. Feldman and G. Stedman Jones (eds.), *Metropolis London: Histories and Representations Since 1800* (1989).

[11] Stedman Jones, *Outcast London*, Part I.

dock workers and those in a range of declining artisan trades has created the general impression, as Jim Gillespie notes, of an East End dominated by 'a fragmented impoverished working class'.[12] This perception, although certainly not completely inaccurate, needs to be tempered.

The historical treatment of the political and social attitudes of such 'impoverished' workers in London, and particularly in the East End, has remained as essentially one-dimensional as these economic analyses. This is largely because work on this area has hardly moved since the ground-breaking, class-informed studies of Henry Pelling, Stedman Jones, and Paul Thompson in the 1960s and 1970s. Much of this work sought to explain the 'failure' of independent working-class politics, or socialism, by reference to the influence of extremely poor economic and social conditions on the world-views of workers such as those in the slums of the East End.[13]

Most influential in regard to the East End was the form of argument put forcefully by Stedman Jones in *Outcast London*, largely informed by Pelling's work:

At a political level, the most striking characteristic of the casual poor was neither their adherence to the left, nor yet to the right, but rather their rootless volatility . . . those who had participated in the great Dock Strike of 1889, fell with little resistance under the spell of protectionists and anti-alien propaganda in the 1890s . . . Constituencies like Limehouse, Mile End, St. George's-in-the-East, and Stepney, generally voted Conservative in the period 1885–1906.[14]

There were a number of 'layers' of analysis implicit within such arguments. First was the assumption that poorer workers in London swung strongly in this period behind the Conservatives, in support of trade protectionism and also, as David Howell puts it, the most 'important [factor] of all . . . the anti-alien, or to be precise anti-Jewish agitation in the East End'[15] (that is, opposition to the increasing immigration of European Jews into East London from the mid-1880s).[16] Such arguments have been

---

[12] J. Gillespie, 'Poplarism and Proletarianism: Unemployment and Labour Politics in London, 1918–34', in Feldman and Stedman Jones, *Metropolis*, 164.

[13] See D. Mayfield and S. Thorne, 'Social History and its Discontents: Gareth Stedman Jones and the Politics of Language', *Social History*, 17:2 (May 1992), 169–73 for a discussion of this; H. Pelling, *Social Geography of British Elections 1885–1910* (1967) and *Popular Politics and Society in Late Victorian Britain* (1968); P. Thompson, *Socialists, Liberals and Labour: The Struggle for London 1885–1914* (1967); and Stedman Jones's works referred to in this section.

[14] Stedman Jones, *Outcast London*, 343 and n. 17.

[15] D. Howell, *British Workers and the Independent Labour Party* (Manchester, 1983), 257.

[16] On this generally see J. Garrard, *The English and Immigration 1880–1910* (1971); D. Feldman, 'The Importance of Being English: Jewish Immigration and the Decay of Liberal England', in Feldman and Stedman Jones, *Metropolis*; and Husbands, 'East End Racism'.

repeated continually in studies of the politics of the period.[17] Electoral Conservatism in the East End has been seen as being based largely upon working-class support for such populist issues, combined with a good helping of popular imperialism, particularly during the South African War.[18]

But this has been linked closely to the argument that amongst the very poorest of workers, particularly the unskilled 'casual poor', there was a political capriciousness, bred by poverty and desperation—a lack of long-term commitment to any cause, the very 'rootless volatility'—which meant that there existed little hope of them ever being brought together in support of a movement for social or economic change. The very poor in areas such as the East End have been characterized, as Jennifer Davis suggests, as 'unorganized, apolitical', and as often only too eager to resort to violence or riot in the way of the 'pre-industrial' urban mob.[19] Such historical portrayal has changed little, even in recent work, as will be seen below.

Stedman Jones also provided much of the next 'layer' of belief about the politics of the London working class. His influential work on their 'remaking' in the late nineteenth century sought to show a 'defensive' and home-focused working-class culture leading to the decline of active politics and the dominance of a fatalism and apathy on social and political questions.[20] In this analysis, the London working class generally in the late Victorian period became 'cut off', both from middle-class interference in their lives, and also in the sense of becoming overwhelmingly 'inward-looking' rather than challenging of social structures, as it had been in the Chartist period. It sought a 'culture of consolation' based around the music hall and similar

---

[17] See e.g. Pelling, *Social Geography*, 42–8, K. D. Wald, *Crosses on the Ballot: Patterns of British Voter Alignment since 1885* (Princeton, 1983), 104; Husbands, 'East End Racism', 7–12; M. Pugh, *The Tories and the People 1880–1935* (Oxford, 1985), 105–6; and the quote from Duncan Tanner later in this section.

[18] See J. Schneer, *London 1900: The Imperial Metropolis* (New Haven, 1999), esp. ch. 3; P. Readman, 'The Conservative Party, Patriotism, and British Politics: The Case of the General Election of 1900', *Journal of British Studies*, 40:1 (Jan. 2001), 133; and J. McKenzie, Introduction to *Imperialism and Popular Culture* (Manchester, 1986), 5–6.

[19] Davis, 'Jennings', 12; and see also E. Hobsbawm, 'The Aristocracy of Labour Reconsidered', in his *Worlds of Labour: Further Studies in the History of Labour* (1984), 244, for a similar comment regarding the 'potentially riotous' nature of the 'unorganised poor'. David Goodway essentially adopts Stedman Jones's descriptions and applies them to his view of the London poor at the time of the Chartists: D. Goodway, *London Chartism 1838–1848* (Cambridge, 1982), nn. 133 and 135 on p. 127, and p. 114.

[20] G. Stedman Jones, 'Working-Class Culture and Working-Class Politics in London, 1870–1900: Notes on the Remaking of a Working Class', in id., *Languages of Class: Studies in English Working Class History 1832–1982* (Cambridge, 1983), originally published in the *Journal of Social History*, 7:4 (Summer, 1974).

forms of escapism, rather than social change.[21] Its lack of support for independent working-class politics, and the condition of 'apathy', Stedman Jones ascribes to such cultural factors.

For Paul Thompson's political arguments regarding the East End, structural poverty was the key issue. In Bethnal Green and Stepney, and in similar areas, says Thompson, politically 'the most serious difficulty was probably the chronic poverty typical of inner working-class districts, breeding a political apathy which made a labour or socialist movement peculiarly hard to establish'.[22] Pelling makes a similar point, arguing generally that 'it was the more prosperous workers who were the more politically militant and radical, while the lower ranks displayed either apathy or conservatism'. The acceptance of a relatively more advanced, progressive stance amongst artisans and other workers in more skilled and secure work has also been a constant in such arguments.[23]

Such themes have been drawn upon by later historians, the subject seemingly requiring little more examination. Usually linked to this perspective was an image of a distinctively fragmented, selfish, industry-based 'sectionalism' of the politics of the London working class, again as had been argued by Pelling, Stedman Jones, and Thompson.[24] Stedman Jones had noted, on the basis of Pelling's psephology, that: 'In a period in which working-class politics was in retreat and trade unionism remained stagnant, it is not surprising to find that large numbers of the working class and poor, when they expressed any political preferences, were motivated by sectional

---

[21] G. Stedman Jones, 'Working-Class Culture', 236–7. Some historians have begun to raise questions regarding the narrow definitions of 'politics' within these perceptions. For a recent discussion, see A. August, 'A Culture of Consolation? Rethinking Politics in Working-Class London, 1870–1914', *Historical Research*, 74:183 (Feb. 2001).

[22] Thompson, *Socialists, Liberals and Labour*, 239 and 84. See also Robert Mckenzie and Allan Silver's famous *Angels in Marble: Working Class Conservatives in Urban England* (Chicago, 1968), which suggested that 'lower income working class voters were more likely to be Conservative in the recent past than in the present' (p. 86), largely on the basis of their 'deference'. While aspects of such a response are discussed in Ch. 4 of this book, the particularities of Victorian and Edwardian East London are sufficiently divorced from the circumstances of Mckenzie and Silver's relatively small voter surveys in the late 1950s and early 1960s to mean that these can provide little of direct relevance for this study.

[23] Pelling, *Popular Politics*, 56. See also Tanner and Joyce later in this Introduction. This of course also responds to the theory of a conservative, prosperous 'labour aristocracy' as put forward by Eric Hobsbawm. For a challenging discussion of this, see T. Lummis, *The Labour Aristocracy 1851–1914* (Aldershot, 1994).

[24] See e.g. Bush, *Behind the Lines*, 1–4, Schneer, *London 1900*, ch. 3; G. Crossick, 'The Labour Aristocracy and its Values: A Study of Mid-Victorian Kentish London', *Victorian Studies*, 19:3 (Mar. 1976), 307; and see Jim Gillespie's summary of historical arguments of this type in 'Poplarism and Proletarianism', 164–5.

rather than class interests.'[25] This 'fragmentation' argument will be discussed at some length in Chapter 4. But all of these, sometimes contradictory, historical conclusions regarding the politics of the London working class and poor were problematic in a number of interconnected ways. First, in regard specifically to the East End, these arguments have been generally informed, as noted above, by an unquestioning acceptance of the complete dominance of casualized and poverty-ridden forms of employment in the area. Simply challenging this assumption, as this book does to some extent, immediately provides an alternative perspective from which to view some of the evidence we have of East End politics. The relationships described between poverty and politics in that area make little sense if the East End was not as unrelievedly and uniformly poor as it is generally portrayed. The somewhat simple point is also made here, that the evidence regarding poverty in the East End, and the evidence regarding the often-Conservative politics of the area, is *not the same* evidence. There were large differences between sections of the working class in East London, both economically and in their connection to politics. This fact has previously been largely simplified and misunderstood, and has distorted analyses of the evidence. A very basic part of this work is an attempt to 'tease out' the material and to make sure that evidence regarding politics in the East End is not being ascribed to the wrong section of the working class, or for the wrong reasons. One very significant, but by no means isolated, example of this concerns the use of electoral evidence in describing the politics of East London.

As described above, Stedman Jones's claim that dockers and other poor workers fell under the 'spell' of protectionists and anti-immigrationists, and the similar claims in much of Pelling's work, are based upon the Conservative dominance of a number of East End parliamentary constituencies in this period. As John Garrard states, pointing to a general problem, the

task of relating electoral swings to the effect of any given issue is a hazardous one even for modern elections. It is even more difficult owing to the size of East End electorates . . . The effect of even a small number of voters on the swing increases proportionately with the decrease in the size of the constituencies. Thus, unless differences between swings are very large indeed, it is almost impossible to make significant comparisons of either the movement of opinion from constituency to constituency within the East End, or the swings in the East End and the country as a whole.[26]

---

[25] Stedman Jones, 'Working-Class Culture', 213.
[26] Garrard, *The English and Immigration*, 73.

Clearly this suggests caution in the use of such electoral material. But more specifically, Garrard's comments begin to bring out the general confusion, or contradictions, regarding exactly whose attitudes election results represented in the East End.

East End electoral registers were often small as Garrard implies, but the percentage of adult males on the register was only unusually low in a few constituencies—in particular Whitechapel, St George's-in-the-East, and Stepney, cases which were all the result of large numbers of non-naturalized Jewish immigrants amongst their populations. But these areas have, incorrectly, been seen as typical by historians.[27] In other areas of the East End, notably Poplar and the Bethnal Green seats, parliamentary voter registration stood at around 50 per cent of adult males for much of this period. This was lower, but not outrageously so, than the national borough registration levels (59.7 per cent in 1892, 56.9 per cent in 1901).[28]

There is also little agreement amongst historians as to whether, within these overall figures, many of the poorer workers in the East End could gain the right to vote. McKibbin, Matthew and Kay, and also Thompson, argue that it was almost impossible for the 'classic slummie' to do so.[29] Others, notably John Davis and Duncan Tanner, argue that the electoral registers, even in areas such as the East End, were much more socially representative than this.[30] The question has thus remained unresolved as to how election results can be used in the analysis of politics in the East End. If these results do not show the attitudes of the most casualized, 'fragmented', part of the working population, what do they show, and also what evidence do we therefore have of the views of this poorest group? Some historians, with similar arguments to Garrard, have simply left the question largely as David Feldman does—'since the proportions enfranchised in the East End were so low, electoral behaviour was not a reliable indicator of popular opinion'.[31] But it is difficult to argue that such behaviour represented nothing of interest in this regard. Chapter 2 tackles this issue by providing a detailed examination of the specific operation of the franchise in the East

---

[27] See Howell, *British Workers*, 257 and 449 n.
[28] For the national figures, see R. McKibbin, C. Matthew, and J. Kay, 'The Franchise Factor in the Rise of the Labour Party', in R. McKibbin, *The Ideologies of Class: Social Relations in Britain 1880–1950* (Oxford, 1991), 76, originally published in the *English Historical Review*, 91 (Oct. 1976).
[29] See ibid. 67, and Thompson, *Socialists, Liberals and Labour*, 70.
[30] J. Davis, 'Slums and the Vote, 1867–90', *Historical Research*, 64:155 (1991), and J. Davis and D. Tanner, 'The Borough Franchise After 1867', ibid. 69:170 (1996).
[31] Feldman, 'The Importance of Being English', 70.

End, and suggests what this means for our understanding of apparent working-class Conservativism in parts of the district.

On this point, certainly the four central East End constituencies named above by Stedman Jones—Limehouse, Mile End, St George's-in-the-East, and Stepney—did very regularly return a Conservative in the parliamentary elections between 1885 and 1906. These results do form much of the basis of the accepted view of politics in the East End. But across the other seven East End constituencies directly surrounding these four, in the forty-two general election contests during this period, the Liberals were successful in thirty-three of these polls, a marked contrast to the results in the central four constituencies,[32] and a figure which weakens the evidence for the existence of a general 'East End Conservatism'. But perhaps of greater significance for our understanding of politics in the district are the very large variations in party electoral support between small areas even within these constituencies. Some possible reasons for these variations are suggested in the examination of ward politics which begins in Chapter 3.

Local-government election results are used in this assessment of ward variations, but inferences are drawn also for our understanding of parliamentary politics. This particular use of evidence opens up an important question raised by John Davis. He has argued that parliamentary elections in the poorest London working-class constituencies were indeed decided in this period largely upon the issues of 'populist Unionism' such as 'jingoism, anti-alienism, the residual protectionism of the riverside districts, and hostility to Home Rule'. London County Council elections, on the other hand, he argues, were fought over municipal action and social reform. This difference in the nature of the election contests, Davis suggests, explains why between 1885 and 1900 the Conservatives won over half of the parliamentary contests in these poorest London seats, but very few of the County Council places.[33] According to this view, the 'populist' issues swung to the Conservatives many working-class voters who were able to distinguish the differences between what the parties stood for in the various levels of government. But I would argue that it is perhaps more likely that much of the explanation for this variation lies more with another suggestion mentioned (but largely discounted) by Davis, that is, that the 'Moderates frequently claimed that the Conservatives were less likely to vote in local elections than Liberals'.[34]

---

[32] Electoral results for all East End constituencies 1885–1914 are given in Appendix 2.

[33] J. Davis, *Reforming London: The London Government Problem 1855–1900* (Oxford, 1988), 188–90.

[34] Ibid. 189.

In comparing the results in nine of the East End seats in the parliamentary and LCC elections of 1892, 1895, and 1910, the three occasions when the elections were only a few months or weeks apart,[35] there is a remarkable consistency in the relationships of votes. In every one of these years, the Liberal LCC vote across the nine seats was equivalent to *precisely* 81 per cent of their total parliamentary vote in the same seats. The very different issues applying in the parliamentary elections between these years clearly did not affect the relationship between the Liberal turnout in the two types of poll.

By contrast, the Conservative LCC vote in these years was equivalent, in 1892 and 1895, to, respectively, 55 per cent and 60 per cent of the parliamentary vote. In 1910, in a perhaps more emotional environment it was somewhat higher, at 72 per cent. On only one occasion, in one seat, did the Liberal LCC vote drop to less than 70 per cent of the its parliamentary vote, and on most occasions it was at least 80 per cent. On the other hand, the Conservative LCC vote was nearly half the time about or below 50 per cent of their parliamentary vote. This suggests that, in these seats, the very explanation made by the Conservatives themselves—that their supporters were far less likely to bother to vote at non-parliamentary elections—was true. It also suggests, given the time-span covering these three election periods, and the very different matters at stake in the parliamentary elections in those years, that the Liberal vote in both types of election was affected much more by general influences on how the party was perceived than the variations in issues between local and national politics. There is further discussion of this in Chapter 4. Generally, this does suggest that local ward electoral results may validly be used to examine at least some factors in East End parliamentary politics in this period.

There remains the general problem of how political attitudes and motivations can be deciphered from any existing evidence. Sarah Williams notes, regarding the historical study of working-class religious belief systems, that the researcher has to

face the most profound challenge of all, that of drawing the dimension of belief out of the fragmentary material available. How exactly do we examine and appreciate the beliefs of historical actors, particularly when the material upon which we rely consists in large part of the socio-religious comment of middle-class observers who attributed a set of meanings to these beliefs which were defined by parameters of their own institutional presuppositions?[36]

[35] In 1892 and 1895, March (LCC) and July (Parliamentary), in 1910 January (Parliamentary) and March (LCC).

[36] S. C. Williams, 'The Problem of Belief: The Place of Oral History in the Study of Popular Religion', *Oral History*, 24:2 (Autumn, 1996), 27.

Interestingly, Williams is referring to much the same period and place (South London in her case) that the present work deals with, and she describes the qualitative material in Booth's work—also a key source for this study—as providing a 'particularly rich example of these problems'.[37] With a time-span for her study which reaches to the start of the Second World War, Williams addresses these difficulties at least partly through the use of direct interviews with her historical actors.[38] But this approach was not available for this study, and similar problems of evidence remain.

Indeed, just such a middle-class observer as Williams mentions himself advised caution in the use of the types of evidence which are of direct relevance to this study. In 1898 a Wesleyan minister candidly told one of Booth's inquirers that the purpose of church mission reports, which often described heart-rending scenes of poverty and degradation in the East End, was to 'bring in the shekels, and though in ours we go through it most carefully to eliminate anything which is untruthful, I don't know that one is bound to tell the whole truth. Still one has to be very careful in accepting the reports of ladies who allow their feelings to run away with them.'[39] This caveat certainly does not apply only to church ladies, and there is little doubt that the historical perception of conditions in the East End has been coloured, at least to some extent, by such human factors.

'Filtered' reports of political feeling could also mislead. Harry Gosling, the London watermen and lightermen's union leader, told of a night-time meeting called by his union about a political issue which, because of thick fog, was attended only by himself and a journalist. The journalist was so grateful to Gosling for presenting his speech regardless, that next morning the paper gave 'a glowing account of the "large and enthusiastic gathering of watermen" who had unanimously condemned the action of the sitting member!'[40]—interesting evidence by which to assess popular working-class sentiment.

Wariness regarding such evidence is clearly common to all historical enquiry. But, as Williams noted, in the case of the working class in poorer districts there exists even less direct evidence of social conditions or political

---

[37] Ibid.

[38] The article relates to work on her thesis, 'Religious Belief and Popular Culture: A Study of the South London Borough of Southwark *c*.1880–1939', Oxford D.Phil., 1993.

[39] Revd John Howard, Wesleyan East End Mission, Booth MSS B184, Charles Booth Collection, British Library of Political and Economic Science, 42–3.

[40] H. Gosling, *Up and Down Stream* (1927), 67–8. See also P. Bailey, '"Will the Real Bill Banks Please Stand Up?": Towards a Role Analysis Of Mid-Victorian Working-Class Respectability', *Journal of Social History*, 12:3 (Spring, 1979), 344, regarding generally how the conventions of Victorian journalism could also lead to similar distortions.

beliefs. Generally, it can be said that there was very little material upon which Stedman Jones, Thompson, Pelling, and others could base their arguments. This remains a limiting factor also for this study. But the approach taken here seeks to value a much wider range of material in examining the important factors in politics amongst the working class. By presenting an alternative view of how economic and social structures, in their specifics, were significant in creating working-class attitudes and responses, this study is also able to draw more deeply upon evidence which perhaps previously seemed of little relevance. While familiar types of evidence are largely used, aspects of 'domestic' arrangements and contacts, for example, and of working-class views on morality are also drawn on here, perhaps for the first time, as relevant to explanations of East End politics.

Recent historical work has, of course, moved away from the necessary and direct association of pure economic structures with political action. To some extent, therefore, the desire to show economic and social reasons for the 'failure' of the pre-war East End to move towards working-class political organization, and also its apparent Conservatism, has become irrelevant. The concern has shifted to the impact of 'politics' itself and the action of parties, governments, and organizations, and their discourses, in creating political 'identities' and constituencies of support. This has been an important and instructive development, yet in many ways it does not go to the heart of political attitudes. As Jon Lawrence states, the danger with this approach to some degree is that 'it risks overthrowing the old social determinism only to impose a new discursive determinism, which ignores not only the social context of politics, but also the whole question of "reception", that is, the question of how ordinary voters actually responded to the party discourses analysed by the historian'.[41] In examining the politics of the East End, this book suggests that it was factors influencing the reception of political ideas by the East End working class which were of the greatest importance—how such ideas were filtered by localized social and economic structures and processes of communication and popular culture. What becomes clear is that what can be termed the 'personal' element was a major overriding influence on the politics of the working class in the East End, and also on how this politics has been perceived.

---

[41] J. Lawrence, 'The Dynamics of Urban Politics, 1867–1914', in J. Lawrence and M. Taylor (eds.), *Party, State and Society: Electoral Behaviour in Britain Since 1820* (Aldershot, 1997), 91. See also Mayfield and Thorne, 'Social History', and also Stedman Jones in the Introduction to his *Languages of Class* (pp. 19 and 21), for his own change of heart on this.

This study is not centrally concerned with assessing what party-political 'issues' were of importance in any particular election result or other manifestation of popular political feeling, partly because of the difficulties described above by Garrard and Lawrence. Instead, it focuses upon showing more fundamental, underlying influences upon the reception and success of political discourse, and the possible importance of these in creating a long-term and persistent perception of Conservatism and apathy in the East End. With this focus in mind, any difference between the support bases for Liberals and socialist candidates amongst the working class is perhaps overly blurred for much of this study. For the purposes of the arguments here—focused, as they are, upon East End Conservatism—the term 'progressive' is used consistently and quite deliberately to signify non-Conservative politics, both Liberal and 'Labour'. I would argue that this 'blurring' does not significantly affect the key points made in this study, and indeed assists its clarity.

The term 'personal' is used here in two senses: the first, and most significant, relates to the importance of personal, local, interaction in the development, and reception, of political ideas and actions. The second sense relates to the importance of assessment of individual, personal, indeed moral, character in working-class political judgements. The significance of the 'personal' in politics is also related in many ways to the continuing importance for the late nineteenth-century working class of concepts inherent in popular radicalism, as has been discussed by a number of writers.[42] These beliefs have been examined in relation to the working class elsewhere in Britain, but are unusual notions to apply to the accepted models of politics in late Victorian or Edwardian London, particularly the East End.[43] A key theme apparent throughout this book is the great significance of specific social structures and milieus in determining the precise effect of these 'personal' influences.

In examining the role of the 'personal' in the juncture of workplace relations and politics, some direct parallels are drawn with the studies of Patrick Joyce and others on work and popular political culture in Lancashire and elsewhere. This comparison is useful, although the unusual employment structures of much of the East End, and its social history, did

---

[42] See generally the contributions in Biagini and Reid, *Currents of Radicalism*, and also J. Vernon, *Politics and the People: A Study in English Political Culture, c.1815–1867* (Cambridge, 1993); J. Lawrence, 'Popular Radicalism and the Socialist Revival in Britain', *Journal of British Studies*, 31:2 (Apr. 1992); and P. Joyce, *Visions of the People: Industrial England and the Question of Class, 1848–1914* (Cambridge, 1991).

[43] Although Vernon does discuss the Tower Hamlets in mid-century.

place quite a distinct slant upon the situation and attitudes there. It also demonstrates again, however, the extent to which the complex social and political dynamics examined in this existing modern body of work have largely not been thought to apply to the situation of late Victorian London, and particularly its poorest parts,[44] even within the context of the more recent studies. Joyce himself, indeed, makes the comment, partially aimed at the capital, that the 'better off, the most skilled, and the best organized and educated among workers were those most attracted to the politics of "opinion" . . . [while] poorer, less politically articulate kinds of workers' were for the most part swayed by 'other considerations . . . the politics of influence and deference, of ethnicity and religion, and of patriotism, beer, bonhomie and corruption'.[45]

With this statement Joyce closely parallels comments made by Duncan Tanner specifically regarding East London. In fact Tanner's comments remain perhaps the most recent comprehensive historical statement of the politics of the East End, and in many ways they take the form of simply a restatement of the analyses we saw above. They show that much of the argument described earlier in regard to the East End has largely not been altered. Tanner argues that, in the period of this study:

There were two Londons. The political/electoral problems which the Liberal party faced were most acute in East End seats, and to a lesser extent in the sink holes of poverty which littered West London. Voters worked in an enormous variety of ill-paid, casual or sporadic occupations. Tory success was built . . . on cultural affinities with working-class social activities, on attendance to ethnic tensions, and, allied to this, on support for the protection of British values, British jobs and British international prestige. The attraction of this appeal was far less apparent in the socially mixed and more affluent artisan and lower middle-class settlements in North and South-West London.

In the East End, says Tanner, 'Ethnic fragmentation and competing economic interests were not easily countered'. Tanner can relate politics in East London specifically, within Britain, only to parts of Liverpool and its surrounding area. In a description clearly applying to the poor of either city, he says, as we heard repeatedly earlier, that the 'combination of casual, unskilled, and dangerous employment, and squalid social conditions,

---

[44] Joyce does suggest some parallels with his work are to be 'glimpsed' in the work of Pelling, Stedman Jones, and Thompson, 'behind the backdrop of class', and argues that this analysis needs to be 'given the attention it deserves' in relation to the metropolis, *Work, Society*, 223.

[45] Joyce, *Visions*, 67.

helped create a conservative and pessimistic culture, based on short-term interest, drinking, gambling, violence, fatalism, the pawnbroker, and an acerbic hedonism'.[46] It is just such a model of the poor and unskilled in the East End that the following chapter sets out to examine.

[46] D. Tanner, *Political Change and the Labour Party, 1900–1918* (Cambridge, 1990), 164–5, 171, and 130–1.

I

Artisans and Dossers

THE TRAFALGAR SQUARE RIOTS

Clubs and shops in the West End of London were attacked on 8 February 1886, by unemployed workers who had earlier gathered at a protest meeting in Trafalgar Square. Friedrich Engels characterized those involved in the attacks as 'the poor devils of the East End who vegetate in the border between working class and lumpenproletariat', mixed with some 'roughs and 'Arrys'.[1] The *Daily News* said the rioters were 'loafers from the docks, and habitual criminals from the East-End'. Most of those involved, said the *Daily Telegraph*, 'were not genuine industrious working men, but members of the "rough" class, largely recruited from the East-end'. This incident has become one of the central pieces of evidence in the historical portrayal of the politics of the very poorest of the East End working class. Adopting the theme of the newspapers, Stedman Jones describes how, after the riot, the crowd 'returned via Oxford Street to the East End'. They were the 'traditional casual poor'. The riot has been used, particularly by Stedman Jones, as evidence of the apolitical and 'pre-industrial' nature of the East End casual poor. Of the crowd, he says: 'their hunger and desperation resulted not in the disciplined preparation for socialist revolution but in . . . frenzied rioting . . . In spirit the crowd was closer to the *Lazzari* of eighteenth-century Naples and Palermo.'[2]

The Trafalgar Square meeting of the unemployed was initiated by the London United Workmen's Committee, one of many bogus working-class organizations set up in the 1880s by the infamous Thomas Kelly, Samuel Peters, and Patrick Kenny, whose role in promoting various employer- and Conservative-sponsored causes to workmen has been well described by John Saville and others.[3] Closely associated with the protectionist Fair

---

[1] F. Engels and P. and L. Lafargue, *Correspondence*, Vol. 1 (Moscow, 1959), 334.

[2] *Daily News*, 10 Feb. 1886, p. 5 col.e; *Daily Telegraph*, 9 Feb. 1886, p. 5 col.c; and Stedman Jones, *Outcast London*, 292 and 345.

[3] See J. Saville, 'Trade Unions and Free Labour: The Background to the Taff Vale Decision', in A. Briggs and J. Saville (eds.), *Essays in Labour History* (1960), 331–6, and the *Critic*, 146 (18 June–9 July 1898), on the history of these organizations.

Trade League, the literature from the LUWC called upon the unemployed to gather at the meeting to generally agitate against their plight, but more specifically, to 'Protest, denounce, and demonstrate against a false commercial system [free trade]', which 'allows the foreigner to rob you'.[4]

The Social Democratic Federation, with a long-standing suspicion of the Kelly–Peters group, and undoubtedly wishing to retain its position at the head of working-class unemployed protest,[5] resolved to disrupt the meeting, or at least to 'attend and place their views before men who were in danger of being misled'.[6] As H. M. Hyndman later wrote, the cause of the LUWC and the Fair Trade League was 'in direct opposition to Socialist palliatives and Socialism as a cure for unemployment, [and] the whole [bogus working-class] movement was used by the capitalists against us'.[7]

The two groups met at Trafalgar Square, with a crowd of at least 20,000 gathering (up to 50,000 according to some reports)—most of whom had not come specifically with either party. After speeches, and some scuffling between the opposing sides, John Burns led part of the crowd—a few thousand—behind a red flag, towards Hyde Park to hold a separate meeting. Whether this was to ease tension in the Square is unclear. On the way, parts of the crowd attacked, after provocation from club members, a number of clubs in Pall Mall and St James's Street, and shops had windows smashed and were extensively looted all along the route. The SDF leaders urged the crowd to stop its attacks, but following speeches at Hyde Park the returning crowd did further damage in South Audley Street and elsewhere. The extent of the panic that beset middle-class London has been described by historians, and the political scapegoating of Police Commissioner Henderson for allowing the attacks to occur is clearly apparent in the records of the Committee of Inquiry established to investigate the 'disturbances'.[8]

There is no doubt that there was a large number of unskilled workmen in the Trafalgar Square crowd. *The Times* said the meeting was made up chiefly of unemployed building and dock workers, some artisans, and 'a very great many of the idle class'.[9] The *Illustrated London News* and *Reynolds's Weekly Newspaper* carried similar descriptions of the crowd, although it is possible

---

    [4] See *Daily News*, 9 Feb. 1886, p. 5 col.e, and *Justice*, 13 Feb. 1886, p. 3 col.a.
    [5] On this see Thompson, *Socialists, Liberals, and Labour*, 114–15.
    [6] *Justice*, 13 Feb. 1886, p. 3 col.a.
    [7] H. M. Hyndman, *The Record of an Adventurous Life* (1911), 400.
    [8] See R. Sindall, *Street Violence in the Nineteenth Century: Media Panic or Real Danger* (Leicester, 1990), 71–4, 99–100, and 122–5; *Report of the Committee on the Origin and Character of the Disturbances in the Metropolis on 8 February 1886*, P.P. 1886 XXXIV; and see Stedman Jones, *Outcast London*, 292–4.
    [9] *The Times*, 9 Feb. 1886, p. 6 col.a.

that these were lifted from *The Times*.[10] Police Superintendent Dunlap believed that at the meeting, of the 'very large number of rough-looking men, many of them were probably working men spending their dinner hour there'.[11] The relatively poor appearance of those in the Square, said the *Daily Telegraph*, showed that they were 'mostly and unmistakably workmen'.[12] The emphasis in all the descriptions of the crowd upon the 'roughness' of those present suggests, given the accepted language of such reports, that they were generally poorer workers, and supports *The Times*'s more specific characterization of the crowd, although there is little evidence to allow one to be more detailed than that concerning its composition.

Stedman Jones uses this same evidence to define those present as 'the traditional casual poor'. He then uses this incident as clear evidence of the politics of this group and much of the East End working class. They gathered to hear 'Conservative-inspired demands for protection as a solution to unemployment, [and then] could riot the very same afternoon under the banner of socialist revolution'.[13] This showed clearly, according to this argument, their weakness for Conservative populism, but also the essentially directionless and 'pre-industrial' nature of their responses.

Even ignoring for the moment such questions as what proportion of the crowd actually participated in the riotous part of this episode, it is possible to see in the events of 8 February a great deal more than just such easy characterizations of the nature of a 'casual poor' crowd. Aspects of the events can suggest a broader perspective on the attitudes of, and influences upon, the London poor, and can help to provide pointers towards a much more variegated view of East End working-class politics.

Some of the most likely audience amongst the unskilled rejected the idea of the meeting entirely. A. S. Krausse spoke to unemployed dockers in Limehouse on the day of the meeting, and asked if they had considered attending:

The last speaker replies for all. 'No, Sir. We are men out of work; many of us with family to keep somehow. None of us go to those things. Do you think a man who really wants work can spare the time to walk to Charing-cross and back, and run the risk of losing a fifteen-penny job in the docks? It wouldn't pay. Times are bad enough, but those meetings don't help to make them better. You be sure, sir, that no working man who wants work ever goes to meetings like that.'[14]

[10] *Illustrated London News*, 13 Feb. 1886, p. 173; and see Sindall, *Street Violence*, 73.
[11] *Disturbances Committee*, P.P. 1886 XXXIV, q. 1374.
[12] *Daily Telegraph*, 9 Feb. 1886, p. 3 col.a.   [13] Stedman Jones, *Outcast London*, 343.
[14] A. S. Krausse, *Starving London: The Story of a Three Weeks' Sojourn Among the Destitute* (1886), 16–17.

The LUWC had perhaps received similar responses amongst dock workers before dropping what appears to have been its original plan to march from the East India and West India Dock gates to the meeting, changing in favour of marches from Clerkenwell Green, Blackfriars Road, and Mile End Waste.[15] Yet of course, from the usually accepted historical view, such responses could be thought to simply provide evidence of the type of fatalism and lack of interest in matters political amongst the working class discussed earlier.

Yet the cynicism of the Limehouse dockers was not necessarily as empty or apolitical—or indeed 'fatalistic'—as it might first appear. The *Daily News* commented that the 'prevailing impression' amongst those who *did* attend the meeting was similarly that 'not much was likely to come of meetings such as this'.[16] But this same crowd also reacted in quite definite terms to the politics displayed at the meeting.

Protectionist measures for English industries were the key demands included in the appeals by the LUWC for workers to attend the demonstration. Yet, again it appears that its leaders may have had to respond to the reactions they received directly from workmen. The *Daily News* reported that in the speeches of the LUWC, ultimately 'little was said on the question of Protection, as there was evidently a very great mixture of opinion on the matter, and any allusion to that or the subject of emigration met with an unmistakably impatient hearing'.[17] This 'impatient hearing' came, said *The Times*, from the crowd surrounding the LUWC platforms, consisting of a large number of '*bona-fide* out-of-work labourers'. Interestingly, both *The Times* and the *Daily News* used the term 'bona-fide' to describe this crowd, seemingly in an attempt to define those around the LUWC platform as the 'more legitimate gathering', as the *Daily News* put it.[18] But the crowd, and its responses, varied little across the Square. It was certainly not a crowd brought by the SDF which was deriding the protectionists. In smaller groups in various 'out-of-the-way corners' of the Square, said the *Daily Telegraph*, other 'fair traders' who attempted to speak also faced 'half-mocking' audiences.[19]

When Albert Charrington, former Conservative candidate for Battersea, attempted in turn to refer to 'fair-trade views' he was simply, and clearly,

[15] See 'Police Orders—Proposed Demonstration at Trafalgar Square', initialled by Police Commissioner Henderson, and 'Draft Replies to H.O. Queries', Public Record Office, MEPO 2/174, also *Disturbances Committee*, P.P. 1886 XXXIV, App. 1, and see earlier unsigned 'Police Orders—Proposed Demonstration at Trafalgar Square', MEPO 2/174.

[16] *Daily News*, 9 Feb. 1886, p. 5 col.f.   [17] Ibid., p. 5 col.e.

[18] *The Times*, 9 Feb. 1886, p. 6 col.a, and *Daily News*, 9 Feb. 1886, p. 5 col.e.

[19] *Daily Telegraph*, 9 Feb. 1886, p. 3 col.a.

'refused a hearing' by the crowd. When his successor as Battersea candidate, Mr Cook, 'declared that the Conservatives had been entirely in favour of giving relief work to the unemployed . . . [he was] interrupted with queries as to the reason they had not done so when in power; and his declarations that the present distress was caused by over production, hostile tariffs, and want of confidence also met with rejoinders'.[20] The crowd did not generally support the arguments of the protectionists. If those in attendance were in large measure the East End casual poor, as was suggested, then this provides little support for one of the central assumptions about this group's politics—that they were easy prey for such populist politicking.

But if we look closely at just that section of the crowd involved in the riot, perhaps we will still find the 'pre-industrial', apolitical responses of this group, as claimed by Stedman Jones. The leaders of the LUWC were based in the East End, and clearly a number of their supporters came from there to the meeting.[21] The major direct evidence used to link the rioters, and the crowd generally, to the East End has been the fact that a number of the group involved in the rioting marched back in that direction, along Holborn and Cheapside. The LUWC had, of course, begun one of its processions to the meeting at Mile End Waste, marching in along Whitechapel Road, Cheapside, Fleet Street, and the Strand.[22] It is the actions of this returning group, more than any other, upon which much of the analysis of the events of the day has been built. Stedman Jones makes a good deal of the fact that: 'Having completed its work, this crowd made its way back to the East End, singing "Rule Britannia"—an eloquent testimony to its confused and limited level of political consciousness.'[23] The selection of this song seems to have been linked to the protectionist rhetoric of the LUWC: that under free trade 'every advantage is given to foreign workmen'.[24]

Is it possible to be more precise about who formed this returning crowd—with its 'classically' confused and violent actions—and, indeed about the social make-up of the rioters generally? SDF supporters are the least likely suspects, although the crowd which contained the rioters had followed Burns out of the Square. One of those arrested was overheard by a

[20] *The Times*, 9 Feb. 1886, p. 6 col.b.

[21] See *East London Advertiser*, 5 Sept. 1885, p. 6 col.e; 19 Sept. 1885, p. 7 col.f; and 9 Feb. 1886.

[22] Police Orders initialled by Henderson, MEPO 2/174.

[23] Stedman Jones, *Outcast London*, 345.

[24] From LUWC circular, *Daily News*, 9 Feb. 1886, p. 5 col.e. See also R. Samuel, *East End Underworld: Chapters in the Life of Arthur Harding* (1981), 262–3.

constable in a pub after the riot to say that: 'About 5,000 of us followed a man from Mayfair, who was carrying a red flag . . . I did not come out to steal, but when I saw them helping themselves I thought I would have my share', suggesting little involvement with the socialists.[25] Hyndman said that, in moving from the Square, 'we called upon the people to follow. Many of the other side came too, and a wholly unorganized mob went rushing down Pall Mall'.[26]

It is likely that the riotous 'East End' group discussed above may have been more in sympathy with the LUWC. The *Daily News* believed generally that the rioters were the 'roughs' 'who had originally followed the procession of the Fair Traders'.[27] On another of those arrested was found 'a [presumably LUWC] ticket for the procession'. The prisoner confirmed to the magistrate that he was not a 'Social Democrat'.[28] Hyndman pointed out, again in seeking to distance the SDF from the riots, that 'Not one of the persons who were afterwards charged at the police-courts was a Socialist.'[29]

One suggestion as to the social character of the rioting crowd was made by Howard Goldsmid, who said that 'Many—nay most—of the men who took part in the riots of that day came from the low lodging houses.'[30] Some of the arrest records support this. A number of men had identifiable common lodging-house addresses or were said to be at present of 'no fixed home'. The *Daily Telegraph* believed that the 'mischief-makers' in the riot were 'that large class of "odd-job men", or nondescript characters, to be seen loitering in the streets'.[31] It is possible, as most commentators believed,[32] that it was the 'roughest' section of the crowd which rioted, and they may have been attracted to the meeting by the LUWC call. This would support much of the thrust of Stedman Jones's arguments.

Yet this interpretation is complicated by the fact that, if we look more closely at the major piece of evidence—the riotous and confused 'East End roughs' returning home—we find that the leader of this group was in fact an unemployed artisan. James Mahoney, a 21-year-old compositor (incidentally from Marylebone, not the East End), was said in court to be 'undoubtedly the ringleader' of this 'mob of some 300 or 400 men' who

---

[25] *Daily News*, 10 Feb. 1886, p. 6 col.c.   [26] Hyndman, *Adventurous*, 401.
[27] *Daily News*, 10 Feb. 1886, p. 5 col.e.   [28] Ibid.
[29] *The Times*, 12 Apr. 1886, p. 7 col.d.
[30] H. Goldsmid, *Dottings of a Dosser: Being Revelations of the Inner Life of Low London Lodging Houses* (1886), 136. On the nature of the common lodging houses, see the third section of this chapter.
[31] *Daily Telegraph*, 9 Feb. 1886, p. 3 col.b.
[32] See e.g. the evidence of Barling, *Daily Telegraph* reporter, at the Hyndman et al. sedition trial, *The Times*, 8 Apr. 1886, p. 12 col.a.

returned to the East End through the City, and who 'undoubtedly would have committed much greater destruction but for the precautions taken by the police'.[33] Police Constable Bush described how he was following the crowd in Newgate Street, and that he 'heard the prisoner [Mahoney] purposely shout as he was passing 33 Newgate-street, a restaurant, and I then heard a smash of glass . . . Every time the crowd slackened he turned round and urged them to come on. He called out "Come on: Rule Britannia", and the cry was taken up by the crowd'.[34]

Just the fact that one group of the casual poor may have been led in their 'political confusion' by an artisan (perhaps a LUWC supporter) does not alter the reality of their participation, or the general argument regarding their 'volatility'. But the situation was more complex than that. In fact, of all those arrested in the 8 February riots, one-third were tradesmen of some type, including a butcher, tailor, printer, plasterer, compositor, shoemaker, and wire-worker. This suggests a much more integral role for the artisans. None of these were socialists, if we accept Hyndman's testimony, and their presence in the riots is interesting.

As was briefly discussed in the Introduction, Pelling, Stedman Jones, and others have suggested a dichotomy between the political and social responses and attitudes of skilled workers and the unskilled/casual poor. Despite a growing political apathy amongst the previously radical artisans, the unskilled were still in a quite different political class, says Stedman Jones. 'Unlike the artisans', he says, 'the unskilled and casual poor were ignorant, inarticulate, and unorganized.' Their political underdevelopment and volatility, and propensity to riot, were due to the 'ever-pressing demands of the stomach, the chronic uncertainty of employment, the ceaselessly shifting nature of the casual-labour market, the pitiful struggle of worker against worker at the dock gate'.[35]

Mahoney's trade of compositing had a large 'seasonal' fringe, perhaps up to 20 per cent of the workforce,[36] who were unemployed for large parts of the year. It is likely that Mahoney was part of this fringe. It is quite possible that the other artisans arrested on 8 February were also from sections of their trades subject to regular bouts of unemployment. Such workers often

---

[33] *Daily News*, 16 Feb. 1886, p. 5 col.f.   [34] *Morning Post*, 10 Feb. 1886, p. 6 col.c.
[35] Stedman Jones, *Outcast London*, 341 and 344. This is repeated fairly much in 'Working-Class Culture', 213–14. As Jennifer Davis argues, it is surprising the extent to which modern historians 'portray that [casual poor] group similarly to nineteenth-century observers—as violent, volatile . . . and, indeed, culturally alien to wider English society', 'Jennings' Buildings', 32, n. 6.
[36] See W. Beveridge, *Unemployment: A Problem of Industry* (1909), 140–1.

swelled the ranks of those seeking casual work in unskilled jobs, in the slack times in their trades. Yet, economically, socially, and politically, what was their relationship to the 'casual poor'?

There were at least four major sources of recruitment into the casual labour market; two of which involved the permanent or temporary entry of skilled workers into unskilled and casual jobs.[37] Yet the implications of this when discussing the politics and other attitudes of this 'group' have barely been touched upon. Jennifer Davis has argued that the 'casual poor' was as much an 'ideological category' as an economic one, constructed in the mid- to late nineteenth century as an 'other' against which the respectable work- ing class—as they became more integrated into the wider community— could be defined.[38] Vague enough as the evidence is for the 8 February incidents, it was, and continues to be, distorted by similar ideological as- pects. One of the most explicit examples of this can be seen in the *Morning Post*'s general report of the meeting. As speeches by the socialist leaders were 'cheered to the echo by the listeners, it will be apparent that the pro- portion of genuine working men amongst them was very small. They in- cluded loafers and idlers of the most unprepossessing cast of countenance.' Similarly, the *Illustrated London News* described how 'fanatical orators, be- longing to the Socialist Democratic faction . . . stirred up the feelings of some part of this vague assembly . . . A rabble of several thousand men and youths, bearing little resemblance to any of the London working classes . . . mere idlers and reckless street vagabonds . . . these were, no doubt, the actual rioters at the close of the meeting.'[39] From these viewpoints, by their very actions the rioters defined their 'class', which of course made it easy to ignore the role of others, such as the artisans, who may have been involved in the events.

Stedman Jones clearly demonstrates that underemployed artisans formed part of the economic 'problem' of casual labour in the East End. Yet in turning his focus on to politics in the area, he delineates a set of shared apolitical attitudes amongst a 'casual poor' which he then carefully defines as 'street traders, porters, riverside workers, casual labourers, vagrants, beggars, and petty criminals'.[40] Yet the possible political importance of an interrelationship between the skilled and the unskilled at a very localized, personal level has been neglected. Mahoney's role in probably

[37] See Stedman Jones, *Outcast London*, ch. 4.

[38] Davis, 'Jennings' Buildings', 12–13. On the 'integration' of the working class into the 'nation', see also Feldman, 'The Importance of Being English', 76–9.

[39] *Morning Post*, 9 Feb. 1886, p. 5 col.c and *Illustrated London News*, 13 Feb. 1886, p. 173.

[40] Stedman Jones, *Outcast London*, Part I and p. 342.

orchestrating the actions of his historically prominent group is one example
of this, although little can be said about the role of an individual in one case.
But the issue is broader, and to what extent the actions of artisans helped to
form part of our historical judgement of the 'casual poor' and their politics
is an important point. The riotous actions on 8 February are not in themselves of great consequence politically, but it is intriguing that the rioters
may have essentially represented a combination of the skilled and the very
poorest of the unskilled. An understanding of the implications and issues
involved in this possibility requires a knowledge of the economic and political interaction that existed between the artisans and labourers in the East
End, and of the 'levels' within the casual labour market. Economic and social structures within each of these separate sections influenced politics in
quite distinct ways.

ARTISANS AND THE CASUAL POOR

The unskilled casual labour market in East London is much easier to delin-
eate and study than one would expect. Essentially this is because, as Booth
clearly stated, in 'East London the largest field for casual labour is at the
Docks; indeed there is no other important field.'[41] Stedman Jones disagrees
with this. In seeking to convey the image of an East End 'casual labour market of almost unparalleled dimensions', he argues that one should not focus
too much upon the docks, on the basis that 'Beatrice Potter estimated that
even in Tower Hamlets there were at least 10,000 casual labourers who did
not depend on dock and waterside employment'.[42] But this is a misreading
of what Potter said, and leads to a false impression of the extent of casual
labour in the East End. What she actually stated was that: 'we believe, from
our general inquiry, that there are 10,000 casual labourers, exclusive of
waterside labourers, resident in the Tower Hamlets, employed principally
at the docks'.[43] She was in fact arguing that, as well as those employed on the
wharves in the port—that is, the 'waterside labourers'—the better part of
10,000 other casual labourers were employed in dock jobs.[44] What this mis-
quotation indicates is the type of misunderstanding of London port
employment which has also led generally to a perception of far greater

---

[41] Booth, *Life*, 1st series, vol. 1, p. 42.   [42] Stedman Jones, *Outcast London*, 100.
[43] Booth, *Life*, 1st series, vol. 4, pp. 25–6.
[44] The docks were the large, specially built areas for the ocean-going ships, the wharves
were those structures built straight onto the river, and which usually dealt with the coastal
trade.

levels of distress than was the reality. Interestingly, at the 1892 Labour Royal Commission, Dockers' Union representatives were continually at pains to explain such differences to the commissioners, although again demonstrating the variety of terms in use. Mortimer Costello was asked how many men came to the up-town wharves 'seeking employment in dock and wharf labour.' He corrected the commissioner quite clearly: 'Wharf and riverside labour; not docker labour.'[45] This, of course, could be seen as indicative of a limited solidarity amongst port workers, and their often-commented-upon obsession with gradations of status.[46] But the distinction made is important in discussing the extent of a casual labour 'problem' in the port, as will be seen below.

It is clear that, contrary to the view that there were 'teeming masses' of the starving, unskilled, casual poor in East London who could swell demonstrations such as that in February 1886, there were in fact relatively few who could be so described. Of the 180,000–190,000 adult males employed in the East End, more than half were in occupations classified as skilled, professional, or trading/merchant (excluding street traders).[47] Only around 55,000 were classified as being in completely unskilled positions. In fact, of all employed adult East End males, approximately 10 per cent (18,000–19,000) were casually or irregularly employed manual workers. As Booth noted of the workers in the area, the 'great body of the labouring class . . . have a regular steady income, such as it is'.[48]

The 1891 census provides some sense of the specific areas in which the 55,000–60,000 unskilled (but not necessarily casual) males in the East End were employed. In round figures, the following are the numbers in each 'labouring' area:[49] 14,000 dock and wharf labourers; 3,500 building labourers; 8,000 carmen and carriers; 6,000 porters; 3,500 gasworkers, stokers, etc.; 1,500 coal porters, coal heavers, etc.; 1,500 factory labourers; 1,000 road labourers, navvies; 500 chimney sweeps, scavengers, etc.; 2,500 warehousemen; 3,000 manual miscellaneous occupations; plus 9,000 'general labourers'.

---

[45] *Royal Commission on Labour*, Group B, Vol. 1, P.P. 1892 XXXV, q. 1932.

[46] See J. Lovell, *Stevedores and Dockers: A Study of Trade Unionism in the Port of London, 1870–1914* (1969), 35.

[47] See Stedman Jones, *Outcast London*, Table 16, p. 389, and comparing this to Table 15, and deducting the number of employed males aged 10–20 as shown in the 1901 census.

[48] Booth, *Life*, 1st series, vol. 1, pp. 44 and 51.

[49] These figures are after the distribution of half of those enumerated as 'general labourers' proportionately across the specific areas. This is on the basis of the calculations made by Arthur Baxter for Booth, see ibid. 469–70.

Booth's division of the working population of East London into 'classes' essentially on the basis of the regularity and the level of their wage, shows, by his calculation, that of 57,000 men normally engaged in manual occupations, around one-third were not in receipt of a completely regular wage.[50] Even of this number, a significant percentage suffered relatively little underemployment.

Many of the manual occupations listed above were essentially very regular in their work. Of the 8,000 carmen and common carriers,[51] for example, Booth noted that the 'great bulk' of employment in this area consisted of the handling of the vans and carts of a 'multitude' of small businesses. The employees of these small businesses found that their 'employment is constant; their pay is ruled by the general standard of remuneration, and as such will undoubtedly be a "living wage"'. There was casual employment with the larger firms, which was at its most extreme for the contractors who competed for Post Office business,[52] but this was only a very small percentage of the total trade. Even for these larger firms the percentage of casual employment was not extremely high—perhaps 20 per cent, indicating that across the trade only a small number were casually employed, perhaps 5–10 per cent.[53] Lizzie Alldridge, of the Ranyard Biblewomen and Nurses, noted that amongst workmen in the poor areas of Whitechapel the 'more fortunate are carmen, and policemen, and postmen', suggesting a distinctly higher social status for the carmen than usually claimed.[54] Undoubtedly there was higher seasonal unemployment amongst the carmen principally engaged in the coal trade, but this was a relatively small number, and will be discussed below in relation to this general issue. Booth noted that his Section 5 of labour categories—those 'who earn from 22s. to 30s. per week for regular work'—'particularly' included the carmen.[55]

The building trade—which Stedman Jones calls 'a major alternative focus of casual employment'[56]—was in fact quite a minor employer in the East End in relative terms. In East London only 3,000 bricklayers and bricklayers' labourers were counted in the 1891 census, one-tenth of the London total.[57] Using Dearle's figures on the proportions of occupations

---

[50] Booth, *Life*, 1st series, vol. 1, ch. 3, Table XVI.

[51] The census lists 10,000, but one-fifth were probably boy 'van-guards'.

[52] Booth, *Life*, 2nd series, vol. 3, pp. 323–34 and 327.

[53] See Charity Organisation Society (COS), *Special Committee on Unskilled Labour*, 1908, report 50–2 and evidence of George Lavington, qq. 1484–8.

[54] L. Alldridge, 'With the George Yard Biblewoman', *Biblewomen and Nurses*, 16 (June 1898), 112.

[55] Booth, *Life*, 1st series, vol. 1, pp. 50–1.   [56] Stedman Jones, *Outcast London*, 125.

[57] See also Booth, *Life*, 2nd series, vol. 1, 402–3.

within the trade,[58] this indicates that the number of building labourers of all sorts in the area was 3,000–3,500. The Charity Organisation Society report on unskilled labour found that, in 1901, East End boroughs had far lower proportions of building labour amongst their populations than most other areas of London.[59] Again, most of the labourers in this trade were quite regularly employed. Reports by employers to the Board of Trade showed that in 1906–7 the numbers of labourers employed only dropped below the average by 8 per cent in the worst seasonal month, December, and only rose above it by 5 per cent in the best month, October. Employment was very steady for the rest of the year.[60] These returns were undoubtedly from larger firms, which did tend to be more regular than the smaller firms which were more prevalent in the East End.[61] But countering this was the fact that, within the East End, these smaller firms were almost solely engaged in repair work, which was far less affected by weather conditions than the new work undertaken by the larger concerns, and so they were less likely to employ significantly fewer men in the winter. But also, unlike repairing builders elsewhere in London, who were badly affected by social factors such as the constant demand by customers for work to be done while they were away on their summer holidays, the East End certainly suffered less—in this respect at least—from such seasonal issues.[62]

The 1,500 factory workers were not subject to much casualness. Male factory workers, at least, were fairly safe. Will Thorne noted that the 'Laborers in ironworks, soap, chemical etc', which were covered by his union, 'have fairly constant work'.[63] The 'professional' road labourers and navvies—quite a small number, and distinct from the seasonal 'relief' road workers—were also relatively regular in their employment.

The general point here is that the 'core' of such occupations provided reasonably regular work. This emphasizes the significant point that there were large numbers of 'professional' labourers or similar in each of these occupations. Such 'professionals' were also much more likely to have a regular pattern of substitute work in their 'off-season'. As Will Thorne said, although the total number employed as stokers and similar at all the

---

[58] N. Dearle, *Problems of Unemployment in the London Building Trades* (1908), 21–2. This is the figure used in the table above.

[59] COS, *Unskilled Labour*, 54.

[60] *Royal Commission on the Poor Laws and the Relief of Distress*, P.P. 1910 XLIX, App. No. XXI(D), 647.

[61] See Dearle, *Problems of Unemployment*, 19.

[62] See E. Aves in Booth, *Life*, 2nd series, vol. 1, pp. 115–18.

[63] Booth MSS B144, 7. See also the evidence of Alexander Horn, directing manager of Clarke, Nickolls & Coombs, confectioners, COS, *Unskilled Labour*, q. 1761.

London gasworks fell from 15,000 in winter to 5,000 in summer, a great many of those displaced went straight to work in repair work on the gas buildings. Figures given to the Poor Law Commission regarding 1906 show that total employment at the gasworks fell by less than 20 per cent in the summer, although this figure was somewhat higher at the very start of our period. With relatively small numbers in the East End, those affected did not form a very sizeable group. But those 'turned away in summer go as bricklayers laborers, brickmakers', and similar work. Others found work in areas of the docks in seasonal peaks.[64] Similarly, some carmen who moved coal in the winter took up shifting builders' rubbish in summer.

Such an analysis of the whole list of unskilled employment areas—excluding port and 'general' labouring work—suggests that 'regularly' employed labourers accounted overall for around 80 per cent of employment in these areas. But in the port as well there were many more 'professional' workers than is usually allowed for. This also relates to the issue noted earlier regarding the difference between dock and wharf employment. On the docks themselves prior to the 1889 strike there was a small number of permanently employed workers at each dock location—in 1887 there were just under 1,000 'permanents' employed across the three northside dock groups, London and St Katherine's, West and East India, and Millwall. Then there were the 'preference' men or 'Royals', who were called first when there was casual work available, and who received relatively regular work. These numbered around 1,500. Then there were the true 'casuals', who had to compete for the rest of the jobs when, and if, they came. The number of these casual jobs varied widely, between perhaps 500 and 5,000, and Potter's estimates suggest that perhaps 7,000 or more casual labourers competed at times for these, so clearly many were often unable to obtain work.

But employment on the wharves and associated warehouses was much more regular. While the fluctuations in dock employment are noted above, Booth's figures showed that in 1891–2, on the northside wharves, the maximum number of labourers employed was 4,800, the minimum 3,300, the average 4,000, a variation far less than that of the docks, and so allowing much greater certainty for the wharf workers. Booth concluded that: 'Work at the wharves is less subject to fluctuation than at the docks, and the variations from day to day, or week to week, are not great . . . The northside

---

[64] Booth MSS B144, 5; *RC Poor Laws*, P.P. 1910 XLIX, App. No. XXI (D), Table VII, p. 647; and W. Thorne, *My Life's Battles* (1925), 90. 20% was 600–700 men. See also COS, *Unskilled Labour*, qq. 828 and 939–49, and F. Popplewell, 'The Gas Industry', in S. Webb and A. Freeman (eds.), *Sweated Trades* (1912), 183–4 and 208.

wharves and warehouses offer pretty fair employment for 4,500 men, and probably 5,000 seek a living at them.'[65]

There has been a concentration on the more obvious situation on the docks, but the East End wharves employed in total more men, on average, than the docks, and far more regularly, and far fewer competed for the work there. Stedman Jones has suggested, using the arguments of Beveridge, that the rise in the number of wharves had a major worsening effect on the lives of the riverside workers, because casual labour was relatively immobile and so an individual surplus of labour needed to be encouraged by each employer to cope with times of extra demand. Stedman Jones continues:

> by the end of the century there were 115 separate wharves employing 41 per cent of the [total London] dock labour force. This dispersion of centres of employment, together with a contraction in the demand for casual dock labour in the upper riverside areas, to a large extent accounts for the peculiar sense of misery and hopelessness conveyed in descriptions of the condition of East End dockers in the 1880s.[66]

Yet the small size of the employing entities, combined with the particular type of work the wharves handled, in fact meant that a more personal relationship developed with those who sought work there, leading to quasi-permanence, or at least 'preference' for a regular large number of men, even if they were officially defined as 'casual'. Booth said that at the wharves there was 'less competition, or less chance of competition, between outsiders and those who, being always on the spot, are personally known to the employers and their foremen'.[67] Union officials explained the system:

> Wharf workers usually follow up one wharf or one ship, and do not go to another wharf unless there is a certainty of a job. There are no hours of call at a wharf. At the end of a job the men are told when to come next . . . This system no doubt tends to keep wharf work in the hands of the same men . . . Work at the wharves is far more regular than at the Docks, because as only certain lines come to particular wharves, their arrival can be approximately timed and the work arranged for beforehand.[68]

The much closer relationship of the casual workers on the wharves with their employers suggests a similar situation to that found by Jennifer Davis in her study of the casual workers of the Jennings' Buildings in Kensington. She concludes that while

[65] Booth, *Life*, 2nd series, vol. 3, pp. 410 and 419.
[66] Stedman Jones, *Outcast London*, 124. [67] Booth, *Life*, 1st series, vol. 1, p. 42.
[68] Evidence of Costello and Driscoll, Booth MSS B141, 102.

almost all of the inhabitants . . . at times suffered periods of under- or unemployment, a considerable gulf existed between the precarious position of those who were
unable to form connections with either employers or their agents inside the slum,
and the relatively secure position of those who could. Some residents maintained
regular and often personal relationships with local employers . . . which lasted over
a number of years. These came to entail mutual obligations, such as an expectation
of re-employment after a seasonal lay-off.[69]

The wharf workers enjoyed at least some of the security associated with
such relationships, just like the 'preference' men. Although technically
casual workers, they were in a quite different social/economic environment
because of this. Remaining in employment with one relatively small concern meant that the men became specialists in one particular area. These
men can be largely equated with what Gordon Phillips and Noel Whiteside
call the 'intermediate class' of port workers, 'earning between 15*s*. and 25*s*.
a week . . . Characteristically, too, they associated themselves with a particular firm . . . and they possessed accordingly a definite, though limited,
market value'.[70] James Sexton said of such port workers that, 'where
specialisation existed, self-respect tended to exist also, and it was from this
class that the most competent workmen, and the most loyal trade unionists,
were drawn'.[71] The issue of unionization amongst the unskilled, and the
political influence of this, will be discussed in a later chapter, but the differentiation made here is important.

Wharf work even remained more far more regular than the docks in the
bad times. Figures from the Board of Trade showed that, between 1897 and
1906, average daily employment on the wharves varied by less than 10 per cent
between the best trade year and the worst, while the average of the rest
of port employment fluctuated by a third.[72] All these factors combined to
mean that there was a relatively small surplus of labour at the wharves, and
that they were not a focus for casual labour. On the other hand, in the East
End they provided perhaps 50 per cent of all riverside employment. This
situation remained essentially the same throughout the period.[73]

There are two significant points to be made here. First, the above shows
that there were a large number of port workers in the East End who did not
have to 'struggle at the dock gates' for work every day. Combining the

[69] Davis, 'Jennings Buildings', 20.

[70] G. Phillips and N. Whiteside, *Casual Labour: The Unemployment Question in the Port
Transport Industry 1880–1970* (Oxford, 1985), 31.

[71] J. Sexton, *Sir James Sexton, Agitator* (1936), 112.

[72] *RC Poor Laws*, P.P. 1910 XLIX, App. No. XXI (D), Table VIII, p. 648.

[73] See *Report to the Local Government Board on Dock Labour in Relation to Poor Law Relief*,
P.P. 1908 XCII, 491 ff. See also COS, *Unskilled Labour*, p. 31 and q. 1248.

wharf workers with the permanents and 'preferables' at the docks, at least half of the labouring jobs in the port went to men quite regularly employed, that is, around 5,000 out of the 8,000–10,000 on average in work. So, as a report on poverty amongst dock labourers (defined broadly) stated in 1908, 'dock labour is by no means a great mass of casual and unorganized labour such as it has often been represented to be'.[74]

But in the port, in addition to those who were regularly employed there were perhaps up to 10,000 others who consistently competed for the extra casual jobs, including both a smaller number of other 'professional' dock and wharf labourers, and a large number of 'general labourers'. In addition to these, there were the seasonally unemployed artisans and others, who came at various times to swell these numbers. It is amongst these groups, then, that we do have the classic 'crush at the dock gate', and, as both Booth and Potter suggested, it is here that it is quite possible to study the 'core' of East End casual labour, and indeed to apply what we find across the area.

We have an overall picture of an unskilled labour market in the East End which is much less desperate and chaotic than that generally portrayed. But having identified a smaller group of the unskilled 'casual poor', and positioned it very much upon the docks, how can this help in looking more closely at our perceptions of the politics of the East End working class, and in particular the importance of their social circumstances in the development of attitudes? Rather than their 'separateness', it is the relationship of this group with other sections of the working class which is of significance here.

Levels within the ranks of casual dock labouring can be defined by their relationship to underemployed artisans. First, we have the often-cited statement of the secretary of the Dockers' Union, Ben Tillett, who told the Select Committee on Sweating in 1888 of the large numbers of those seeking casual work at the docks in London who were not 'dock labourers by trade'. At 'least 25 per cent of them had been at some trade; and they were pretty well divided between the tailoring and the shoemaking', with some bakers and costers.[75] Tillett was using this argument to emphasize his view of the ill-effects of the heavy Jewish immigration into the East End. Artisans were being pushed out of their jobs by the 'undercutting' immigrant tailors and bootmakers, he argued, and the English artisans were being forced into dock work as a last resort.

---

[74] *Report on Dock Labour*, P.P. 1908 XCII, 500, and see also Lummis, *Labour Aristocracy*, 55–60.

[75] *Select Committee on the Sweating System*, P.P. 1888 XXI, qq. 12658–68.

Booth's figures on male artisans show that probably fewer than 20 per cent of these skilled workers across the East End were not in receipt of a regular wage, and that two-thirds were in a 'comfortable' or better position.[76] This suggests that perhaps around 14,000 artisans across the district were underemployed or suffered seasonal unemployment. But those 'artisans' seeking work at the dock gates can be divided into two groups. First there were those, as above, who sought work simply because their own trade was slow. This was one 'level' of the casual labour market. Tillett himself noted that, in 'the winter . . . a large number of men in the building trade are turned off, and men in the tailoring trade, and the bootmaking, and the costermongering; we get them from all these various sources',[77] and as Edward Steward, a dock labourer for sixteen years, also told the Sweating Committee, that when the 'season' came around again for these various trades, they returned to them: 'the painters, when the sun is out we lose them; and the tailors, when they improve in their styles and fashions, we lose them; so that we are left by ourselves as dock labourers at certain times'.[78]

Certainly these underemployed artisans had little ongoing contact with those who remained attached to casual dock work throughout the year. This can be shown particularly by the results of a survey of 189 casually employed East End riverside workers applying to Mansion House for relief in 1893. All of these men were, or had been, members of a trade union (they were part of a total of 372 applicants). The survey showed that only 10 had at any point previously been members of unions representing artisans. This was reinforced by a similar result in a survey in 1909, amongst 107 dock-worker applicants to the Poplar Distress Committee—again, almost none of the applicants had previously been in a skilled trade, although many had come from other labouring areas.[79]

Yet it was also continually claimed that the poorest end of the dock workforce included very many who permanently drifted into the work from

[76] Booth, *Life*, 1st series, vol. 1, ch. 3, Table XVI. The figures were not quite as favourable in some specific areas, in particular in Bethnal Green, where only 70% of artisans were in totally regular employment: ibid., Table IX.

[77] *SC Sweating*, P.P. 1888 XXI, q. 12828.

[78] Ibid., q. 13213.

[79] *Board of Trade Report on Agencies and Methods for Dealing with the Unemployed*, P.P. 1893–4 LXXXII, 625–6, and *RC Poor Laws*, P.P. 1909 XLIV, 769–72. A survey undertaken by Llewellyn Smith for Booth, of permanent labourers at the India Docks has generally been seen as evidence of the 'residual' nature of dock work—see Stedman Jones, *Outcast London*, 74. But there were specific factors regarding the permanent labourers at that time related to the recruitment of many from outside the dock workforce after the 1889 strike, as discussed later in this chapter.

other trades—in contrast to those who merely went there in their 'off season'. Arnold White wrote of the many amongst the labourers who 'gravitate to the riverside' who were 'artisans who have dropped their subscriptions to their unions and societies through want, who have sold their tools for bread, and who have thus been driven down the ladder of life from the exercise of skill to the exertion of brute force'.[80] The key reason why this did not show in relief committee surveys is that these committees, had specifically excluded all men who lived in common lodging houses from their schemes, usually arguing that these 'irresponsible characters' did not deserve their help. As Alexander Paterson, who investigated their conditions by temporarily becoming such a character, noted: 'To the Distress Committee, and similar agencies for the unemployed, we of the lodging-house are outcasts. No man who gives this as his address will be allowed to enter his name upon the register of unemployed persons.'[81]

It was these 'dossers' amongst the casual dock labourers who were most likely to be men who had lost positions in their own trades. It was also mainly this group which obtained only occasional work at the docks. They were the unattached casuals—those most likely to have called themselves 'general labourers'[82]—and were most typically, but of course not exclusively, single men who lived in the cheapest common lodging houses. Phillips and Whiteside state that:

The lowest stratum of dock labour, made up of men earning less than 15s. a week on average, may have constituted as many as 40 per cent of the work-force [6,000–7,000 men in the East End] . . . It included . . . unfit and elderly workers . . . general labourers and odd-job men to whom the waterside was one of several sources of an exigious income, men driven to the docks by long spells of unemployment in their normal trade, and the 'workshy'—willing to accept only the kind of short term jobs on offer in this industry. Though all these elements remained in the docks because they had some chance of employment there, both employers and other workmen sought to keep them at the back of the queue.[83]

This last point is made clear if we look at the situation directly after the great dock strike. After 1889 a 'list' system was established by the Dock Company whereby labourers were registered according to their value to the company. There were first the permanents, then the 'A' list of those who

---

[80] A. White, 'The Nomad Poor of London', *Contemporary Review*, 47 (May 1885), 717–18. See also Potter in Booth, *Life*, 1st series, vol. 4, p. 31.

[81] See H. V. Toynbee, 'A Winter's Experiment', *Macmillan's Magazine*, 69 (Nov. 1893), 56, and 'A.P.' [Alexander Paterson], 'The Common Lodging House—III', *Toynbee Record*, 21: 6 (Mar. 1909), 95.

[82] See Beveridge, *Unemployment*, 93.   [83] Phillips and Whiteside, *Casual Labour*, 30.

were employed on a weekly basis, and who for all intents and purposes were also permanent. After this followed the 'B' list, who equated with the 'preferables' of before. The next group was the 'C' list, of those who would also be chosen in order but only when a number of extra men were wanted.[84] Then there were the completely 'unlisted' casuals. But although this structure was very similar to that existing before the strike, if more formalized, the position of a great many individuals employed at the docks had now changed. In most areas, particularly in the India Docks, union leaders told Booth's inquirers in 1892 that the men in their branches were usually in no higher than the 'C' class, although these men had often been 'preferables' before the strike. This was both because of the 'grudge' held against those who had participated in the strike, and because the union had advised its members to reject offers of the increased numbers of permanent positions which began to be created in 1890.[85] A regulation whereby permanence would only be given to those under 30 years of age also worked against the established dock workers. As a result, as John Lovell explains, 'the committee brought in a number of outsiders to fill the new [permanent] vacancies, and, once started, this process went on relentlessly. The consequence was that unionists were largely confined to the lower ranks of the classified lists, and so received an ever decreasing share of employment'.[86]

Many of these union branches complained of the 'dossers' competing for work against their own members on the 'C' list. Such distinctions were continually being made by the casually employed unionists in the early 1890s. A number of branch representatives told Booth's interviewers of the 'trouble' they were having with the 'dossers', or 'single men living in lodging houses'. They compared these men, who only wanted 'about 3 days' employment a week, with the 'older men, having a family to keep', who had remained in the union after the strike, and who 'work hardest'.[87]

Significantly, such a telling distinction was also made by F. A. McKenzie in his descriptions of the unemployed dockers parading the streets in the very mild winter of 1903. About one-half were 'loafers and inefficients', he said, 'bachelors living in casual wards and common lodging-houses', but of the others there were many 'men eager to work, but unable to find work to do, and often with hungry wives at home. Many had joined the processions after trying, in the early morning hours, at the dock gates for work. They

---

[84] The 'C' list was slowly abolished by the Dock Company over the next decade, and shipowners became the direct employers of a higher percentage of dock labourers in this period. Their method of employment in fact was very similar to that in existence before 1889.

[85] See Booth MSS B141, 5, 44, 53–4, and 58.

[86] Lovell, *Stevedores*, 136–7.   [87] Booth MSS B141, 44, and 83–4 and B140, 57.

had their certificates or dock cards. "We're all good union men here," said one, with strange pride."[88]

At least four groups can now be identified within the East End casual labour force concentrated at the docks. There were the underemployed artisans and others who came to dock work at times of slowness in their own employment; the B- or C-list 'professional' dockers, who were either 'preferables' or in the higher levels of the casual workforce; and the lowest level typified by the 'dossers', who themselves had at least two components—the very poorest of the casual labourers, and those men who had 'declined' from their own trades into unskilled work and the lodging house. Politically, these divisions are important.

Amongst those artisans who had been forced out of their trades by lack of work, it seems probable, as is suggested below, that the protectionism promoted by the LUWC and others was an appealing policy. How this related to the taking up of this issue by some of the very poorest of the casual unskilled must also be considered. The 'professional' labourer, on the other hand, had little contact with such views, and there is little direct evidence of protectionist views being put forward by these workers. Certainly it can be argued that it is likely that much of the anti-protectionist comment at the Trafalgar Square meeting came from the professional labourers who undoubtedly formed a large part of the crowd—in the terribly hard winter of 1886 even the best-placed 'preferable' was out of work. Making distinctions between the views of labourers in different 'levels' of work makes sense, as we shall see below that in the political influences upon them, as well as in their social, and economic circumstances, 'professional' dockers were quite distinct from those of their fellow workers who 'dossed' in the lodging houses.

Lodging Houses and Politics

We can calculate that perhaps as many as half of the casual/irregular labourers in the East End lived at least part of the time in the common lodging houses or casual wards of the area. There were around 8,500 beds for males in common lodging houses registered in the East End throughout this period, with an occupancy rate of 80 per cent.[89] But in addition to these

---

[88] F. A. McKenzie, *Famishing London: A Study of the Unemployed and Unemployable* (1903), 10–11.

[89] See the Report by London County Council Medical Officer on the Census of Homeless on the night of 8 February 1907, London Metropolitan Archives, LCC/CL/PH/1/261, 2; figures on common lodging houses included in *London Statistics* throughout the period,

numbers there was a 'floating' population who spent some of their time in the lodging houses and part in casual wards or other shelters, or on the streets.[90] Howard Goldsmid showed how thin the dividing line was between those who happened to spend the night in a lodging house and those who did not:

> When you enter the 'kitchen' of a 'doss-house', it would be a mistake to suppose that all the people you meet there are going to spend the night under its roof. Many of them are 'reg'lar'uns', who, in consideration of their constant patronage are permitted to spend the evening, or a portion of it, before the blazing coke fire . . . glancing towards the door at each fresh arrival to see if a 'pal' has come in from whom it may be possible to borrow the halfpence necessary to complete their doss-money. At last, their final hope being gone, they shuffle out into the streets and prepare to spend the night with only the sky for a canopy.

He noted that many in this situation had 'hung about the docks or the markets the whole day, and very possibly have not even earned a penny'.[91] The London City Mission's worker in the East End lodging houses reported that 'Unskilled labourers who obtain a precarious livelihood' comprised the majority of the lodging-house population in his area.[92] Henry Davids, secretary of the Mariner's Friend Society, wrote in 1886 of the dock labourers in the poorest areas of St George's-in-the-East, the 'living mostly in lodging houses . . . and sleeping indoors when they can find 4*d*., at other times in the street'.[93] The available descriptions of residents are remarkably consistent, and confirm this assessment. Police Superintendent Mulvany, of the Whitechapel Division, in 1905 described the occupants of the lodging houses in his area as 'labourers, dock labourers, itinerant traders of all sorts, men selling toys about the streets, and newspaper lads'.[94] Nearly twenty years earlier Goldsmid had provided almost exactly the same description from his experiences as a 'dosser' in Brick Lane, Whitechapel. Most of the residents were 'dock labourers, a few are pickpockets; some work in various markets; some are hawkers, some only "cadgers", while a shoe-black box or two lying about show that there are some few members of the boot-cleaning fraternity'.[95] The extent of lodging generally amongst dock workers was shown by the fact that of 567

---

particularly Vol. 15 (1904–5), 217; and the evidence of Superintendent J. Mulvany, *Report of the Departmental Committee on Vagrancy*, P.P. 1906 CIII, qq. 9632–3.

[90] See C. B. Marshall, 'The Homeless Poor of London', *Economic Review*, 2: 2 (Apr. 1892), 260, discussing the COS report on the homeless.

[91] Goldsmid, *Dottings*, 72–4.   [92] *London City Mission Magazine*, 60 (1 Feb. 1895), 32.

[93] *East London Advertiser*, 9 Jan. 1886, p. 7 col.f.

[94] *Report on Vagrancy*, P.P. 1906 CIII, q. 9634.   [95] Goldsmid, *Dottings*, 18.

St George's-in-the-East working-class men who said they were living in a 'shared room' when surveyed in 1887, almost exactly 50 per cent described themselves as dock workers (although dock workers formed only just over 20 per cent of the total workforce surveyed). The next largest group in this form of accommodation were those generally 'engaged in rough labour requiring no special skill'.[96]

The labourers living in the lodging houses were those with the most intermittent employment. Booth noted that the 'common doss houses contain a casual class very few of whom are regular labourers'.[97] A. S. Krausse described how very few of the labourers in the lodging house in Limehouse he visited in 1886 had obtained work that day.[98] Missionaries reported at the start and end of our period that not more than 5 per cent of lodging-house residents were regularly employed.[99] R. A. Valpy reported for Booth that in 'the Whitechapel district many porters and dock labourers would seem to reside permanently in these houses, which, there as elsewhere, are the resort of the most brutal of their class'.[100] The lodging houses were concentrated in Whitechapel and surrounding areas, and were closest to the London and St Katherine Docks where, by far, casualness of employment was at its worst.[101] The cause of the casual worker coming to live in the common lodging house was well described by Edward Steward to the Select Committee on Sweating:

A man with a small amount of money, such as 10*d.*, could not go and pay a deposit for lodgings; and it is the shortness of work that gets him out of respectable lodgings . . .

Q.13198. And you think that the men are compelled to live in these common lodging-houses because they cannot earn enough in the short spell of work they get to make a deposit?—Yes.[102]

Although there were some married lodgings available in these houses, these descriptions applied almost exclusively to single labourers (or those who claimed to be single).

It was an accepted fact that a large number of the residents of the lodging houses and similar accommodation, even though now reduced to casual

[96] See *Statements of Men Living in Certain Selected Districts of London*, P.P. 1887 LXXI.
[97] See section from Booth's notebook in Beatrice Webb's MS Diary, Passfield Collection, British Library of Political and Economic Science, vol. 11, p. 56, typescript 830.
[98] Krausse, *Starving*, 14.
[99] *London City Mission Magazine*, 58 (2 Oct. 1893), 227; 76 (May 1911), 83.
[100] Booth, *Life*, 1st series, vol. 1, p. 211.
[101] See Dock, Wharf, Riverside and General Labourers' Union, *The Sweating System: The Draft Report prepared by the Earl of Dunraven, K.P.* (n.d. [*c.*1890]), 29.
[102] *SC Sweating*, P.P. 1888 XXI, qq. 13195–8.

labour, had previously been in 'good' positions. Of the inmates of the Whitechapel casual ward in 1904, who were 'recruited' mainly from the common lodging houses,[103] the residents nearly all described themselves at that time as casual dock and general labourers. Yet 40 per cent had worked at at least one relatively skilled occupation.[104] Interestingly, only a small number were from the tailoring or bootmaking trades, which may explain why anti-immigration arguments seem not to have figured heavily in the lodging houses. A similar percentage was found in the St George's ward, and was undoubtedly repeated in the common lodging houses, and indeed on the streets. Goldsmid said that large numbers of the residents of low lodging houses were 'respectable artizans whom the waves of trade depression have overtaken and submerged; clerks . . . small shopkeepers . . . even professional men'[105] (although the majority of residents had still come from labouring backgrounds). Montagu Williams said many were 'broken-down tradesmen, decayed gentlemen'.[106] Paterson summed up the situation neatly for the lodging house at which he stayed:

We are almost entirely the riverside crowd, the shuffling figures that throng the wharves [docks?] each early morning. By one route or another we have come to be casual labourers; with some it is a destiny inherited (with little else) from riverside fathers, but many have been cast out on the river-bank by an economic tide from the land. We do not belong to the upper class of riverside labourer, who is regularly attached to some factory and wharf.[107]

There are two ways in which the social composition of the lodging houses is important to this discussion of politics. First, only as a minor issue, it is possible that in events such as the disturbances of 8 February, men described as the poorest 'labourers' could have been from backgrounds such as those described above. One of the 'lodging-house labourers' arrested on the day, at least, admitted to the court that he had previously been a clerk who had 'declined' to the lodging-house life.[108] Although, again, the riots themselves were not of great political significance, what does it mean for our perceptions of the 'casual poor', if an even larger number of those involved in the riots were underemployed or had 'declined' from other positions?

---

[103] See Marshall, 'Homeless Poor', 260.

[104] H. Thorp, 'The Casual Ward System—III', *Toynbee Record*, 17: 10 (July–Sept. 1905), 80–1.

[105] Goldsmid, *Dottings*, 10.   [106] M. Williams, *Later Leaves* (1891), 378.

[107] 'A.P.', 'The Common Lodging House—IV', *Toynbee Record*, 21: 8 (May 1909), 130.

[108] *The Times*, 11 Feb. 1886, p. 6 col.f.

Not only is it possible that ex-artisans could influence our perceptions of the politics of the 'unskilled, casual poor' directly through their actions, but it is also very likely that, by their presence in the common lodging houses, they strongly influenced the views of their fellow residents. As Kellow Chesney remarked regarding the mid-century London lodging houses, there 'was a good deal of club spirit about some of the smaller lodging-house kitchens, a sense of membership',[109] and like any club, this could lead to a sharing of views. As Valpy wrote for Booth, in the lodging houses men were seen 'recounting anecdotes and experiences . . . and [there was] discussion—political and theological'.[110] The London City Mission had missionaries throughout this period specifically assigned to the common lodging houses of the East End. One of these complained in 1895 that, at his services every Sunday in the houses, not only might the 'quality or quantity' of the hymn-singing be criticized, but also that after his address he could 'be confronted with quotations from men of various views (Paine, Tyndall, Huxley, McCheyne, and Farrar)'.[111]

Other missionaries reported similar experiences of the discussions amongst the lodging-house men themselves. One found a 'broken-down university man' denouncing the Bible and asserting that man 'is only one of the higher order of brute', while giving a lecture on physiology to about fifty men 'as low and brutal as himself'.[112] Booth commented that mission services had had to be curtailed in some East End lodging houses, because

theological wrangling of too animated a character followed the introduction of some debateable doctrine. Those who frequent these places are by no means unintelligent, and are so mixed [it is said] that 'a good deal of discretion has to be shown, and an unsectarian and non-combative stand-point adopted by the speakers.' And this among the people who are often referred to as having never heard of Christ![113]

Yet battles over theology tell us little about the politics of these people. They do indicate that the lodging houses were not themselves the intellectually dead or hopeless places assumed from their association with the most casual and most depraved of the London poor. But what was the process or pattern of discussions in these places, and how does it affect our impressions of the politics of the working-class poor?

[109] K. Chesney, *Victorian Underworld* (1989), 110.
[110] Booth, *Life*, 1st series, vol. 1, 209.
[111] *London City Mission Magazine*, 60 (1 Feb. 1895), 36.
[112] J. Hunt, *Pioneer Work in the Great City: The Autobiography of a London City Missionary* (1895), 101–2.
[113] Booth, *Life*, 3rd series, vol. 2, 17–18.

Clearly those who held forth on complex issues of theology and similar issues were some of the men who had 'declined' from better days, and in this case were often well educated. But apart from these occasionally ex-professional residents, there were many who had previously been in artisan or similar callings. One striking thing shown by the examination of the attitudes espoused amongst the casual labourers in the lodging houses is how much the issue of protection was dominant—and that this issue was being introduced by those who had been displaced from other trades.

Howard Goldsmid, in his journeys in the East End in 1886, whilst criticizing the political ignorance he found among many in the low lodging houses, nevertheless discovered that those

> who do talk serious politics in a sensible fashion, generally discuss the fair-trade heresy, and I am bound to say that I never, during all my experience of the doss-'ouses, heard a single man who had a good word to say for our system of free imports. This made a remarkable impression on me; for, opposed to them as I was, I could not fail to notice that every man who had formerly occupied a good position ascribed the stagnation in trade which had ruined him to Free Trade.[114]

This issue of protection continued to be a major topic of discussion in the doss-houses. In 1912 Thomas Holmes found that in the lodging houses the residents 'speak very much like other people, and speak on subjects upon which other people speak . . . Here are a couple of wordy excitable fellows who are arguing the pros and cons of Free Trade and Tariff Reform.'[115] L. Cope Cornford, in 1905, discussing with an East End homeless and lodging-house crowd whether the distress at that time was largely due to the militancy, independence, or other 'faults' of the workman, received no response: 'A pause. Then an old man with thick, white whiskers rose up and said:—"In my opinion, it is entirely want of Protection what has done it." Murmurs of assent . . .'[116] Despite the arguments that artisans supported the free-trade system, while the unintelligent labourer could fall under the 'spell' of the protectionists,[117] it seems very clear that the protectionist views were being promulgated by those who had seen better days. The white-whiskered man who spoke in favour of protection above had been 'a skilled mechanic'.

Lionel North found on the Embankment a homeless man from the carpet trade who told him, 'I sometimes think there'll be nothing more to

---

[114] Goldsmid, *Dottings*, 133.   [115] T. Holmes, *London's Underworld* (1912), 72–3.

[116] L. C. Cornford, *The Canker at the Heart: Being Studies from the Life of the Poor in the Year of Grace 1905* (1905), 77–8.

[117] See R. McKibbin, 'Why Was There No Marxism in Great Britain?', in id., *Ideologies of Class*, 31, and Stedman Jones, *Outcast London*, 343.

do for me in this country, unless we get Protection—or something.' North commented that it 'was quite astonishing how many men I met that night who shared his views', noting particularly the statements of an old farrier.[118] An optician in the Whitechapel casual ward blamed 'French and Austrian competition'.[119] Direct statements of support for protection by the unskilled were not mentioned, which is not surprising, given that the artisans and others were the more articulate, but this is also interesting in terms of what evidence historians have for this attitude amongst the unskilled poor. This articulacy in itself is very significant, because it gave these 'protectionist' men influence.

The 'orators' in the common lodging houses had great sway amongst their listeners. Paterson wrote in 1909 that the ordinary resident of the lodging house was accustomed to 'seize' upon any expression of opinion which seemed informed on matters of public interest, and 'having chosen a fitting shibboleth, to close the discussion by repeating the aphorism'.[120] The man who had travelled before finding himself in the East London lodging house, said G. Holden Pike, 'exercises an influence which they cannot hope to command who have not enjoyed similar privileges . . . [he] is proud to have his opinion quoted in the uproarious disputes around the kitchen fire, as coming from the final court of appeal'.[121] Clearly the most intelligent or best orators won the day and the arguments. Goldsmid found 'remarkable . . . the strained attention with which such oracles are listened to by their companions'.[122] In another case, the speaker 'gave the table another thump, while his companions cheered him for his cleverness'.[123] Those best able to relate their opinions, and whose views were most clearly formed, developed a following in the lodging houses, where the men seem to have been keen to hear 'explanations' of their plight. Goldsmid wrote of the many who 'ponder over social inequalities . . . their real grievances and aggravating them by dreaming of imaginary wrongs'.[124]

The question arises as to whether this situation indicates that the casual poor were just 'easy targets' for such ideas. But an important point is that the common lodging house was indeed like a 'club', which made such opinions much more easily accepted than if they were merely expounded from the street corner. The arguments of John Davis regarding the London

[118] L. North, *Human Documents: Lives Re-Written by the Holy Spirit* (n.d. [1909]), 223 and 227–8.
[119] H. Thorp, 'The Casual Ward System—I', *Toynbee Record*, 17: 5 (Feb. 1905), 80.
[120] 'A.P.', 'The Common Lodging House—II', *Toynbee Record*, 21: 5 (Feb. 1909), 81–2.
[121] G. H. Pike, *Pity for the Perishing* (1884), 133.   [122] Goldsmid, *Dottings*, 132.
[123] Hunt, *Pioneer*, 103.   [124] Goldsmid, *Dottings*, 134.

working-men's clubs are relevant here. It seems undoubtedly true that politics within the lodging houses could also 'draw upon partisanship and "clubability" without requiring political erudition or sophistication . . . The strength of associationalism—the ability of social loyalties to generate a shared political partisanship—remained . . . associational politics still required opinion formers, and it is likely that their expertise and articulacy gave them a greater influence.'[125]

The lodging houses were not just somewhere for the homeless to sleep. These were homes and centres of social life for many people. James Greenwood described a Spitalfields lodging house in 1890:

everybody seemed to know and to be on terms of easy familiarity with everyone else . . . This is a feature of common-lodging house life that is not generally understood. The popular supposition is that those who patronize such places as a rule require but one night's lodging, and that in cases where it is their ordinary mode of life they go indiscriminately from one to another. On the contrary, by far the greater number—say sixteen in every twenty—fix on a particular house, and there they remain as regular lodgers summer and winter, sometimes for many years, and by right of user claim one particular bed, with a certain seat in the kitchen, and a place no one else may take at the table.[126]

Edward Barnett, the London City Missionary to the lodging houses, found that at '11 o'clock in the morning you will find some 200 men gathered together' in the kitchen of the house,[127] clearly ensuring social interaction. Paterson noted the 'tendency to fellowship and forgiveness . . . a oneness' amongst the residents of the houses, and described the particular social structures that developed, with their 'rules of forms and manners'.[128] Francis Smiley commented upon the 'practical sympathy' that existed amongst those in a Spitalfields house, while another observer spoke of the 'bonhomie' he saw in a house in St George's.[129] The development of 'communities'[130] in the lodging houses provided the basis for the trust

[125] J. Davis, 'Radical Clubs and London Politics, 1870–1900', in Feldman and Stedman Jones, *Metropolis*, 116–17.

[126] J. Greenwood ['One of the Crowd'], 'Sleep of the Homeless', *Daily Telegraph*, 26 Dec. 1890, p. 7 col.g. The regularity of the lodgers was commonly mentioned in reports. See, in particular, the survey of East End common lodging-houses in *RC Poor Laws*, P.P. 1909 XLIII, App. XXI, pp. 263–4; also Cornford, *Canker*, 23; Goldsmid, *Dottings*, 16; and 'A.P.', 'The Common Lodging House—II', 81.

[127] *London City Mission Magazine*, 71 (1 June 1906), 159. See also 64 (1 Nov. 1899), 245–6.

[128] 'A.P.', 'The Common Lodging House—II', 81.

[129] F. Smiley, *The Evangelization of a Great City: Or the Churches' Answer to the Bitter Cry of Outcast London* (Philadelphia, 1890), 141; Anon., 'Leaves from the Life of a "Poor Londoner"', *Good Words* (Aug. 1885), 532.

[130] 'A.P.', 'The Common Lodging House—II', 81.

placed in the 'orators' who put forward their views. As undoubtedly long-term residents, like many of their listeners, they were accepted as speaking from the same position as their audience, with the additional influence that this brought, just as the club lecturer could attract loyalty to his cause.

This clearly was likely to be an important influence on the views of what was a large section of the East End casual poor. The consistent support for protectionism given by many of the 'declined' artisans and tradesmen in the lodging houses must have encouraged their fellows to at least adopt these views as 'shibboleths', as Paterson said. This specific influence may go some way toward explaining the 'mixture of opinion' amongst the unskilled on this issue, such as appeared to be the case at the February 1886 Trafalgar Square meeting.

The background to this meeting and its aftermath, then, begins to suggest the very great significance of the local, the personal, in the development of the ideas of the working class in the East End, factors which, as we shall see, had importance well beyond this one specific case. Economic and social circumstances were important here in establishing the basis for the attitudes of these unskilled workers. But the connection between poverty and politics was a much more complex, and varying, process than is usually described.

This chapter has looked at the evidence regarding the attitudes of the poorest members of the East End working class. There is little evidence to suggest that they were 'easy prey' for protectionist discourse in a standard sense. But that they did respond very quickly, given the right circumstances, shows the vital importance of looking at issues related to the context of 'reception' in analysing the impact of ideas and political language. However, those who discussed protectionism in the lodging houses were undoubtedly not those who delivered to the Conservatives the electoral victories which are said to have been based upon this and like issues. The next chapter looks at that key form of evidence of working-class Conservatism—the electoral result.

2

A House Divided

A parliamentary general election was held in 1886, five months after the West End riots. It became one of the most violent and bitterly fought elections seen in the East End. But the poll was not contested on issues of protectionism or the distress of the unemployed. Its bitterness came from its central issue of Home Rule.

Gladstone's Irish Home Rule bill was lost in the House of Commons in June 1886, and parliament then dissolved. Of the eight Liberal members who had won East End seats in 1885, none joined the ninety-three of their number who opposed the bill in parliament and ensured its defeat. But local divisions clearly existed, with party splits appearing most obviously in Poplar and in Stepney.

In Poplar, the Liberal member, Henry Green, as the Home Rule issue was developing in the parliament, was said to have undertaken 'a study of the bill, and after due consideration of its meaning and likely consequences, he announced himself an opponent of the measure and one of those who would vote against it at the proper time'.[1] But local party members could not accept this, and resolved to demand that Green support Gladstone's proposals. This he ultimately did, but, clearly affronted by this assault on his conscience, he then refused to be nominated for selection as candidate for the election. He continued, however, to show his support for the Liberal campaign in the area. His successor as candidate, Sydney Buxton, won narrowly, with the Liberal vote dropping by more than 25 per cent.

In Stepney the signs of disunity were even stronger. The Liberal member, Durant, had attended meetings with Joseph Chamberlain to discuss opposition to the bill, although Durant did also subsequently support the bill in the House. His constituency party, however, (with other concerns about his performance) resolved not to invite him to contest Stepney again.[2] The candidate they chose, Sir R. S. Wright, lost the seat, it being said that the party was 'hopelessly divided as to his candidature'.[3] In one constituency, Bethnal Green North East, the sitting member, George

[1] *East London Advertiser*, 12 June 1886, p. 6 col.a.
[2] Ibid., pp. 3 col.b and 6 col.b. [3] Ibid., 26 June 1886, p. 6 col.c.

Howell, was opposed by a Liberal Unionist, but retained his seat, although with a greatly reduced majority.

The bitterness of the local campaign clearly had a good deal to do with the existence of a large Irish population in the East End, particularly in districts near the docks, where in some parts this may have reached 20 per cent of the population of an area. It was reported that in St George's C. T. Ritchie—subsequently Conservative Chancellor of the Exchequer—had election meetings severely disrupted, and was often followed down the street by a 'howling mob' or was 'most grossly insulted' in his journeys around the constituency.[4] In September it was said that: 'One of the outcomes of the late election has been the boycotting of certain tradesmen who gave their support to Mr Ritchie. A gang of ruffians who took a lively interest in the Radical cause . . . have used threats and intimidations towards tradesmen, going so far in one case as to dictate what one should sell and what he should not, besides gathering near his shop to intimidate customers from shopping there.'[5]

Similar passion and violence was apparent in the campaign in other areas of the East End. In Limehouse, fist-fights and forcible ejections seem to have been common at election meetings, with an aftermath of legal battles. Certainly the Irish support for the Gladstonian Liberal cause added the most colour and vigour to the election. In Poplar, 'Mr Sydney Buxton's supporters—the Irish Separatists . . . paraded the borough with brass bands and torches, accompanied by all the rough element of the neighbourhood'.[6] Of the likely effects of this support it was said that, in Limehouse, for example, 'as in fact in all the others, the Irish vote will be cast for the Radical candidate; but this will be more than counter-balanced by the votes of Liberals, so many of whom will vote at the forthcoming election for the Conservative candidate, or else abstain from voting altogether'.[7]

As Liberal candidates reflected on the outcome of the election, they would have entirely agreed with the very last part of this assessment. Of the eight East End constituencies the Liberals held prior to the election (all except Mile End, Limehouse, and St George's-in-the-East), they lost two—Bow and Bromley, and Stepney—and in other areas had close escapes. Their total vote in these seats on average dropped by 20 per cent. Significantly, the reason for the poor Liberal performance in the East End was essentially no different to that in the rest of Britain in this election[8]—the Liberals lost because Liberal voters stayed at home.

[4] Ibid., p. 3 col.e., and 14 Aug. 1886, p. 5 col.b.   [5] Ibid., 4 Sept. 1886, p. 5 col.d.
[6] Ibid., 3 July 1886, p. 3 col.d, and 10 July 1886, p. 6. See also *Eastern Post*, 20 July 1895, p. 5 col.b, on Whitechapel.   [7] *East London Advertiser*, 26 June 1886, p. 6 col.d.
[8] See N. Blewett, *The Peers, the Parties and the People: The General Elections of 1910* (1972), 21–2.

The poll in St George's in 1886 was said to be 'a very small one, principally caused by Liberal abstentions'.[9] George Howell, whose support dropped significantly in Bethnal Green, made a similar claim: 'The returns show that the "Unionists", as they were called only polled 62 more than at the previous election in 1885, but my poll was fewer by 817, showing that there were many abstentions as well as removals. My opponents had not gained by secession, but I had lost through secession.'[10] In Bow and Bromley, which the Liberals lost, it was said of former Liberal voters that 'their abstention from polling in 1886 placed Sir John [Colomb, Con.] in the seat'.[11] In that constituency, and in many others, total voter turnout dropped by around 10 per cent, and this essentially all came from the Liberals.

This clear picture of abstention in 1886 is quite different from the normal view of the electoral results in the East End of the period. The results did not flow from an East End working-class poor consistently voting Conservative on the appeal of populist issues, but from former Liberal supporters making a decision not to turn out. To gauge the implications of this for our overall understanding of the politics of the East End, we need first to know more about exactly who possessed the vote in Victorian East London.

As in the rest of urban Britain, the vast majority of householders in the East End in the late nineteenth century were tenants of rented accommodation.[12] The intricate franchise processes by which tenants could become voters in this period have been well described, most recently and comprehensively by John Davis and Duncan Tanner, and there is little point in repeating these details here. But to be able to use election results as evidence of political feeling in the East End, it is important to have a more developed and detailed understanding of precisely who did manage to gain a place on the electoral register. The discussion below is an attempt to describe as accurately as possible the typical characteristics of the East End voter in the late nineteenth century, and the implications of this for our understanding of politics in the area.

---

[9] *East London Advertiser*, 10 July 1886, p. 6 col.d.

[10] 'MS Autobiography of George Howell', Howell Papers, Bishopgate Institute, Vol. D, Section DL—Elections 1885–1895.

[11] *East London Advertiser*, 2 July 1892, p. 8 col.b.

[12] Avner Offer's work suggests perhaps 15% owner occupation across urban Britain in this period. Other studies argue for a lower figure than this. Certainly in the East End owner occupation was low. Although not stating categorically how many premisses were owner occupied, figures from Poplar in 1908 suggest clearly that out of 22,730 dwellings, at least 20,000 were not lived in by their owners. Taking into account multiple tenant occupation, this suggests that far fewer than 10% of households were owner-occupiers. A. Offer, *Property and Politics 1870–1914* (Cambridge, 1981), 119; *RC Poor Laws*, P.P. 1910 XLIX, qq. 91594 and 95746; and see J. Harris, *Private Lives, Public Spirit: A Social History of Britain* (Oxford, 1993), 113.

Davis and Tanner have rightly pointed out that various modifications to the electoral laws after 1867 meant that, in even the poorest urban constituencies, voters could be much more representative of the area's male population than either was envisaged by the legislators or than has been allowed for in many historical studies. Davis and Tanner argue that, although the effects of the franchise law were 'capricious', its result was voter registration with 'an unexpectedly wide social variation'.[13] But a detailed analysis of the census returns and electoral registers for three areas of the East End in 1891[14] suggests that, while the enfranchisement criteria did not 'systematically discriminate' against specific groups of voters,[15] the great majority of those enfranchised were clearly from amongst the more regularly employed and prosperous within each occupational category.

The vast majority—approximately 85–90 per cent—of parliamentary voters in all East End constituencies in this period were enfranchised under the 'householder/occupier' category. These were adult males who owned a property or, much more commonly, were tenants with non-resident landlords. They occupied a dwelling, or part thereof, that was liable to be separately rated, even if they paid their rates only indirectly, through their rent.[16] They then could be entered into the local rate book and so automatically onto the electoral register, provided that they satisfied the other franchise requirements, such as length of residence. The discussion below concentrates upon this group. I will discuss the only other significant parliamentary voter group, lodgers, later in the chapter.

Three groups of census enumeration districts were examined, one from the North Ward of St George's-in-the-East, and two in Mile End Old Town—one group of Mile End districts being located at the eastern end of the parish, near Limehouse and Bromley, and the other in the north, near

---

[13] Davis and Tanner, 'The Borough Franchise', abstract 306 and *passim*, and Davis, 'Slums and the Vote'.

[14] The 1892 register, which was used for this analysis, came into effect on 1 January 1892, and included those voters who qualified by twelve months' residence within the same parliamentary borough (or, for lodgers, at the same address) between July 1890 and July 1891. The 1891 census was conducted on 5 April 1891 and so was within the residence qualification period for the 1892 register. See N. Blewett, 'The Franchise in the United Kingdom 1885–1918', *Past and Present*, 32 (Dec. 1965), 35–6 and 40, and E. Higgs, *Making Sense of the Census: The Manuscript Returns for England and Wales, 1801–1901* (1989), 105.

[15] See D. Tanner, 'Class Voting and Radical Politics: The Liberal and Labour Parties, 1910–31', in Lawrence and Taylor (eds.), *Party, State and Society*, 114.

[16] See Davis, 'Slums and the Vote', 378, 383, and *passim* for details. As Davis says, the major distinction between a 'householder' and a 'lodger' in franchise terms was that the lodger's landlord was also resident in the house. The householder and occupier franchises were related but distinct qualifications which were not separated on the registers. I will be using the term 'householder voter' throughout to refer to these franchises. See also Blewett, 'Franchise', 32–3.

Bethnal Green.[17] The general areas within which each district was contained were described by Booth as having, respectively, 51 per cent (one of the higher levels in the East End), 31 per cent, and 22 per cent of their population in poverty.[18] While significant social variations could occur within small areas, and these specific enumeration districts may not necessarily represent the average conditions of the larger Booth blocks, the broad differences between the areas suggest that they can be taken to represent a wide range of conditions for the East End. There were 18,000 people in the districts studied, including 1,400 identifiable male parliamentary voters and 200 Division 3 voters (essentially, female voters entitled to vote only in local-government elections).

What is strikingly clear from examining the accommodation, employment, age, and family situation of each householder voter in these areas is that most were in a better-than-average financial situation and most likely represented the most regularly employed and skilled in their occupation. Poorer, or less skilled, workers were able to become householder voters, but tended to be on the register for a significantly shorter period. Generally, voters possessed relatively common social characteristics across all three districts studied. This begins to suggest the key importance of localized influences over simple economic differences, in political variations between areas of the East End in this period.

Regularity of work was one of the most important factors in determining who would or would not gain the vote in the East End. This was because the chance of becoming a householder voter was in most cases very clearly based upon whether one could afford to become the 'principal tenant' of one's rented dwelling.

Davis and Tanner have shown that every tenant who lived in a dwelling without a resident landlord theoretically had the right to be entered into the local rate books as a 'rate compounded' tenant (i.e. with rates paid as part of their rent), and to be automatically entered onto the electoral register. This was the case even if their house was divided into four, five, or even more separate tenements.[19] But it seems from the electoral registers and other evidence that the entry of more than one 'compounded' tenant into the rate book for a dwelling in the East End was relatively rare. This was almost certainly because, as noted by Davis and Tanner, landlords had the

<hr />

[17] See RG12/285, St George's-in-the-East North Enumeration Districts 7–13, RG12/313 Mile End Old Town Eastern Enumeration Districts 42–4, and RG12/306 Mile End Old Town Eastern Enumeration Districts 7–9, Public Record Office.

[18] See Booth's descriptions of areas 73b and 74c; 78a; and 84a and b: *Life*, 1st series, vol. 2.

[19] Davis, 'Slums and the Vote', and Davis and Tanner, 'The Borough Franchise', *passim*.

responsibility of filling in the forms that notified the authorities of who should be included in the rate books as their 'compounded' tenants, and the 'landlords who completed the forms might know little about their tenants, particularly if they collected rent through one "chief tenant" in a multiply-occupied building'.[20] The practice of one tenant taking a whole dwelling and sub-letting parts of it to other tenants was much more common in London than a landlord letting out separate parts of a building and having a direct relationship with all tenants.

Maud Pember Reeves found that landlords 'insist on letting a whole house to tenants who are invariably unable to afford the rent of it . . . [and so] contract out half of the landlord's risk'. She described the normal housing situation for the working class in Lambeth in 1913, which undoubtedly mirrored much of that in the East End:

small houses are let at rents varying from 10s. to 15s. [a week] . . . They are let to a tenant who is responsible to the landlord for the whole rent, and who sublets such rooms as she can do without in order to get enough money for the rent collector . . . The ordinary housing for 8s. a week consists generally of three rooms out of a four-roomed house where the responsible tenant pays 10s. or 11s. for the whole, and sub-lets one small room for 2s. or 3s., or of three or four rooms out of a five or six-roomed house where the whole rent might be 14s. or 15s., and a couple of rooms might be sublet at 6s. or 7s.[21]

Such arrangements were widespread across the East End. Very similar conditions were reported in St George's, Bethnal Green, Poplar, and elsewhere.[22] Such sub-letting, where the principal tenant became the 'landlord' for the other tenants, was claimed to be occurring in three-quarters of London houses in the middle of the century, and it seems unlikely that this figure decreased as the century went on.[23] It was reported for Stepney borough in 1905 that, for most houses, sub-letting 'is the very general rule'.[24]

It is clear that there was a very common division between the 'principal', 'chief', or 'responsible' tenant, who had a direct relationship to the owner or

[20] Davis and Tanner, 'The Borough Franchise', 319. See also Lawrence, 'The Dynamics of Urban Politics', 87–8.

[21] M. Pember Reeves, *Round About a Pound a Week* (1913; repr. 1979), 29–30 and 37. The rents given, for Lambeth in 1913, are higher than for the same size dwellings in the East End in the period under discussion.

[22] See *London City Mission Magazine*, 53 (Nov. 1888), 249, Booth MSS B316, 9 and *Report of the Board of Trade Enquiry into Working Class Rents, Housing and Retail Prices*, P.P. 1908 CVII, p. 418. See also further examples from South London in A. Paterson, *Across the Bridges* (1911), 19.

[23] See A. Wohl, *The Eternal Slum: Housing and Social Policy in Victorian London* (Montreal, 1977), 24.

[24] See *Board of Trade Enquiry*, P.P. 1908 CVII, p. 421.

the owner's agent, and the other sub-tenants in a dwelling, who, for the reasons mentioned above, had little chance of appearing in the local rate book or on the list of householder voters. As Anthony Wohl further suggests, even if the landlord knew of all the tenants in a dwelling, an unwillingness to admit to overcrowding to local authorities meant that 'both landlord and tenants had very good reasons for concealing the amount of subletting'.[25] The legal uncertainty as to whether the real 'landlord' of sub-letting tenants was in fact the principal tenant to whom they paid their rent, or the absent rate-paying owner or lessee of the house, also on occasion caused confusion for authorities as to how such residents should be regarded for the franchise.[26]

Local-government figures from 1891 show that in nearly all areas of the East End the total number of rated households in each area was quite close to the total number of inhabited houses, indicating an average close to one rated household per house. But the total number of *all* households was in all cases at least 60 per cent more than the number of inhabited houses, and often 100 per cent more—indicating a much higher average number of separate households existing in each house.[27]

How this was then also transferred into enfranchisement levels is shown decisively by the evidence from these three East End areas. Of the 639 houses in these areas which were divided into at least two separate dwellings, and which contained a registered household voter, only twelve out of the 639 had more than one such voter. The pattern was consistent across all of the areas. More than 98 per cent of these divided houses supported only one householder voter.

Which of the tenants in these divided houses would be the lucky one to gain the vote was also very clear. Of the 654 household voters, 509 (78 per cent of cases) had more rooms in the house than *any* of the other tenants. In 111 cases the voter was in the equal-largest set of rooms. In only thirty-four cases was the householder voter *not* in the largest accommodation available in the

---

[25] A. Wohl, 'The Housing of the Working Classes in London, 1815–1914', in S. Chapman (ed.), *The History of Working-Class Housing* (Newton Abbot, 1971), 24.

[26] The important point, as noted earlier, was that if their 'landlord' lived on the premises, tenants could only claim the vote under the stricter 'lodger' franchise rules which will be discussed below. See *The Times*, 19 Sept. 1905, p. 5, for a report of differing interpretations of this point by revising barristers in West Ham.

[27] Census, P.P. 1893–4 CIV, pp. 80–1 and 256–7. These figures are distorted to some extent in some areas, such as Whitechapel, where there was an extremely large number of block dwellings, with each apartment within these being separately rated under compounding. Whitechapel had the most significant deviation from a close to 1:1 ratio of houses to rated households. This did not result in a higher level of enfranchisement in Whitechapel, because many of the tenants were unnaturalized immigrants. See J. White, *Rothschild Buildings: Life in an East End Tenement Block 1887–1920* (1980), 2.

house. In the clear majority of cases in all of the areas, the only person registered as the householder voter for the house was the one who could be regarded as the 'principal tenant', that is, the one with the greatest 'stake' in the house.

The general characteristics of principal tenants (including those cases where the house was not divided and there was a sole tenant or owner) can be at least suggested from the census evidence. Again, these tenants comprised the vast majority of voters in these East End areas.

First, it is important to show clearly, as mentioned earlier, that indeed there was not a significant bias in the householder electoral register against any particular occupational group. Tables 1 to 3 illustrate this point.[28]

TABLE 1. *Voter occupational comparison, total locally born adult male population and householder voters. St George's-in-the-East, North ward*

Occupational group	% of the population	% of the register
Labourers	37.1	28.9
Artisans		
Building	5.9	6.3
Furniture	2.3	2.9
Footwear	2.9	2.2
Metal	5.3	8.1
Textiles	5.8	6.3
Total artisans	22.2	25.8
Shopkeepers, publicans	5.1	12.8
Cabmen, carmen	10.8	9.2
Watermen/foremen etc.	5.2	6.3
Shop workers/food industry/		
messengers	8.1	5.1
Professionals/white-collar	3.5	4.5
Home workers	2.7	2.9
Hawkers etc.	1.2	1.6
Miscellaneous	1.2	1.1
Policemen/soldiers	0.6	0.0
Not given	2.2	1.8

[28] I am using 'locally born' in these tables to refer to those born in Britain and Ireland, and my comparisons throughout regarding the adult male population involve only this group. This is because the percentage of other (non-Irish) immigrants who were on the registers was so small (12 voters out of an adult male immigrant population of 1,017 in the St George's North area), that to have included the entire immigrant population in the calculations would have greatly reduced the clarity of the arguments regarding the range of other important factors involved in gaining enfranchisement.

The figures in these tables show that the occupational structure of the householder electoral register did not vary very widely from that of the general population, even in the poorest of areas, such as St George's North ward. In St George's, labourers comprised 29 per cent of householder voters, compared to their 37 per cent of the adult male population, and shopkeepers/publicans formed 13 per cent of the electorate, while being only 5 per cent of adult males. This certainly started to skew the electorate away from the poorer working class to some extent, but the overall occupational structure does not differ vastly from what would have been expected from a fully inclusive franchise. Artisans and labourers combined made up 55 per cent of the register, compared to 59 per cent of the adult male population. The electoral registers in the other areas, Mile End North and East, were similarly occupationally representative of the populations of their areas. But it is very clear that, while the registers may have been reasonably occupationally representative, they were not similarly socially representative.

TABLE 2. *Voter occupational comparison, total locally born adult male population and householder voters. Mile End North*

Occupational group	% of the population	% of the register
Labourers	21.9	17.6
Artisans		
Building	7.0	8.6
Furniture	5.2	6.8
Footwear	5.8	3.5
Metal	10.2	12.7
Textiles	3.0	4.6
Total artisans	*31.2*	*36.2*
Shopkeepers, publicans	2.2	4.1
Cabmen, carmen	11.1	8.1
Watermen/foremen etc.	3.6	4.9
Shop workers/ food industry/ messengers	11.5	11.1
Professionals/white-collar	7.2	8.1
Home workers	2.8	2.2
Hawkers etc.	2.7	3.5
Miscellaneous	1.7	1.9
Policemen/soldiers	1.5	0.5
Not given	2.7	1.9

TABLE 3. *Voter occupational comparison, total locally born adult male population and householder voters. Mile End East*

Occupational group	% of the population	% of the register
Labourers	16.6	11.8
Artisans		
Building	11.9	16.7
Furniture	2.0	1.2
Footwear	0.8	0.9
Metal	10.0	9.1
Textiles	3.1	1.8
Total artisans	*27.8*	*29.7*
Shopkeepers, publicans	2.7	7.0
Cabmen, carmen	3.8	3.6
Watermen/foremen etc.	10.6	12.1
Shop workers/food industry/		
messengers	8.9	5.5
Professionals/white-collar	22.8	23.3
Home workers	1.4	1.8
Hawkers etc.	0.3	0.3
Miscellaneous	0.5	0.9
Policemen/soldiers	0.7	0.9
Not given	3.9	3.0

In the St George's area the clear majority (66 per cent) of householder voters lived in accommodation of three rooms or more. But only 25 per cent of the total locally born adult male population did so.[29] Three-room accommodation was, by the standards of this part of the inner East End, very spacious. Booth and other investigators described single-room accommodation as the dominant housing form in St George's. The 1891 census summaries suggest that, of 10,211 separate tenements in the St George's registration district, 6,171 (60 per cent) were of one or two rooms, although the method of defining and calculating these overall figures left much to be desired.[30]

[29] Calculated from the census manuscript material. The 25% figure seems to have been relatively consistent, for the working class at least, across the entire St George's parish. See *Statements of Men*, P.P. 1887 LXXI, pp. 306 and 322.

[30] Booth MSS B333, p. 23 and Census, P.P. 1893–4 CIV, p. 62, and see P.P. 1890–1 XCIV, pp. 5–6. The issue of the varying status given to 'lodgers' and 'boarders' as 'heads' of separate households, and definition of tenement size, by different enumerators is a difficult one, which can to some extent be adjusted for when working with the manuscript material. See Higgs, *Making Sense*, 56–62.

That those on the electoral register lived in much larger than average-size dwellings for the area was not simply a statistical result of the fact that those adult males necessarily living in small accommodation, such as those boarding or living with parents, found it more difficult to obtain the vote.[31] This is shown by comparing the accommodation for adult male household heads only, and across specific occupational groups.[32]

Such a comparison shows that, in St George's North, 41 per cent of the total locally born artisan household heads lived in three rooms or more, but 65 per cent of artisan householder voters did so. More dramatically, only 18 per cent of labourers in the area headed that many rooms, but such men comprised nearly half the labourers on the householder register. Amongst both artisans and labourers in St George's, of those men heading households of at least three rooms, 75 per cent were householder voters. Of those heading a household in one room, only 8 per cent were on the register.

In the Mile End districts one- or two-room accommodation for households was far less common, but the relative difference between the housing of voters and non-voters was similar. In the Mile End North area, 51 per cent of labourers headed three or more rooms, but they comprised 89 per cent of labourer householder voters.

The chance of being on the householder electoral register in the East End in this period essentially depended upon one's position as a tenant. Occupational bias in the register was not extreme, but there was a significant under-representation of those male household heads living in separate dwellings of one or two rooms.

But what is also clear from this evidence is that a move to larger accommodation, and to being a 'principal' tenant, understandably occurred largely as families needed extra space. Only the most wealthy in the East End in this period would rent rooms for which they did not have an immediate need. Single men usually rented very small accommodation, newly married couples slightly larger, and the number of rooms taken did tend to increase as the number of children in the family grew. In St George's North, of those married couples whose children were all below working age,[33] the percentage

---

[31] Cf. Lawrence, 'The Dynamics of Urban Politics', 88, and Tanner, *Political Change*, 119–20.

[32] The method used for distinguishing household 'heads' followed the conventions established, by Michael Anderson especially, for such studies. See Higgs, *Making Sense*, 61, and W. A. Armstrong, 'The Census Enumerators' Books: A Commentary', in R. Lawton (ed.), *The Census and Social Structure: An Interpretative Guide to Nineteenth Century Censuses for England and Wales* (1978), 52–3.

[33] The significance of making a distinction between those with and without children in employment will be seen later in the chapter.

who lived in three or more rooms jumped from 19 per cent for those with one child, to 29 per cent for three children, to 53 per cent for those with four or more children.[34] Enfranchisement levels, for the reasons discussed above, closely followed this increase in accommodation size, as Table 4 shows.

TABLE 4. *Household heads with all children under working age voting in St George's-in-the-East, North ward—percentage on the householder electoral register, by number of children in the family*

Number of children in family	%age on electoral register
1	22
2	28
3	43
4+	58

Nevertheless, families did not rent larger dwellings (and by doing so increase the chances of the father becoming a voter) simply because they had more children. Obviously they also needed to be in a position to afford the extra space. Certainly, very many could not. Of the families in St George's with two, three, or four children, large numbers (44 per cent) still lived in only one room. The heads of these families had very little chance of getting onto the electoral register.

Amongst families who had the same number of children, there is little doubt that there was a very significant difference between the economic position of those on and off the register. As a stark example of this, in St George's North non-voters who had two children lived, on average, in 1.3 rooms per family. But householder voters with exactly the same number of children lived on average in the considerably larger space of 2.9 rooms.[35] There was obviously a substantial difference between the average weekly rent being paid by each group.

[34] This to some extent probably also reflected a greater earning capacity as the father aged and became a more experienced and skilled workman.

[35] A very important point to take into account regarding these averages is that the census only provided for the enumerator to indicate the number of rooms in a dwelling when it was *less than 5*. Therefore, those dwellings larger than 4 rooms could have had any number of rooms from 5 upwards. For these averages I have used 5 as the number of rooms in all these cases, as it is likely that very few households in these areas had many more rooms than this, particularly those without adult children at home. But the average number of rooms for those on the register in particular would certainly have been in reality slightly higher than that given here. The important issue for this study, however, is the comparative aspect of these figures. All the analyses also exclude those with boarders living with them, to provide a clear comparison.

From the figures gathered by Booth, statistically the rent payable for '1.3 rooms' in St George's at that time was around 3s. 3d. For '2.9 rooms' it was double that—approximately 6s. 6d. Significantly, a rental of 6s. or above represented the top 30 per cent of all rents paid by the 6,000 working-class men surveyed in St George's in 1887.[36] Wohl suggests 4s. or 5s. as the limit for lower-paid workers.[37] Being on the householder electoral register in the East End largely depended upon one's family size and relative prosperity.

The social distinction between non-voters and those on the householders register is also shown by a comparison of the respective levels of overcrowding in their housing. Public authorities defined overcrowding as existing if there were more than two persons per room in a dwelling.[38] Only one-third of these householder voters lived in overcrowded conditions, compared to the three-quarters of non-voters who did so. The higher enfranchisement levels amongst those with larger families clearly represented only those who could afford to rent more space as their family grew. This is also shown by a comparison of the enfranchisement levels of labourers and other workers in St George's. Of labourers with two children, 19 per cent were on the householders register. Amongst non-labourers with two children, 36 per cent were on the register. Clearly, size of the family was not the sole criterion here.

In St George's, amongst labourers, only the regularly employed were able to pay the rent required for larger accommodation. Ben Tillett described the situation for dock labourers at the end of the 1880s: 'the majority of the labourers live in back rooms, the more respectable living in two and three rooms. What we call the more respectable would be the "Royals", or permanent hands working at the docks, but the ordinary man . . . is unable to pay more than 3s. or 3s. 6d. a week rent, and that, of course has to be contributed to by his wife and his children.'[39] As this implies, any uncertainty of employment made it extremely difficult for a family to commit itself to a larger rent. Rental arrears were commonplace amongst those who were irregularly employed, and although in a good week reasonable rents could be paid, a few weeks of falling behind with a high rent posed too much of a risk. Most commentators agreed that casual workers could afford only the lowest of rents.[40] That the householder voter was generally a principal

[36] *Statements of Men*, P.P. 1887 LXXI, pp. 306, 323, 423.

[37] Wohl, *Eternal Slum*, 40 and 308–9.

[38] Ibid., p. xv and *Royal Commission on Alien Immigration*, P.P. 1903 IX, App. Table XLIX.

[39] *SC Sweating*, P.P. 1888 XXI, q. 12832.

[40] See Pember Reeves, *Round About*, ch. XIV, and evidence of the Revd Billings of Spitalfields, *Royal Commission on the Housing of the Working Classes*, P.P. 1884–5 XXX, qq. 5039–42.

tenant, who took the risk of a whole house, further excluded any of the irregularly employed.[41]

Most typically, householder voters in these areas of the East End were regularly employed workers within each occupation, usually with at least a few children. In addition, it can be said, importantly, that there was indeed a 'typical' voter across most areas of the East End. Table 5 shows, for all of the census areas studied, the difference in the average number of rooms rented by all labourer and artisan householder voters and non-voters. The difference between the situation of voters and non-voters was quite consistent across all the areas. When comparing the Mile End figures to those of St George's, it is important to remember that average rents in areas slightly further from the centre of London, such as these on the northern and eastern edges of Mile End, were much lower than those of 'inner' zone areas such as St George's. The Board of Trade estimated that rents for one-, two-, and three-room accommodation were, on average, more than 20 per cent cheaper in what it called the 'middle' zone ring around London. This differential meant that accommodation with one extra room could often be afforded in the 'middle' zone, compared to the 'inner' zone, for minimally more rent.[42]

TABLE 5. *Average number of rooms rented by labourer and artisan householder voters and non-voters, by area*

Census area	Labourers		Artisans	
	Household voters	Non-voters	Household voters	Non-voters
St George's, North	2.5	1.3	3.1	1.8
Mile End North	3.7	1.9	3.8	2.3
Mile End East	3.9	2.6	4.4	3.0

[41] See Pember Reeves, *Round About*, 30. See also comments by Lummis, *Labour Aristocracy*, 150.
[42] See *Board of Trade Enquiry*, P.P. 1908 CVII, p. 421, and *Report of the Board of Trade Enquiry into Working Class Rents and Retail Prices*, P.P. 1913 LXVI, map on p. 412 and table on pp. 508–9. Although Mile End North is just within the defined 'Inner Zone' in the 1913 map, its characteristics certainly would not have put it there in the 1890s. By 1891 neither Mile End North nor Mile End East had experienced the level of overcrowding, exacerbated by immigration, which had pushed rents up in St George's and in other parts of Mile End adjoining that district and Whitechapel. Both the census areas studied were within the eastern part of Mile End Old Town, which was said in 1901 to have 19.8% of its population living in overcrowded conditions compared to 27.4% in the western part of Mile End Old Town and 48% in St George's North Ward. See *RC Alien*, P.P. 1903 IX, App. Table XLIX. On rent differentials between areas, see also Wohl, *Eternal Slum*, 295–6.

The average rent paid by an artisan on the register in Mile End North for '3.8 rooms' is likely to have been very little different to that paid by the artisan in St George's for an average '3.1 rooms', that is, from around 6s. 6d. to 7s. Similarly, the closeness of the ranges of rents given by the Board of Trade for two rooms in St George's, and three rooms in outer Mile End suggest that there would have been not a great deal more to pay for the labourer voter's average 3.7 rooms in Mile End North compared to his 2.5 rooms in St George's—perhaps 6s. 6d. instead of 5s. 6d.

The Mile End East area was certainly more prosperous in terms of average accommodation size—an average accommodation of nearly four rooms for the labourers on the register was exceedingly large by East End standards—but even these figures would suggest an average rent for labourer and artisan voters of 7s. to 7s. 6d. for the 'middle' zone.

So across the three areas the *average* rents for householder voters probably ranged between 5s. 6d. and 7s. for labourers and 6s. 6d. and 7s. 6d. for artisans. These two occupational groups made up close to half the householder voters in all the areas. This relatively limited range in average rents for these voters between very poor and comparatively well-off areas is an important point.

The overall consistency of voters between the areas is best shown by the fact quoted earlier, that 66 per cent of all householder voters in St George's were living in three rooms or more, an astonishing figure for one of the poorer, and high-rent, areas. From the evidence of rent relativities above, we can see that this compares reasonably well to the 75 per cent of householder voters in Mile End North who lived in four or more rooms, or the 89 per cent who did so in Mile End East.

Undoubtedly, in the area of Mile End East analysed there were more 'wealthy' voters on the register than in St George's. But the important point is that the majority of voters across the areas can be seen to have been relatively consistent in their economic circumstances, and that their circumstances indeed seem quite prosperous. This consistency in the average standing of voters in the poorer and wealthier areas of the East End is significant for the themes taken up in other chapters. It suggests, again, that localized, rather than directly economic, differences may have been more important in determining the political variations between areas of the East End.

The consistency between areas, in this 'core', relatively well-off, group of voters is understandable, given that the electoral register was being drawn generally from the most prosperous sections of each area. Although the extent of poverty in each may have varied widely, there appears to have been within each area of the East End a relatively consistent 'top' section of the society. This is shown in Booth's figures. Comparing the total registration districts of St George's and Mile End, for example, he found that in St George's 29 per cent of the population were very poor or in receipt of irregular earnings (Classes A to C). In Mile End this figure was only 14 per cent. But in the categories of 'Highly Paid Work' and 'Lower Middle Class' (Classes F and G) he found the difference between these areas was only 13 per cent against 19 per cent. It was those in these categories—along with the better paid of the very large group Booth calls Class E immediately below them—who would have provided much of the 'core' of householder voters in both areas. In fact, the consistency in the size of these 'Classes F and G' was remarkable across the areas of the East End, according to Booth's figures. In Shoreditch they were 13 per cent of the population, in Bethnal Green 14 per cent; Whitechapel 16 per cent; Stepney (Limehouse) 18 per cent; Poplar 17 per cent.[43]

How principal tenants could differ from the rest of the population in an area was also shown in Bethnal Green, where Booth's investigator found that, in the poorer areas, 'Most of these houses are taken by a better class workman or artizan, who occupies one or two rooms himself, and sub-lets the others.'[44] In a report for Christopher Addison, the Liberal member for Hoxton, on housing conditions in his constituency, it was suggested that it was a 'Mistake to think or speak of the "typical slum-dweller". In the same street (and in the same house very often) may be found families quite well-to-do and also families in the extreme of poverty and filth . . . A street average of earnings tells nothing, a house average, where there are 4 or 5 families in the house, little.'[45] With households of quite different economic circumstances, even within the same occupational group and in the same house, it is quite clear from the earlier evidence which tenant would be more likely to gain the vote.

But the point made earlier, that labourers and other generally poorer occupational groups were not markedly under-represented in the registers, seems to conflict with this argument. This is largely explained by the fact that there were essentially two distinct categories amongst working-class male householder voters. First, there were those men—the majority of parliamentary voters as described above—who simply because of their employment situation could afford accommodation, as required, that was generally much larger and more expensive than that in which most of the working class in the area lived.

[43] Booth, *Life*, 1st series, vol. 1, 36.   [44] Booth MSS B316, 9.
[45] 'Housing Notes' [*c.*1910], Addison Papers, Bodleian Library, Oxford, Box 84, File No. 2 6ce3, 2.

The second, smaller, group of working-class householder voters were those who were able to live in large enough accommodation to be on the register only because they had older or adult children living with them. They most typically moved to larger accommodation as their children became older, began work, and could contribute to this larger rent. This second group of voters included a larger percentage of those in lower-status occupations, such as labourers. This process is well described by Arthur Harding, who told how in 1902, as he and his sister started to earn money and contribute to the family budget, the Hardings 'moved to Queen's Buildings . . . We were a wee bit higher in the social ladder. We paid 7s. 6d. rents—at Bacon Street the rents was much smaller, 2s. 9d. or 3s. My mother said we'd have to look a bit more respectable . . . the people were more posh around here.'[46] As Jose Harris notes, the contribution of working-age children 'to the domestic budget was the single most powerful factor that could raise a working-class family into affluence and comfort'.[47] (And possibly lift the father into the status of voter.[48])

Although only 24 per cent of all labourer household heads in St George's had working-age children living with them, such men constituted 46 per cent of labourers on the householders electoral register. This group of voters did not necessarily need to be in as secure an employment situation to gain the right to vote. These men gained the vote not because they had always been in a better individual economic position, like those in the first group of voters, but instead could be said to have had the responsibility of voting thrust upon them as their children reached adulthood.

Labourers, in particular, found this to be the case. The highest level of enfranchisement amongst the labourers in St George's was for those aged 51 to 60, and in fact this was higher than for artisans in this age group, the only age group where that was the case. The reason for this seems to be that the adult children of labourers stayed at home longer for economic reasons, and so there were *more* adult children in the family group at a time, requiring larger accommodation. This same factor would mean, of course, a likely lower enfranchisement rate amongst the male children of labourers in the younger adult age groups. Enfranchisement levels for labourers dropped somewhat after the age of 40 for those without children, because the earning capacity of heavy manual labourers declined as they aged. So at that stage of life the importance of adult children for family welfare became even

---

[46] Samuel, *East End Underworld*, 62–3.

[47] Harris, *Private Lives*, 71. See also Lummis, *Labour Aristocracy*, 150.

[48] In addition, also possibly changing the family's social milieu—seen to be of importance in a later chapter.

greater. Variations in enfranchisement levels for labourers with different family structures are shown in Table 6.

TABLE 6. *Householder voters as a percentage of all those with the same parental status, by age. St George's-in-the-East, North ward, labourer household heads*

Age	% age on householder voter register of all		
	Married—no children	With children	Adult children at home
31–40	26	40	53
41–50	19	29	59
51–60	21	40	75

So one group—of poorer voters in particular—was gaining the vote at a relatively late age. A significant aspect of this was that these voters had not had to make an electoral choice earlier in their lives. This point is important politically, because of the apparent importance of the longevity of party attachment in the political responses of voters. The work of David Butler and Donald Stokes makes this point strongly. They argue that younger voters are more likely to switch allegiances on the basis of either national political trends or very localized factors. But they also state that:

There is evidence that what determines the strength and unchangeability of partisan ties is not so much the voter's age in years as the duration of his attachment to one party. Younger voters tend to be more plastic because their party preferences tend to be more recent. But older voters who have supported a party for as brief a time prove to be just as weak and changeable in their partisanship.[49]

Those who were becoming voters in their forties and fifties because of their move with adult children to larger accommodation had not had to choose parties in elections before this. Butler and Stokes argue that it is the process of having to choose that is very important in hardening party allegiances. The more often this is done, the stronger the partisanship.[50]

A significant point regarding all pre-1918 voters is that they were on the register, on average, for a much shorter time than those under modern universal franchise provisions. This was particularly the case for less

---

[49] D. Butler and D. Stokes, *Political Change in Britain: Forces Shaping Electoral Choice* (1971), 79–80. See also I. Crewe, 'The Politics of "Affluent" and "Traditional" Workers in Britain: An Aggregate Data Analysis', *British Journal of Political Science*, 3 (Jan. 1973), 33, and Tanner, 'Class Voting', 115.

[50] Butler and Stokes, *Political Change*, 81.

prosperous voters such as those noted above, many of whom came on to the register as their children reached adulthood. But voters generally before the First World War, at least in London, gained the vote only as their family size increased (and indeed probably as their own earning capacity increased with work experience). It is possible to calculate the maximum average period of voters on the register from their age breakdown. For the St George's North area, for all non-labourer voters this period was around twenty years, suggesting that the total electorate changed, on average, every four general elections, or that around 25 per cent of voters were new voters in each five-year cycle. But, as noted in Appendix 3, this method underestimates the rate of change, and it is more likely that the figure would have been closer to 33 per cent of new voters at each scheduled general election.[51]

But in the case of labourers and other poorer workers in that area, who, as noted above, often came onto the register at a later age than other voters, the average period was somewhat shorter, at just over sixteen years. This suggests, with all the relevant factors taken into account, that perhaps up to 40 per cent of labourer voters at each general election in St George's North were new voters. In terms of what could affect the way they voted, this is likely to have been extremely significant.

These profiles of the two groups of voters can greatly assist our understanding of electoral politics in the East End. The householder voters, although occupationally still representative in broad terms of their areas, varied from the average in a number of ways. First, for perhaps at least three-quarters of them, they were not the poorest, and more clearly represented the better-paid section of each occupational category. The socio-economic standing of such voters seems to have been surprisingly consistent across areas in the East End. Second, other voters were those who were not as economically advantaged, but who had become voters late because their children began to bring money into the household. These facts, as touched upon above, suggest strongly the importance of localism and non-party influences in East End politics.

These profiles appear to represent a common pattern for householder voters in the East End. But there certainly was not an absolute consistency in the way the franchise system worked across all areas. Some inconsistencies occurred because of variations in housing stock. Quite obviously, given the importance of being the 'principal tenant', if all tenants were sole occupiers of, say, small two-roomed houses, then universal male enfranchisement would have been much closer. This can be seen through variations

---

[51] See Appendix 3 for a discussion of the method of calculation of these figures.

within the areas analysed. In Waterloo Place, which contained two-roomed houses in a poor part of St George's, each with a single household occupying, of fourteen male household heads, twelve were on the electoral register, an 86 per cent enfranchisement. There were eight labourer household heads amongst the fourteen, and every one of these eight was on the register.[52]

By comparison, a labourer may have taken, for much the same sort of cost as a house in Waterloo Place,[53] two rooms sub-let in a divided house of five or six rooms, and most likely not have been able to gain the vote. As an example, in Sheridan Street, St George's, many of the houses were of five or six rooms, and many were divided into three or even four tenements. Of seventy-three male household heads in part of that street, only sixteen were on the register as householder/occupiers. Of thirty-five labourer household heads, only five were registered occupier voters. Even of those labourers in tenements of two rooms or more, paying probably as much as those in Waterloo Place, only one-third were registered. So becoming enfranchised was based both upon what one could afford and also on the dominant housing conditions in the area in which one lived. Those 'lucky' enough to live in areas of smaller houses usually had a much greater chance of getting on the electoral register.

The importance of housing type and size in the franchise process added another very localized dimension to political dynamics before the First World War. It is difficult to demonstrate the effect of this across broader areas than individual streets, as housing types and conditions did vary enormously even within small sections of the East End. But, interestingly, two areas stood out in the East End for their unusual housing stock and a high level of enfranchisement, and, significantly, also a generally high level of support for progressive politics in this period. These areas were Poplar and part of Bethnal Green.

Between 1891 and 1901 the constituencies of Poplar and Bethnal Green South West had the highest level of householder voter enfranchisement of any of the East End seats. Bethnal Green South West averaged over 46 per cent of its adult male population as *householder* voters across this period.[54] Poplar

[52] Separate two-room cottage accommodation did not imply that an area was better off in any part of the East End. See also *Public Health*, 2: 20 (Dec. 1889), 244, and *Select Committee on Artizans' and Labourers' Dwellings' Improvement*, P.P. 1881 VII, qq. 93–4.

[53] Compare 15—a description of Yule Court, St George's—with 9 and 23 in Booth MSS B333.

[54] Across Britain, borough *householder* voter enfranchisement in this period was between 52% and 55%. See McKibbin et al., 'Franchise', 75–6, in conjunction with *Return Relating to Parliamentary Constituencies*, P.P. 1901 LIX, p. 126.

had the next highest level, averaging around 43 per cent across the period. The reason why these two areas had higher levels of enfranchisement for householder voters may have been that the houses in many parts of these constituencies were smaller than in most areas of the East End, this meaning that there were fewer tenants per house and so a greater percentage of the population were principal tenants.

The deputy town clerk of Poplar told the Poor Law Commissioners in 1908, in reference to the large Stepney borough, that there 'you do not get the same number of small houses occupied as in Poplar or Bethnal Green'.[55] In this context, 'small houses' meant those with four rooms or fewer.[56] Small houses were relatively common in poor waterfront areas.[57] Parts of St George's also had small houses, but the rents in that area were so high that even these houses were usually let to very many tenants.[58] But Poplar seems to have had many more of them, and rents were low enough in that area, being further from inner London, to allow for less subdivision within the houses, and also for relatively less prosperous workers to take the risk of renting these whole houses as principal tenants, and sub-letting. A four-roomed house in Poplar in 1897 could be had for 4s. 6d. per week upwards, and again, 'in many cases the tenants of four-roomed houses sub-let one or more of the rooms'[59]—in this case, most likely both upstairs rooms. The dock labourer who may have taken the house, and sub-let part, perhaps to a workmate, could have been the principal tenant, and the compounded ratepayer, for 3s. or so a week.

Two-roomed houses were also available in Poplar, and in St George's, as noted above, but that size of house was far more common in Bethnal Green, at least before the turn of the century. Booth said that, in 'Bethnal Green are found the old weavers' houses . . . In some cases the houses had originally only one room on each floor; and each floor, partitioned, now accommodates its family.'[60] It was reported in 1888 that there remained in Bethnal Green 'many two-roomed houses occupied by one family'.[61] Duckworth

[55] *RC Poor Laws*, P.P. 1910 XLIX, q. 95782.

[56] See Booth MSS B331, 'Poplar', 11–17, and T. Burke, *The Wind and the Rain* (1924), 15, for examples of areas of small houses in Poplar.

[57] See description of Bermondsey in the *Board of Trade Enquiry*, P.P. 1908 CVII, p. 407.

[58] See Booth's description of area 74c, *Life*, 1st series, vol. 2, App. 30.

[59] See Booth MSS B331 'Poplar', 15; and see also W. Southgate, *That's the Way it Was* (Oxted, 1982), 20, for Bethnal Green; and *Board of Trade Enquiry*, P.P. 1908 CVII, p. 418.

[60] Booth, *Life*, 1st series, vol. 1, p. 71. They were also common in Spitalfields of course, but the size of the immigrant population there meant that this fact was less relevant for franchise purposes.

[61] *Report of an Inquiry as to the Immediate Sanitary Requirements of the Parish of St Matthew, Bethnal Green*, P.P. 1888 LXXXI, p. 539.

found a number of small weavers' houses there still in 1898, mainly in the south-west corner of the borough and on the boundary with Spitalfields. A local-government representative in Bethnal Green said in 1898 that it 'is a peculiarity of Bethnal Green that we have a multitude of little houses—little boxes you might call them'.[62] Two-roomed dwellings averaged 5s. per week rent for the house.[63] Four-roomed cottages were also very common. Walter Southgate reported that North Street, Bethnal Green, where he was a child in the 1890s, comprised around 100 cottages all of a similar pattern, each having 'four rooms, two up and two down'. The Tent Street area of Bethnal Green was said to be 'composed entirely of streets of two, three and four-roomed cottages'.[64]

Again, like Poplar, relatively poorer inhabitants could afford to take a small house in Bethnal Green, having to pay perhaps 4s. or 5s. a week, and possibly as low as 3s. or less when part was sub-let. For this sum they could become enfranchised ratepayers. These factors may suggest at least part of the reason why both Poplar and Bethnal Green had relatively high percentages of their adult male population as householder voters, at least until the turn of the century. In Bethnal Green different factors, such as large-scale Jewish immigration, came into play after that time, as did the replacement of small houses by block dwellings.[65] By 1911 Bethnal Green had 16 per cent of its population housed in block dwellings, with Stepney not far behind this figure with 13 per cent and Shoreditch with 8.5 per cent. Poplar at that time still had only 3.5 per cent of its population in blocks.

These factors again emphasize the importance of gaining a very detailed local understanding before conclusions are reached as to whose opinions voting patterns in parts of the East End, or other parts of London, represented.

This chapter has been fundamentally concerned with the issue of identifying exactly who gained a place on the East End electoral registers, and the implications of this for our perceptions of politics in the area, rather than with the details of why many East Enders did not obtain the vote. But it is clear that the effects of multiple occupation, sub-letting, and owner negligence significantly reduced the number of men eligible for the householder parliamentary vote, and that this meant that the 'lodger' franchise was the only voting option remaining for perhaps half the adult males in these areas.

[62] *London City Mission Magazine*, 63 (Apr. 1898), 65.
[63] See Booth MSS B350, 3 and 131, and B351, 149, 167, and 213.
[64] Southgate, *That's the Way*, 18, and *London City Mission Magazine*, 54 (Apr. 1889), 70.
[65] See the following chapter regarding block dwellings.

However, it was also too difficult for many of them to meet this franchise's requirements.

Lodger voters comprised 12.4 per cent of parliamentary voters in the East End seats in 1894, and were 13.5 per cent of voters across London in 1911 (the other significant separate category was 'service' voters, who were only a handful in these areas). The requirements to become a lodger voter were so rigorous that the category has become well known by Neal Blewett's phrase as a 'mere agent's franchise'.[66]

Potential lodger voters essentially were those tenants who had not been placed on the ratepayers' list, and so were perhaps 50 per cent of adult males in the East End. But there were a number of difficulties in becoming a lodger voter. These have been very well described by others but, briefly, lodger voters were required to make a new application to remain on the register each year, had much tighter restrictions on their ability to move from place to place within the twelve-month franchise-qualifying period, and had to be living in a dwelling with a rateable value, unfurnished, of at least £10. How this last condition was interpreted varied. But, as Blewett and others have argued, it was the organizational ability of local parties that often determined how many lodger voters there would be in the constituency.[67]

Blewett's description of the 'agent's franchise' seems to be confirmed by the situation in 1891 in the area around Bloomfield Road, Mile End East, where registration levels seem most liable to have been affected by personal influences, probably of a party operative resident in the area.[68] On the side of Bloomfield Road which was within the census area analysed, a very high 55 per cent of adult males were enfranchised, and an astonishing 40 per cent of these voters were 'lodgers'. In the three enumeration districts within the neighbourhood of Bloomfield Road, a total of 29 per cent of voters were lodger voters. As mentioned above, the average in London, even in the later period, was 13.5 per cent, and in the other areas of the East End examined the percentage ranged from 6 to 15 per cent of voters being lodger voters.

---

[66] Blewett, 'Franchise', 40–1. See McKibbin et al., 'Franchise', 80, and Davis and Tanner, 'The Borough Franchise', 326. This franchise was it seems, however, first described in this way by Charles Seymour in *Electoral Reform in England and Wales: The Development and Operation of the Parliamentary Franchise, 1832–1885* (1915; repr. Newton Abbot, 1970), 381.

[67] See Blewett, 'Franchise', 41–3.

[68] See RG12/313 Mile End Old Town Enumeration District No. 42. It seems most likely that John Bartlett, who lived at 2 Bloomfield Road and was described in the census as a 'canvasser', was a party worker.

Those who became lodger voters in the East End areas generally followed the same occupations as those on the householders' register, as shown in Table 7. But there were two major exceptions to this. First, quite obviously shopkeepers and publicans were not likely to be lodger voters, as their premises would without doubt be rated. The very low figure for this group as lodger voters shows this. But in class terms this was more than compensated for by the very high percentage of white-collar workers amongst the lodger voters. This reflects a very large number of young clerks taking lodgings, after moving away from home very early in their working life. Comparing the economic position of lodger voters to householder voters by means of their average accommodation size is difficult, given that some number of lodger voters were young males living at home with their parents (if they occupied a separate section of the home), and that generally many were single and so, regardless of income, needed less accommodation

TABLE 7. *Occupational comparison by voter type. All three census areas*

Occupational group	As % age of population or voters in category		
	% age of adult male pop.	% age of householder voters	% age of lodger voters
Labourers	26.9	20.3	20.8
Artisans			
Building	7.9	10.0	10.0
Furniture	3.0	3.7	1.3
Footware	3.1	2.3	1.3
Metal	8.0	9.9	7.5
Textiles	4.2	4.4	3.8
Total artisans	26.2	30.3	23.9
Shopkeepers, publicans	3.6	8.3	1.3
Cabmen, carmen	8.9	7.2	5.8
Watermen/foremen etc.	6.3	7.5	7.9
Shop workers/food industry/messengers	9.3	7.1	11.3
Professionals/white-collar	10.0	11.1	20.8
Home workers	2.3	2.4	2.9
Hawkers etc.	1.4	1.8	0.4
Miscellaneous	1.1	1.3	1.3
Policemen/soldiers	0.9	0.9	0.4
Not given	2.8	2.2	3.3

space. Also, by definition, those families who needed large accommodation would be much more likely *not* to be living with a resident landlord, and instead be principal tenants and potential householder voters. The most effective comparison in this regard is between voters married but with no children, and this shows that the average number of rooms taken by those on the lodger register was somewhat higher than that for non-voters, but slightly below that for those who had made it onto the householder register. We can assume that the lodger voters, on average, probably represented the next financial 'slice' below the householder voters in each occupational group.

In terms of rent paid, the £10 rateable value for the dwelling occupied by the lodger was interpreted in most areas as meaning that the yearly rental (or assumed rental) needed to total £10—therefore just under 4s. a week[69]—and so this was a minimum rental for lodger voters. But even this was significantly above, for example, the average rental paid by those labourers in St George's who were not on the register.

In the Mile End East area, which was seen above to have had an extraordinarily wide range of lodger voters, the average-size accommodation in which they lived was perhaps somewhat closer to the average for those not on the register in the area. It can be assumed that in Mile End East the lodger voters were therefore more socially representative of the area. By working harder on this issue, it seems that party officials had perhaps reached 'below' the economic level of the usual voters. But this, to some extent, would have only been possible because the Mile End East area studied was generally somewhat more prosperous than, say, St George's, and more 'lodgers' would have met the basic rental requirements for the franchise. But the work of the officials would certainly still have been needed to 'shepherd' them through the process. In most other parts of the East End, it seems, lodger voters were nearly as unrepresentative of the population as the householder voters.

All the factors above are difficult to compare from area to area, but variations within them undoubtedly played a complex role in helping to determine some of the differences at a local level in voting patterns and support. The importance of specific housing type and size in gaining the vote, in particular, suggests that there was indeed what John Davis calls a 'random and vexatious' nature to some aspects of the franchise.[70] But there was also an overall consistency in how the franchise operated in terms of the social

---

[69] There seems to have been some variations to this. See evidence in *RC Poor Laws*, P.P. 1910 XLIX, qq. 91670 and 95747 and App. No. XXXIII(B), and *East London Advertiser*, 18 Nov. 1905, p. 8 col.a.

[70] Davis, 'Slums and the Vote', 388.

structure of the register, and the great majority of voters were from the most prosperous and regularly employed sections of their occupation.

In the pre-war period no women were allowed the parliamentary vote, and few were able to gain the local-government franchise. Women comprised around 15 per cent of local-government voters. In the areas of the East End analysed, as noted above, there were around 200 female voters in Division 3 of the electoral register, indicating that they were on the county council register but not the parliamentary. The major criterion for inclusion in this division (there were a number of small special cases) was that they were woman—spinsters or widows only—who 'would have been entitled to vote at parliamentary elections . . . but for the fact that they were women'.[71] Essentially, the women who gained the local-government vote were again 'principal tenants', most commonly widows who had adult children living with them. In St George's and the Mile End areas, females on the register were living in accommodation of a size similar to, or larger than, that occupied by those male artisans on the register without adult children, indicating a similar, relatively prosperous family economic situation.[72] Again, because of their necessity to have working adult children to contribute to the rent to be a 'principal tenant'—or because they had been widowed only a short time—in most cases these women would not have been on the register for very long. Like their male counterparts who gained the vote as their children grew, it is likely that they would not have had a strong party-political allegiance.[73]

Of course, all arguments regarding the composition of the register are of little value unless that percentage of voters who actually cast a ballot in each election was representative of those on the register. There were, in fact, for East End parliamentary elections in this period, two issues that were overwhelmingly important in determining the percentage of voters who participated in each poll—'removals' from the constituency, and the apparent level of abstentions from voting by Liberal supporters.

---

[71] See *London Statistics, vol. 25, 1914–15*, 22. The other grounds for inclusion were: peers, who were excluded from the parliamentary vote; occupiers (owners of property) who lived between 7 and 15 miles from the parliamentary borough (7 miles being the parliamentary franchise limit); householders who had moved from one parliamentary borough to another but stayed within the county; married women who occupied qualifying property in respect of which their husbands were not qualified. In the East End areas there was not a large number of persons qualified under any of these categories.

[72] See also P. Hollis, *Ladies Elect: Women in English Local Government, 1865–1914* (Oxford, 1987), 31–2.

[73] Issues such as whether their husband had been on the register clearly could also be important here.

Voter turnouts did vary widely from election to election, and between and within constituencies. In parliamentary elections the percentage turnout in the East End seats averaged across the period in the low seventies, dropping into the sixties (or even lower) in 1885, 1886, and 1900 in particular, and peaking in the low eighties in 1906 and the two 1910 elections. Turnout was slightly lower than the average for the rest of London, although in some constituencies, notably St George's, turnouts were always amongst the best in the metropolis.[74]

The effect of 'removals', a voter shifting out of the area between the time of the drawing up of the register and an election, was an issue of great concern to election agents. It is commonly argued that in London 20–30 per cent of voters may have moved before an election was held on the relevant register, a figure consistent with the evidence from East End seats.[75] It was said that poll turnouts in London were lower than in the counties, because 'many of the London electors have but a slender hold on their residence'.[76] Undoubtedly, many voters had moved before being called to exercise their vote. But usually a great deal of effort went into tracing these voters, and the parties could be very successful in this task.[77] In 1910 it appears that the parties in St George's were able to trace more than 50 per cent of removals,[78] and such results seem to have been achieved in other constituencies earlier in the period, although there is probably little doubt that party efficiency improved as time went on.[79] The fact that party workers suggested that the locally 'available' vote (that is, excluding removals, etc.) could be maximized at about a 90 per cent turnout indicates that an overall percentage turnout in the mid- to high seventies represented at least half of the removals being brought to vote.[80] This

---

[74] See e.g. *East London Observer*, 20 July 1895, p. 6 col.c., and *East London Advertiser*, 9 Mar. 1895, p. 5 col.f.

[75] See Thompson, *Socialists, Liberals and Labour*, 72; Blewett, 'Franchise', 36–7; and e.g. *East End News*, 3 Oct. 1892; *Daily Telegraph*, 28 July 1908; *Morning Leader*, 11 Jan. 1910; and *The Times*, 25 July 1911, p. 13. Thompson's quoted evidence from the *Daily News*, of 4,000 removals out of 8,000 voters in Haggerston in 1906, seems excessive against the other evidence.

[76] J. E. Thorold Rogers, 'Confessions of a Metropolitan Member', *Contemporary Review*, 51 (May 1887), 687.

[77] See *The Times*, 25 July 1911, p. 13 and *Daily Herald*, 22 Nov. 1912, Tower Hamlets Local History Collection, Bancroft Library, cuttings file 321.5.

[78] Press cutting, Feb. 1910, newspaper unknown, Stansgate Papers, House of Lords Record Office, ST/11, cuttings 17.

[79] See *East End News*, 3 Oct. 1892, and *East London Advertiser*, 6 Aug. 1892, p. 8 col.b, which show that despite a large numbers of removals in Poplar and Stepney, high polls were achieved. See Davis and Tanner, 'The Borough Franchise', 318, on party efficiency generally in tracing potential voters.

[80] See the comments of E. H. Kerwin, agent for F. N. Charrington in Mile End in 1892: 'I do not think we could have polled many more at Single Street; they came up splendidly, street

percentage turnout was achieved in St George's, Stepney, Poplar, and Lime-house in the Liberal victory of 1892. Whitechapel, Mile End, Bethnal Green North East, and Bow and Bromley were only marginally behind these figures. The overall percentage votes in the low to mid-eighties in 1906–10 suggest even more effective work.

But of course in general, the whole question of 'removals' is only relevant to the analysis of electoral results if it meant that there was a substantial dif-ference between the social composition of the total electoral registers and the group who actually voted. Politicians of the time disagreed over who was more likely to move in the cities, and indeed, for whom those 'removed' would have been likely to vote. Liberals argued that the artisans, whom they claimed as supporters, were 'more migratory than any other human being . . . But the permanent Tory elector of the poorer classes is generally on the spot.'[81] Conservatives argued, conversely, that large numbers of re-movals in the cities were to their advantage, because they were 'in the vast majority of cases the lower classes of citizen, and the unskilled labour people—and their absence from the poll is to be desired as they are not of our kidney at all'.[82]

Some historians have asserted, similarly, that it was the 'classic slum-mies' who were the most 'frequent flitters'.[83] The evidence earlier in the chapter suggests that the poorest tenants were far less likely to be on the electoral register, and so this last factor would have had little impact on turnouts. But indeed, there is little doubt that all sections of the working class were relatively mobile in this period, even if that meant only moving between adjoining streets or even houses or rooms.[84] David Englander has shown that frequent removal 'was not restricted to the lowest stratum . . . The high rate of residential mobility in part represented the respectable

after street had 90 per cent of voters', *East London Advertiser*, 12 Mar. 1892, p. 8. Method of calculation: average 25–30% removals, leaving 70–5% 'available' × 90% turnout = 63.0–67.5%. Assuming some of the 'removals' were dead, then a 50% recovery of removals would have added 12% to the poll = 75.0–79.5% overall turnout. See also the com-ments of the Liberal candidate for Stepney, *East London Advertiser*, 6 Aug. 1892, p. 8 col.b.

[81] Rogers, 'Confessions', 687. Seymour also makes this point: 'the Radicals have long com-plained that the franchise is often a myth, and that thousands of the best citizens are effectu-ally deprived of their rights, while the stationary classes of the slums are favoured', *Electoral Reform*, 318.

[82] Letter from Powell-Williams to Joseph Chamberlain, 15 May 1892, Balfour Papers, British Library Add. MSS 49773, fo. 41, quoted in E. H. H. Green, 'Radical Conservatism: The Electoral Genesis of Tariff Reform', *Historical Journal*, 28: 3 (1985), 680.

[83] McKibbin, et al., 'Franchise', 69.

[84] See Booth, *Life*, 1st series, vol. 1, pp. 26–7, and Davis and Tanner, 'The Borough Fran-chise', 317–18. For examples, see A. Linton, *Not Expecting Miracles* (1982), and E. M. Page, 'No Green Pastures II', *East London Papers* (Winter 1966), *passim*.

working man trying to remain respectable'. He quotes the view of a Poor Law official who thought that the 'better class of artisans' moved very often, as 'it was the only chance of getting repairs done'. They would move across the street if a house became vacant that had just been put into repair.[85] Localized moving would not have been as significant a problem for the party organization, or the committed voter, as long as they met the franchise residence requirements, although it is possible that some voters tried hard to hide their new address because of unfinished business with their previous landlord.[86]

It seems unlikely that there was a common pattern whereby the actual vote at elections was skewed by the fact that a particular group of working-class voters was more likely to have 'removed' and not voted. But it is likely that working-class voters were generally more mobile than the shopkeepers and similar individuals who did form a significant part of the electorate in some seats, such as St George's. Those shopkeepers and middle class who did move may also perhaps have been easier for the parties to trace.[87] This, at least in a minor way, would have tended to emphasize the importance of this group in the vote. But this may have been countered, to some extent, by the fact that poorer workers with adult children living at home, as discussed earlier, may also have been one of the least likely groups to move, given the complications of a number of family occupations. That, for example, over 80 per cent of all those on the register voted in *all* the East End constituencies in the 1910 elections (up to 86 per cent in St George's), and that turnouts close to this were achieved in various elections earlier in the period, suggests that 'removals' were not the primary cause of small votes. From the calculations noted above, we can suggest that untraceable removals generally reduced the poll by not much more than 10 per cent of the register. Given that the 'removals' were unlikely to have been overwhelmingly skewed to one side of politics, the percentage effect on the results was not large.

Much more significant politically were the very low voter turnouts of 60 per cent or less at some elections up to 1900. As was mentioned earlier in relation to 1886, these were largely the result of other factors, and in particular the abstention of Liberal supporters from voting. This factor will be discussed in greater detail in a following chapter, but it is useful here to give a brief summary of the evidence suggesting that variations in turnouts were political in nature, rather than functional.

---

[85] D. Englander, *Landlord and Tenant in Urban Britain 1838–1918* (Oxford, 1983), 8–9.
[86] See ibid. 9–10.
[87] See Thompson, *Socialists, Liberals and Labour*, 72.

The importance of abstention generally in election results in this period has been emphasized by a number of historians. David Dutton, for example, has argued the significance of the fact that 'it was a feature of the Liberal party's electoral support between 1885 and 1910 that its vote fluctuated sharply, while by contrast that of the Unionists remained relatively stable even in 1906', and that victories for either side were not caused by 'mass conversions' from one party to the other.[88] Most East End seats followed this pattern closely. The Mile End constituency showed the best example of a stable, solid Conservative vote. Its average Conservative vote across the eight elections in the twenty-two years 1885–1906 was 2,239. The lowest Conservative vote in this period was 2,091 (in 1885) and the highest 2,440 (in 1900). So the variation from the average was only −7 per cent and +9 per cent. This was a rock-solid vote. The Liberal vote in this seat, on the other hand, fluctuated dramatically at times, going as low as 1,280 in 1886 and 1,516 in 1895, and being maximized in 1906 at 2,295. It varied each side of the average by −30 per cent and +26 per cent. The situation in Limehouse was similar, with the Conservative vote varying around the average by only +12 per cent and −15 per cent, while, for example, the Liberal vote in 1906 was nearly double that of 1885. Of other seats, the figures in St George's and Stepney, for example, are harder to calculate, due to the declining size of their total electorates as a result of immigration, but broadly the patterns are the same. These figures demonstrate that the social 'representativeness' of voting patterns in the East End was dependent not only upon the effects of the franchise requirements, but also upon the political fickleness of many potential Liberal voters. Who these may have been is, again, discussed in a later chapter.

This chapter has attempted to put into context the electoral evidence from the East End constituencies in this period. It has demonstrated that voting patterns in the East End should be seen as more closely representative of the views of the most prosperous within each area of East London. But there was also an overall consistency across areas in the economic circumstances of voters, which suggests that the obvious variations in electoral results between constituencies or wards may be best explained by localized or other factors rather than broad economic or class circumstances. This is further emphasized by the shorter time that voters remained on the registers in this period, particularly a significant group of poorer voters who gained the vote quite late in age. This suggests, as well,

---

[88] D. Dutton, *'His Majesty's Loyal Opposition': The Unionist Party in Opposition, 1905–1915* (Liverpool, 1992), 2. See also Green, 'Radical Conservatism', 678–9.

3

'Politics stirs them very little'

'COMIN' DAHN 'ERE TALKIN' ABOUT SLUMS!'

In an oft-quoted and influential statement, Alexander Paterson said of the working men in riverside London that:

Politics stirs them very little . . . They have but the vaguest notion of the issues before the country, or the meaning of party catchwords. Old scandals sink deep and live for ever; anything that affects the reputation of the candidate is likely to prove a more potent influence than the gravest flaw in his cause . . . from the muddle of party cries and untrue scandals he plucks a tangled skein which he calls opinion, and is whirled away in a motor-car by a grateful party.

Stedman Jones uses this statement as a key piece of evidence in arguing for the existence of 'political apathy among the unskilled and the poor' in London.[1] But this connection certainly cannot be made very directly, given that there was a relatively small number of the poor amongst working-class voters, as we saw in the previous chapter.

Yet the lack of party-political commitment implied by Paterson does sit well with the view, also put in that chapter, that amongst poorer voters in particular there may have existed little allegiance to party, with this being at least partly as a result of the relatively short time that they were on the electoral register. Paterson is, in fact, suggesting that such limited party allegiance was widespread amongst working-class voters, and that its effect was indeed to encourage an excessive interest in the 'personal' and 'scandal' above policies.

But if this was the case, such interest in the personal behaviour of candidates need not automatically also suggest the ideological apathy argued by Stedman Jones. It is possible, as will be argued below, that this interest in fact indicated a very active awareness of the social and economic position of the working class, and also of at least one way in which they could respond to this. It is worth analysing Paterson's comments more closely, and also comparing them to two widely differing statements describing the responses of the London working class to 'class' relations in the eighteenth and nineteenth centuries.

[1] Paterson, *Across the Bridges*, 215; Stedman Jones, 'Working-Class Culture', 214.

In describing the political struggles which took place upon the streets of eighteenth-century urban Britain, Edward Thompson emphasized the importance of symbolic victories. With how power was perceived being vital in the fragile balance that existed between the actions of rulers and the reactions of the crowd, Thompson says of 'mob' challenges to the elite that:

> the contest for symbolic authority may be seen, not as a way of acting out ulterior 'real' contests, but as a real contest in its own right. Plebian protest, on occasion, had no further objective than to challenge the gentry's hegemonic assurance, strip power of its symbolic mystifications, or even just to blaspheme. It was a contest for 'face', but the outcome of the contest might have material consequences.[2]

Margaret Loane, a district nurse in Edwardian London, said of her work with poor working-class mothers that:

> In dealing with the backward poor, one needs to recall the Chinese maxim as to the duty of 'saving a man's face', and in doing so long words are of incalculable value. If I told an umbrageous matron that her little daughter was troubled by pediculi, I always found her ready to adopt means of cure; if I had used a homelier term [lice], she would have vehemently denied the fact and utterly ignored my advice. I never told the careful housekeeper that the stuffiness of her rooms was mainly responsible for her children's anaemic condition; I spoke of the necessity for regular ventilation and occasional perflation.[3]

Any connection between the concepts of 'saving face' in these two passages may seem tenuous. But reading these statements in conjunction allows some alternative ways of thinking about working-class politics and thought. Evidence from the East End and elsewhere suggests that one constant in attitudes and responses across the working class was the desire for a measure of self-esteem.[4] Just as importantly, as we will see, this could encompass a striving for a feeling of at least symbolic empowerment in their dealings with the world, just as in Thompson's example of conflict on the streets.

Looking at the message implied in the domestic case described by Loane, there is little doubt that the mothers she spoke of knew that their children had lice. This fact was not going to change, regardless of Loane's use of a technical term. What seems more apparent is that these mothers were forcing Loane to act out a charade, however transparent to both sides, to 'equalize' the relationship between the poor mother and the middle-class visitor. The situation was transformed from one where the middle-class nurse was

---

[2] E. P. Thompson, 'Eighteenth-Century English Society: Class Struggle Without Class?', *Social History*, 3: 2 (May 1978), 159.

[3] M. Loane, *Neighbours and Friends* (1910), 83.

[4] See e.g. Joyce, *Visions*, 52–3 and 110–12.

coming in to 'cleanse' away the diseases caused only by working-class poverty and squalor, to one where the afflictions of the children were described in 'neutral', untainted, classless medical terms, discussed as equals between mother and nurse. This should be seen as an exercise in power by the mothers over the intruder, although one in which Loane willingly acquiesced.

Loane's writings provide numerous examples of this same type of 'equalization' by the poor. She noted that 'it rarely enters the mind of the poorest labourer to doubt that he is of as much consequence in heaven and on earth as his social superiors'. She encountered this belief in equality put directly in her own class terms: 'The one French word in frequent use among my patients is *dishabille* and to borrow from the advertiser's phrase-book, "it meets a felt want". A few days ago a repulsively dirty matron clasped me warmly by the hand, exclaiming "You're a lady like meself, though I'm a bit in my dishabeels".'[5] Loane was perhaps more sensitive than many to the acceptable social dealings of the working class. She advised new visiting nurses that: In all the preliminary conversation the voice should be lowered. Although the poor commonly speak to one another with what might be considered unnecessary loudness, they resent this tone in their social superiors, not only because it enables inquisitive neighbours to hear too much, but because they know it is not how a lady speaks to a friend.'[6]

In these examples, the women would be dealt with as 'equals' or not at all. Jerry White argues that in the extremely poor Campbell Bunk in Islington, after the First World War, 'egalitarianism' was one central plank of the residents' social and political views, based upon 'an alternative structure of self-esteem. This averred that Bunkites were as good as other people. When the young Walter Spencer wanted to leave a lunchtime gaming school in Campbell Road to return to work and his "Guvnor", another punter exclaimed, "Do what? You *got* no Guvnor!" No one owned you in that way, no one was your better, you were all equal.'[7]

The difficulty for the poor was, of course, to act out such a fundamental

<hr />

[5] Loane, *Neighbours*, 194 and 76. See Bailey, 'Bill Banks', 339, for the use of this term in this way.

[6] M. Loane, *Outlines of Routine in District Nursing* (1905), 141, quoted in R. McKibbin, 'Class and Poverty in Edwardian England', in his *The Ideologies of Class*, 180. See also the similar comments of Emilia Kanthack quoted in J. Lewis, 'The Working-Class Wife and Mother and State Intervention, 1870–1918', in J. Lewis (ed.), *Labour and Love: Women's Experience of Home and Family, 1850–1914* (Oxford, 1986), 111. On Loane generally, see McKibbin, 'Class and Poverty'.

[7] J. White, *The Worst Street in North London: Campbell Bunk, Islington, Between the Wars* (1986), 103.

belief in equality. Amongst the more fortunate working class, some were able to assert their 'independence' in the workplace to show they had control over their own lives. As John Rule describes the typical desire amongst skilled workmen earlier in the century for employers to respect them and have 'mutual regard', this 'proper treatment' included 'no interference in the way in which they did their work'.[8] In 1897 the Revd Richard Free said also of the very skilled East End working man that: 'Lofty independence in regard to the daily toil . . . is one of his most marked characteristics', and recounted the story of a 'typical' employee who had 'excellent places', but who 'left them one after another in the most reckless fashion. When I remonstrated, he would excuse himself thus: " 'E says I wasn't a doin' of it right. I says, 'Yus, I am'. 'E says, 'No, you ain't'. I says 'Very well, then, do it yourself'; an' aut I come".'[9]

But other workers clearly knew that they simply had no such option. The unemployed in Bethnal Green, said a London City Missionary in 1888, had 'a feeling of more than half developed indignation against the wealthy and well-to-do "who", they say, "do not care a rush for the worker at other times, so long as they can make labour machines of them when they happen to require their services"'.[10] The complete and arbitrary power of the foreman or the contractor in labour-crowded industries to overlook for employment a potential 'troublemaker' was clearly a disincentive for asserting independence or claiming 'respect'—an important issue that will be discussed further in the next chapter. James Welsh, an outspoken dock labourer, told the Sweating Select Committee that:

I do not think any notice reached the dock company itself as to my doings individually, but certain men are appointed in office in the position of contractors, foremen, and others, who think it is in their interest to do this sort of thing by preventing men of my description from working . . . I happened to be one of the particular kind they have a great objection to. Of course, whenever intelligence exists among men . . . however small it might appear, it is obnoxious.[11]

But it seems that perhaps equally galling for these workers was not only to have their independence taken from them, and be treated as a 'labour

---

[8] J. Rule, 'The Property of Skill in the Period of Manufacture', in P. Joyce (ed.), *The Historical Meanings of Work* (Cambridge, 1987), 109. See e.g. on the issue of 'independence', K. McClelland, 'Some Thoughts on Masculinity and the "Representative Artisan" in Britain, 1850–1880', *Gender and History*, 1: 2 (Summer 1989).

[9] R. Free, *Seven Years Hard* (1904), 79.

[10] *London City Mission Magazine*, 53 (Jan. 1888), 3.

[11] *SC Sweating*, P.P. 1888 XXI, q. 13036. See also the evidence of William Salter, *RC Labour*, P.P. 1892 XXXV, qq. 2823–4.

machine', unable to assert any 'intelligence', but also to be given constant reminders of the degraded, barely human state in which they were assumed by their 'superiors' to live. Their inferiority, not only socially and economically but also morally and spiritually, was commonly held up to them.

A workman in Poplar said of his pious and wealthy employer: 'Look what church does for 'er . . . Makes 'er 'ard on everybody what don't do like she does . . . it's people like 'er makes people ippacrits.'[12] A dock labourer complained that ' "Dock-rats", people call us . . . The public . . . "Only a dock-rat", that's what I've been called ever since I . . . became a docker'.[13] The quiet resentment of a group of unemployed East End workers in 1905 was clear, when they were asked by a social investigator whether it was true that the nation's current economic ills could be ascribed to 'the fact, as they very well knew, a few years ago, when trade, especially in the building trade, was prosperous, [that] the British workman . . . habitually scamped his work . . . and drank the better part of his wages[;] the visitor would be glad to know if the men there present were inclined to attribute any measure of the prevalent distress to the consequences of the conduct described. Dead silence.'[14] Such assumptions were clear amongst the 'old women and earnest young men from the Universities who want to leave the world better than they found it', who were described by Thomas Burke in Poplar as making the East End of London their 'hunting-ground', and causing the deep resentment of the working-class poor, 'who were the victims of the whims and theories of the educated'.[15] As Reynolds and the Wooleys described the response of the working class in Devon to exactly such visitors, there was 'a bitterness . . . when he is made to feel, without being able to distinguish or explain, a confusion of such attitudes hemming him in round about, each containing some good and more good intentions, coupled with a contempt mostly unspoken, but none the less perceptible'.[16]

These 'whims and theories', and their implied contempt, were hard to reject when they were applied in circumstances such as the relief of distress caused by unemployment. The strict application in the East End of the framework established by the Charity Organisation Society[17] for assessing an individual's need for relief was deeply resented by the local working class. The COS in Poplar was liked 'as the devil likes holy water . . . the

---

[12] Burke, *The Wind*, 49.
[13] John Law [Margaret Harkness], 'The Loafer: What Shall We Do With Him', *Labour Elector*, 21 Sept. 1889, p. 180.
[14] Cornford, *Canker*, 76–7. [15] Burke, *The Wind*, 26.
[16] S. Reynolds and B. and T. Wooley, *Seems So! A Working Class View of Politics* (1911), 286.
[17] See Stedman Jones, *Outcast London*, Part III.

enquiries make them averse to it'.[18] George Acorn in Bethnal Green thought that this and similar bodies were 'mysterious inquisitors, whose one object was to get us all into the workhouse'.[19] Another put the common, and not unexpected, view that the hatred of the local Poor Law and its judgements 'is a bitter instinct among the men'.[20] The harshness of rules applied by local committees—such as the practices of making unemployed men from common lodging houses 'disappear' from lists of those requiring support, as noted earlier, or the provision of relief only for married men[21]— was felt by many. For such bodies, for example, '[w]e of the lodging-house are outcasts', said Alexander Paterson; belittled and inferior like the resentful 'dock-rats' mentioned above.[22]

As Stedman Jones has argued, the continuing efforts of the COS and other bodies to promote 'respectability' amongst the London poor were relatively futile.[23] They achieved little except an increased perception by the poor of a patronizing attitude accorded to them by the 'old women and earnest young men'. Poorer workers and their families did often accept the conditions imposed by charities and other groups (often in relation to such requirements as their children attending Sunday or day schools), but fitted only by necessity into the models expected of them.[24] Interestingly, Michael Childs has written on the effects of such school attendance that:

As a formative influence, the school could not compete with the omni-present realities of working-class life in the home, the street and the workplace. Social control, or ideological indoctrination by the middle class, paradoxically had little overt success because of the pervasive economic control exercised by the same class and because of the responses to this environment created by the working-class family.[25]

Women at home, as we saw above, in such responses to the middle-class visitors they encountered could exhibit a greater degree of control, and in their reactions had less at stake, than those in the workplace or the relief queue. They therefore had the ability to exercise a form of power, and to force an at least symbolic 'equalization' of their relationship with visitors

---

[18] The Revd W. Joynes, Minister of Cotton Street Bapist Church, Poplar, Booth MSS B171, 34.

[19] G. Acorn, One of the Multitude (1911), 80.

[20] 'A.P', 'The Common Lodging House—III', 94.

[21] Board of Trade Report on the Unemployed, P.P. 1893–94 LXXXII, p. 620.

[22] 'A.P', 'The Common Lodging House—III', 95, and see Toynbee, 'A Winter's Experiment', 56.

[23] Stedman Jones, 'Working-Class Culture', 202.

[24] See Free, Seven, 74–5. Andrew August touches upon such issues in 'A Culture of Consolation?'.

[25] M. Childs, Labour's Apprentices: Working-Class Lads in Late Victorian and Edwardian England (1992), 50.

and others. But in the circumstances of work, or its absence, there could exist less control. Such responses were often dangerous, and perhaps unthinkable, in these contexts. Other methods of the working class trying to gain some degree of respect, or to respond to either overt or unspoken 'contempt', were necessary.

When in employment, workers in even the most unvalued occupations often tried to establish self-respect by repositioning themselves within the workplace. They emphasized to the world any greater training or responsibility in the workplace that they possessed, so claiming the mantle of 'skilled workman'. This has led to the often-repeated historical claims of skill-based 'fragmentation' and lack of solidarity amongst the East End working class.[26] The clear neighbourhood equivalent of this method of claiming self-esteem, the practice of 'inter-personal competition' in trying to 'out-do' the neighbours, has been emphasized by Paul Johnson in his work on working-class economics.[27] This response was also important in the often-observed failure of the COS and other charitable and middle-class bodies to encourage 'thrift' amongst the poor.[28] Such reactions were indeed important, and will be discussed further below. But working-class responses to statements of their 'inferiority' were clearly not limited to these. Anna Clark has argued that male workers' needs to reassert their humanity against the deprecation of the middle and upper classes led to them seeking consciously to demonstrate their adherence to moral 'norms'. She suggests that this response was at the base of some of the shift in Chartist language earlier in the century towards sexual division and female domesticity. Responding to elite suggestions of their 'overbreeding' and other moral failings,

Chartists declared, we are 'treated like beasts of burden—mere animated machines, without hearts, without minds of our own, whose only privilege is to labor and die'. When the manhood of political power and the femininity of domestic seclusion were seen as class privileges by working men denied the vote and unable to support their families, stressing sexual difference was a way of representing themselves as fully human rather than animals or machines.[29]

---

[26] See e.g. Lovell, *Stevedores*, 35–6.

[27] P. Johnson, *Saving and Spending: The Working-Class Economy in Britain 1870–1939* (Oxford, 1985), 231–2, and see also E. Ross, '"Not the Sort that would Sit on the Doorstep': Respectability in Pre-World War I London Neighbourhoods', *International Labor and Working Class History*, 27 (Spring 1985).

[28] See Stedman Jones, 'Working-Class Culture', 200–1.

[29] A. Clark, 'The Rhetoric of Chartist Domesticity: Gender, Language and Class in the 1830s and 1840s', *Journal of British Studies*, 31: 1 (Jan. 1992), 69. See also Vernon, *Politics and the People*, 312–13.

'Fragmentation' and such gender division were perhaps 'inward-looking' responses to the desire for self-esteem and to the pervasive negative characterizations of working-class life. But as a resident of the very poor Campbell Bunk succinctly commented, on the issue of status difference in such areas: 'That was between ourselves.'[30] There could concurrently exist quite different types of response by the working class. Not all their energy needed to be expended on a concern for displays to outdo one's neighbours. They could also simultaneously display an outward-looking, more 'political', response.

Patrick Joyce and others have argued that a central part of earlier Gladstonian Liberal tactics to gather electoral support from working men was 'playing up this sense of insult and exclusion' amongst those who 'were so used to the rude and insolent treatment of their "betters"'. The 'flattery' the Liberals used, says Joyce, put an emphasis on the working-class men being 'perhaps the truest citizens of all', and that the 'poor were better and wiser than the rich'.[31] Perhaps this attracted a number of the working class amongst the 'popular audience' whom Joyce argues gave a 'ready response' to this discourse. But it was certainly not the 'poor' within an East End context who were the targets of such flattery. It was emphasized by Bright and others that it was the 'very cream' of workmen who were being addressed, and that they were to be morally distinguished from the 'residuum'.[32] This was a continuing distinction, and one that was applied even more clearly (even by Radicals) in the East End, as we shall see in the next chapter. But, by later in the century, the Conservatives were in any case competing well in the continuing contest to flatter and show respect for the working-man voter. In Stepney the Conservative member proclaimed that the workers in his constituency formed 'the very backbone of the artisan classes of London'.[33] In Limehouse the Conservative candidate urged trade unionists on towards the 'attainment of that position which he and every friend of labour felt it ought to assume'.[34] When the Tory member for Bermondsey addressed a meeting in the East End, he declared it was a 'great pleasure to visit Poplar and meet so many men of his own class . . . if ever there was a bona-fide working man he was one'.[35] Also in Poplar the chairman of the Conservative-based Municipal Alliance told his members that the

[30] White, *Worst Street*, 79.

[31] Joyce, *Visions*, 52–3. See also Vernon, *Politics and the People*, 323–4, for an East End example of this rhetoric.

[32] Joyce, *Visions*, 53 and 57.   [33] *East London Advertiser*, 16 Oct. 1886, p. 5 col.a.

[34] Ibid., 4 Feb. 1893, p. 6 col.f.

[35] *East End News*, 21 Dec. 1909, Tower Hamlets Local History Collection, newspaper cuttings file 320.2.

'most satisfactory feature' was the majority of working men amongst their number.[36]

But in the East End it appears unlikely, particularly amongst poorer voters, that the 'insult and exclusion' they continued to feel could be turned by such rhetoric into simple political support for either party. In fact, Paterson's comments noted at the start of the chapter begin to suggest this, and there is little doubt that the local politician's attempts to show his 'respect' for the worker could fall on deaf ears. A working-man speaker outside the East India Dock gates during the 1900 election amused his crowd with a description of 'the special attention and civility shown the working classes at election times. He went on to state that the letters sent to them by the election agents were addressed "Mr. So-and-So, Esq".'[37] Masterman noted that the rich man was often 'fair game' for acts of 'tit-for-tat' retaliation by the poor: '"An 'orrible lie!" between two poor people is fair play from a poor man to a wealthier, just as, for instance, the wealthy man considers himself at liberty to make speeches full of hypocritical untruth when he is seeking the suffrage of the free and independent electors, or is trying to teach the poor man how to make himself more profitable to his employer'.[38]

The image of the hypocritical politician fitted in well with the general perception of the middle and upper classes held by many amongst the East End poor—a perception which may have had an important political effect. Masterman had also noted that the 'multitude' of the urban working class had 'their own codes of honour, their special beliefs and moralities, their judgement and often their condemnation of the classes to whom has been given leisure and material advantage'.[39] While suggesting something of a 'separateness' of working-class culture, this condemnation was clearly also at least partly based upon a perception of, and reaction to, this moral hypocrisy.

Walter Southgate's father worked in a Bethnal Green workshop, where the sanctimonious employer every morning insisted on prayers, and then screwed down his vulnerable workers during the day: 'It is no wonder then that his work people, with the exception of . . . the foreman, were a scoffing, irreligious crowd once outside the premises. Father said often enough to me that religious humbugs like [the employer] Mr Dale did more to drive people away from the Bible religion than all the rationalist literature that ever was printed.'[40] This was a continuing preoccupation of the urban

[36] *East London Advertiser*, 13 Oct. 1906, p. 5 col.e.   [37] Ibid., 15 Sept. 1900, p. 8 col.a.

[38] C. F. G. Masterman, *The Condition of England* (1909; republished 1960), 90.

[39] Ibid. 89.   [40] Southgate, *That's the Way*, 40.

working class—'Letters frequently appear in the newspapers, alike pathetic and passionate, from those who have been sweated by "Christian" employers'.[41] Booth suggested of the working class and religion:

Working men have a far more exacting conception of its ethical obligations. They expect a religious man to make his life square with his opinions . . . the step to denounce as hypocrites those members of religious bodies who lead mundane lives is easily made. And they are, as might be supposed, especially prone to observe instances of a lack of Christian conduct or of just dealing amongst their employers, who may at the same time figure prominently as Church members.[42]

It was said of the chairman of the South Metropolitan Gas Works, during a strike in 1889, that 'He is a prominent advocate of Total Abstinence, and is, we believe, the president of the Lambeth Baths Temperance Society. As one man put it—"He would not let us go for half a pint of beer, if it would save our lives; but now he would wash the blacklegs in it, to satisfy his obstinate lust for power".'[43]

That central part of Stedman Jones's 'culture of consolation' for the London working class—the music hall—was perhaps where claims of hypocrisy could best be heard, and appreciated, by the working class. As Michael Childs has argued:

It was noted that 'you can always make pretty sure of a music-hall audience by attacking the vices of the aristocracy'. . . Teetotallers and the clergy provided other favourite targets for the songwriters, the first group for their notorious sanctimoniousness, the second group for their hypocritical conduct and rich living. The lower middle class also came in for its share of ridicule, primarily for its pretentiousness . . . In the 'popular' halls, the songs often contained 'some very broad compliment to what are called the "working classes" as the base—the inevitable, priceless, base of society's column'.[44]

Peter Bailey has discussed the role of elite discourse, in perhaps 'oppressing' the poor, but certainly undermining any claim by them to self-esteem, and also the role of the music hall as being where at least a symbolic 'equalization' could take place. The music hall, says Bailey, was one place where the working class could enjoy a unique 'knowingness' of the language and symbols being used in performance, and music-hall language 'was often a parodic echo of the formal language of officialdom and elite culture'. This,

---

[41] Masterman, *The Condition*, 210.   [42] Booth, *Life*, 3rd series, vol. 1, pp. 89–90.
[43] *Labour Elector*, 14 Dec. 1889, p. 373.
[44] 'The Music Hall', *Cornhill Magazine*, 60 (1889), 74, and F. Wedmore, 'The Music Halls', *Nineteenth Century*, 40 (1896), 134, quoted in Childs, *Labour's Apprentices*, 125–7. See Joyce, *Visions*, 246–53, for these same images repeated in northern popular ballads.

he argues, was 'a qualified reach for the power that these codes represented, while . . . also a form of retaliation in kind against the linguistic oppressions of the period'.[45]

It was similar forms of 'retaliation', the 'reach for power' against the oppressions of 'insult and exclusion', that were perhaps the most available response to unorganized and vulnerable poorer workers in this period. As we saw in these music-hall examples, those 'retaliations' involved reclaiming a measure of 'outward' self-esteem by establishing their moral superiority—by emphasizing whenever possible the hypocrisy and failings of their social 'betters'. Working-class responses to a desire for 'respect' could take many forms—'independence' in the workplace, symbolic 'equalization' such as in the contact by women with middle-class nurses, or language-based 'retaliation' against hypocrisy in the case of the music-hall. But such retaliation could also take more concrete forms. An interesting example of working-class reaction from earlier in the century can be seen in Jim Hammerton's analysis of the 1850 'Haynau incident', when draymen and labourers at Barclay and Perkins's brewery on the south side of the Thames chased and attacked the visiting Austrian general Haynau. Haynau had been involved in a brutal repression of rebellions in Hungary, and was best known for his ordering of the public flogging of a female member of the Hungarian aristocracy. This punishment gained widespread reporting in Britain, including graphic representations likely to be seen by the working class.[46] Reports of the actions of the workers suggest that their main cries while on the attack were 'we'll teach him to flog women' or something similar.[47] Why this event should have caused such passion amongst these brewery workers is a matter for some debate, but Hammerton notes that:

In his autobiography, Eric Bligh, the grandson of one of Barclay and Perkins' managers, speculated that Haynau's woman flogging may have incensed the draymen so much because they were 'tired of upper-class jokes about wife-beating'. . . Bligh's suggestion does at least acknowledge that the assumption of ubiquitous husbandly brutality was a sensitive one for the respectable working-class, that it could simultaneously embody both a sense of guilt about their own behaviour and resentment of upper-class hypocrisy about theirs.[48]

[45] P. Bailey, 'Conspiracies of Meaning: Music-Hall and the Knowingness of Popular Culture', *Past and Present*, 144 (Aug. 1994), 160.

[46] A. J. Hammerton, 'The Targets of "Rough Music": Respectability and Domestic Violence in Victorian England', *Gender and History*, 3: 1 (Spring 1991), 28–9.

[47] Ibid. 30.

[48] Ibid. 36–7. This appears to have similarities with violence during the Cotton Famine which, Joyce says, 'owed much to insults directed at the pride and independence of the operatives', *Visions*, 111.

As has been suggested, such resentment of their portrayal by the upper and middle classes was clear amongst many workers late in the nineteenth century and into the twentieth. The Revd Jay said in 1896, of the poor in lodging houses in Shoreditch, that:

> no statement appears in print about themselves or those they know, without it being quickly passed round to all . . . Many cannot read, but what does that matter, the news is soon read to them in little groups. At many different times little accounts of the church and so on have appeared in the papers, they have always been read by our people at once, though they are very severe on those who describe them as 'roughs', or 'thieves', or 'English barbarians'.[49]

Such tainted terms, particularly 'roughs', which was almost interchangable with 'poor' in elite discourse, were rejected in the same way as those spurned by the women to whom Loane spoke. In a similar way to these women, East End men could also 'retaliate' by using what power they had to control how they were approached. Showing a clear, and perhaps obvious example of this, Masterman, repeating a common complaint of the political activist, commented that the 'Socialist uses the sweated women and starving children as material for inflaming to pity and anger. But he rarely obtains adherents from the husbands of the women or the fathers of the children thus broken at the basis of society.'[50] Some of the dynamics of this can be seen in the response to the socialist orator, apparently in Limehouse, who referred to the number of houses in the area condemned by the Medical Officer of Health, and then heard from the crowd: '"Wot sort ov a place does 'e live in, comin' dahn 'ere talkin' abaht slums!" growled a hearer, voicing the general feeling.'[51] The charge of hypocrisy was clear in this reaction. But in the same way as mothers knew their children had lice, it is hardly suggested that the poor thought their housing was in good shape, only that they could, in this context at least, exercise their power to demand some respect.

The ability of the working class to respond to politicians and their discourse had been altered in late nineteenth-century urban Britain, at least nominally, by the fact of a number of the working class gaining the vote, although this was somewhat restricted, as discussed in the previous chapter. It is apparent, as we saw above, that many voting workers were well aware of the extra attention and power they gained, at least temporarily, from politicians as a result. Generally, as we have seen, the East End working class were conscious of their usual expendability in the eyes of the middle and upper classes. Elections and the language used by candidates

---

[49] A. O. Jay, *A Story of Shoreditch* (1896), 80.   [50] Masterman, *The Condition*, 119.
[51] R. Fox, *Smoky Crusade* (1937), 38. For a similar response see also Jay, *A Story*, 11–13.

could even act to emphasize to the working class the normal lack of respect they were shown by their 'betters', contrasting this with the high level of hypocrisy displayed during campaigns. Potentially, a number of working-class voters may have felt that they now possessed the most direct way of responding 'in kind' to the hypocritical politician, such as in the quote from Masterman above. It is clear that Paterson's argument that the importance of 'scandal' and 'reputation' grew markedly in these circumstances makes some sense.

By focusing upon scandal, the 'reputation of the candidate', the poor voter could be argued to be fighting on his own ground, claiming self-esteem and symbolic power. Vernon has noted a similar fascination in the mid-century regarding political 'heroes', perhaps even those Liberal heroes who gathered support by 'flattering' the working class: 'The people may have created their own leaders and endowed them with heroic qualities, but . . . they always reserved the right to bring them back down to earth with a bump. This popular passion for unmasking heroes may help to explain the undeniable appetite for scandalously satirical street literature. Heroes were never allowed to live up to their expectations, for it was their failure and fallibility which reminded the people of their common humanity.'[52] Pulling the rug, by appreciating scandal, from under those who became too 'full of themselves'—reminded politicians that we are, after all, all equal.

In St George's in 1910, the continuing key importance of such things as 'scandal' in the political life of areas of the East End was suggested: 'It is the little things that carry weight here, and a man might have an excellent chance of election, when a little point is raised which may turn everything against him and place him at the bottom of the poll.'[53] John Brewer has noted, like Edward Thompson, the importance of the 'theatrical' to eighteenth-century politics, such as:

ceremonies of state, the festive celebration of royal birthdays and political anniversaries, the costume, pomp, and circumstance of the judicial process . . . Patrician spectacle had to dazzle, aristocratic theater had to be well performed, for they were not so much an expression of authority, or authority manifesting itself in symbolic form, as the direct exercise of authority itself.[54]

Richard Free said of the reaction of East Enders to exactly such spectacle in the 1890s that 'he reads sarcastic paragraphs about them in his Sunday

[52] Vernon, *Politics and the People*, 279.

[53] *East London Advertiser*, 12 Mar. 1910, p. 8 col.b.

[54] J. Brewer, 'Theater and Counter-Theater in Georgian Politics: The Mock Elections at Garrat', *Radical History Review*, 22 (Winter 1979–80), 35.

newspaper, and he puts them all in his pipe, as it were, and smokes them. The great ones of earth are to him so many marionettes, who go through a series of clever, but stilted and unlifelike performances, and succeed in making sensible folk laugh immoderately.'[55] This demonstrates little engagement with the 'issues' of public life, and all of the above suggests that we should see politics for the East End working class at least partly as 'entertainment', with powerful themes of 'morality' and 'scandal'—combining perhaps as the 'melodrama' Vernon suggests.[56]

In judging 'scandal' amongst the upper and middle classes, workers were imposing not their own moral standards but turning the stated morality of those classes back on themselves. The issue itself could be viewed from 'outside', like watching the marionettes. Any suggestion of 'scandal' itself may not necessarily have been important, but the hypocrisy of it was, in its role in allowing the opportunity for a feeling of moral superiority, and empowerment. It must remain speculative, electorally, how important 'scandal' was for at least some of the poorer of working-class voters. But putting Paterson's suggestion of this into a different political and social context to that applied by Stedman Jones, allows it to take on much more meaning than in its usual simple use as a decisive indicator of the 'apathy' of the London poor.

The dynamics of some political attitudes amongst the poorest of the casual poor, located in the common lodging houses, were suggested in an earlier chapter. The section immediately above has dealt generally with those of a slightly less poor group, perhaps represented by the economically 'lower end' of the enfranchised working class. But of those with the vote in the East End in this period, most were more prosperous workers, and the rest of this chapter will examine factors acting upon their politics more closely. The theme of 'morality' was again quite clearly central to the political responses of this group, although they perhaps accepted to a greater degree the more specific definitions and influences, in this regard, of religious belief and its established forms.

RELIGION AND PARTY

The responses of the nineteenth-century urban working class towards religion and politics have often been linked by historians. Attitudes in both spheres have been portrayed as being the result of feelings of powerlessness or vulnerability, resulting in apathy or simplified 'populist'

[55] Free, *Seven Years*, 104–5.   [56] See Vernon, *Politics and the People, passim.*

reactions. Hugh McLeod has described the consequences for both religion and politics of such a view of life:

> the secularism and parochialism that pervaded working-class London . . . was a typical proletarian response to a world in which most decisions were made by other people . . . only the most intent parochialism could save the individual and those who depended on him from disaster . . . little neighbourly encouragement was likely to be offered to those who concerned themselves with matters of abstract principle or world interpretation . . . In politics, the result was an ad hoc approach, consisting of the use of direct action to remove particular grievances, together with the lack of any long-term commitment.[57]

Clearly this argument fits easily within the relevant broad historical representations of the poor that were described in the Introduction and Chapter 1 above. In a similar fashion to McLeod, Bush has also linked together conceptually an apparent failure of the churches in the East End and what she sees as the political representation of this phenomenon in the 'paradox' of Conservative support in the area before the First World War.[58]

The concept of an apathy towards, or total rejection of religion amongst the urban working class generally has recently been challenged in many ways,[59] to some extent breaking the nexus between this and any assumed working-class political torpor. But this section, and the following, will suggest that a historical connection between religion and politics, for at least parts of the working class in the East End, should be recognized, though perhaps with a very different meaning to that normally given.

The more detailed understanding provided in Chapter 2 as to the effects of the voting franchise provisions allows us to view more accurately the evidence of electoral results in the East End. But what can this material tell us about the dynamics and social bases of politics in the area? Without wishing to engage too heavily in electoral sociology,[60] a relatively simple comparison of voting patterns between local areas in the East End can in fact suggest a number of themes.

Parliamentary constituencies are too large and diverse and, as seen in the previous chapter, the effects of the pre-war franchise are often too 'capricious' between areas to allow for a historically meaningful comparison of

---

[57] H. McLeod, *Class and Religion in the Late Victorian City* (1974), 57–8.

[58] Bush, *Behind the Lines*, 1–2.

[59] By studies showing greater working-class attendance, particularly at Nonconformist chapels, e.g. H. McLeod, *Religion and Irreligion in Victorian England: How Secular was the Working Class?* (Bangor, 1993), 31, and also through an understanding of other forms of working-class religious belief—see Williams, 'Religious Belief', 160.

[60] See Lawrence, 'The Dynamics of Urban Politics', 89–90, for a discussion of the limitations of electoral sociology.

results on that scale, despite the worthy efforts of Paul Thompson and others.[61] This is particularly the case if one is attempting to determine some differences in responses between groups within the working class in an area such as the East End. As suggested, and undertaken, by Duncan Tanner and others,[62] a study of voting ward politics can perhaps indicate a much greater localized diversity, and illustrate much more clearly political influences and allegiances. For a number of reasons, which are discussed in Appendix 4, the only useful evidence of the small-scale political variations in the East End in this period comes from the series of ward votes for the borough council elections of 1900, 1903, 1906, 1909, and 1912, although of course there are a number of qualifications that need to be made in using even this evidence.[63]

To classify the economic character of whole London constituencies for his study, Paul Thompson primarily used the social class calculations Booth made for each of the small residential 'blocks' into which he notionally divided London. Thompson, as closely as possible, aggregated this data into each constituency boundary. He used this analysis to argue very generally, amongst other things, that 'the very poorest constituencies were less resistant to the Conservatives than those in which the middle-class element was slightly larger'.[64] As noted in the Introduction, Booth's 'poverty' figures have often similarly been used by historians in their general descriptions of the character of the pre-war East End and its politics.[65]

A relatively simple test, which has not been carried out, is to determine whether Booth's very localized small-block data can be used to show any connection between more detailed, small-scale economic conditions and party political support in areas of the East End. Booth's 'blocks' were very similar in size to electoral wards, but in fact a number of difficulties arise in attempting to use this material in relation to the 1900–12 ward results. First, the ward boundaries rarely line up exactly with Booth's areas. But perhaps more seriously, Booth's East End material was over a decade old even by 1900 and the start of the borough council voting figures, so raising the possibility of significant social change in areas in the intervening years. As mentioned above, and detailed in Appendix 4, suitable electoral material is not available for the same period as Booth's calculations.

---

[61] See Thompson, *Socialists, Liberals and Labour*, 299–303, and Wald, *Crosses*, and the previous note.

[62] D. Tanner, 'Elections, Statistics and the Rise of the Labour Party, 1906–1931', *Historical Journal*, 34: 4 (1991), 904–5; Joyce, *Work, Society and Politics*, 204–11.

[63] See Appendix 4 for details of all issues regarding the following correlations.

[64] Thompson, *Socialists, Liberals and Labour*, 299 and 20.

[65] See e.g. Bush, *Behind the Lines*, 1–2, and Wald, *Crosses*, 32–40.

It is not possible to adjust Booth's figures at an individual area level on the basis of the further work of Booth's assistants in 1897–8, as Thompson has attempted to do regarding the constituencies.[66] But we can at least attempt to test the continuing usefulness of Booth's material by looking at the two constituencies which, in this period, were probably the most socially stable in the East End—Bow and Bromley, and Poplar. As an example of stability in these areas, in George Duckworth's re-examination of Bromley for Booth in 1898, he walked along 110 streets, covering parts of six of Booth's earlier areas, and recommended changes in the wealth-coded map colours for only twelve of these streets. Of these, six were improved and six were marked down, and in all except one case the difference was one shade.[67]

Large-scale Jewish immigration had not begun to affect these areas by the turn of the century, although clearly the migration of workers to parts of these constituencies from more central districts, because of increased crowding or other factors, was continuing. But it is reasonable to suggest that most of the wards in these seats at least would have retained their relative socio-economic positions vis-à-vis each other for most of this period. Of these constituencies, in parliamentary elections in the period, Poplar always elected a Liberal member, and Bow and Bromley elected the Conservatives six times, the Liberals three, and was Labour for a short time under George Lansbury.

I have attempted to align Booth's areas as closely as possible with the electoral wards, dividing and joining areas as necessary. As a rough examination of the issue of poverty and politics, for each area the percentage of the population that Booth calculated to be under his specific 'poverty level' was compared to the percentage of 'Conservative' vote in each ward.[68] Poverty levels in the wards ranged from 55 to 20 per cent, and the Conservative vote varied from 69 to 38 per cent. This exercise in fact provided results of very little value. They are shown in Figure 1, with no obvious trend in the relationship between the figures.

In fact this is what should largely be expected, because of the effects of the franchise provisions described in the earlier chapter. It was argued there that the great majority of voters across the East End constituencies were of at least a minimum level of relative prosperity, and that the size of

[66] See Thompson, *Socialists, Liberals and Labour*, 301.

[67] See Booth MSS B346, 29–63 and D1 district 12.

[68] See Appendix 4, for details of the use of specific Booth 'blocks', and where the use of the term 'Conservative' is also discussed. Those above the poverty line Booth termed 'comfortable'.

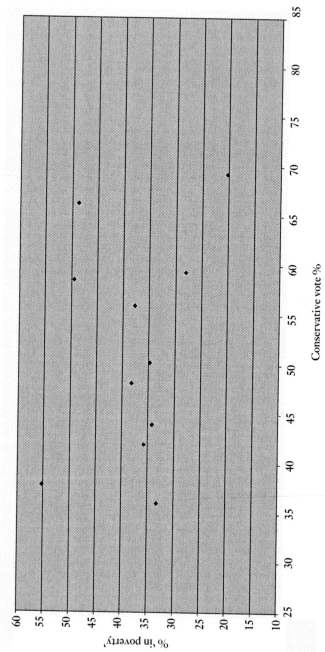

Fig. 1. Poverty levels/Conservative vote

that segment of the population was not necessarily affected by the general poverty level of an area.

But if, instead, the percentage of 'middle class' (Booth's Classes G and H) in each ward is correlated in the same way, a clearer connection seems to emerge between increases in the Conservative share of the vote and a larger percentage of middle-class residents in a ward, as is shown in Figure 2. This is quite useful information, but by itself it tells us relatively little about these areas. The variations in the relatively small numbers of middle-class residents cannot directly explain the much larger differences in Conservative voting percentages between wards. The greatest increase in apparent Conservative support seems to occur as the percentage of middle class rises from 2–3 per cent to 5–6 per cent, with the Conservative share of the vote increasing with this from less than 40 per cent to between 50 and 60 per cent. After that the level of Conservative support, with one or two exceptions, seems largely to level off.

Nearly half of Booth's 'middle class' in Poplar and Bow and Bromley were shop- or eating-house keepers. This does not suggest that they were necessarily located in 'wealthier' areas, or that the economic position of the rest of the area can be directly inferred from the percentage of middle class residents. It is possible that such relatively small pockets of middle-class residents were in commercial districts with surrounding areas of poverty. But trying to extend this class analysis for each area from Booth's figures merely takes us back to the fruitless 'poverty'/'comfort' division examined in Figure 1.

A greater understanding of the implications of this rough socio-economic measure of politics can perhaps be gained by looking at other quantitative evidence, which provides possibly a more subtle indication of social and attitudinal differences between areas of the East End. If we remain with Poplar and Bow and Bromley, we find that, largely because of the historical structure of local government, the local entities which shared the most common boundaries with the electoral wards were the ecclesiastical parishes in the area. Of the fourteen wards in these two constituencies, ten were almost conterminous with parish boundaries, and only two included parts of more than two parishes. Any data available for the parishes can be applied to the relevant ward areas. The survey undertaken in 1902–3 by the *Daily News*, of church attendance in all parishes of London, allows us to relate this measure directly to the wards in these constituencies, and to compare it to the electoral data.[69] When this is done, a very significant result is

[69] The results of the survey are given in R. Mudie-Smith (ed.), *The Religious Life of London* (1904).

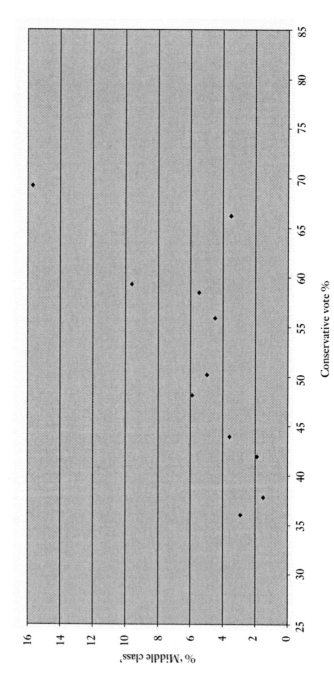

Fig. 2. Middle-class levels/Conservative vote

obtained. Plotting the same ward measure of party support against total Protestant church attendance in the relevant parishes shows a very strong connection between church-attendance levels and apparent support for the Conservatives, as is shown in Figure 3.

In comparison with the other figures, the apparent inclination towards the Conservatives here seems to increase relatively regularly and directly with increases in church attendance. The technical 'correlation coefficient' for this graph—0.73—is larger than that for the middle class/Conservative correlation, and is mathematically defined as 'high'.[70] Of the available data, church attendance indeed seems to provide the most direct predictor of voting patterns in these areas of the East End in this period. The question is why, and how might this finding relate to class or other social influences?

The strength of this result does suggest that the weaker link between middle-class residence levels and Conservatism was not merely a statistical coincidence. This second correlation could perhaps be taken as merely confirming something of a class-based relationship, given the well-established connection between the wealth of an area and the level of church attendance in this period.[71] But the material is far more informative than this, and the relationship is far more complex.[72]

While in wealthier areas it would seem natural for religious display and strong Toryism to be linked, this is a far less usual model to be applied to East London, where Conservatism has more often been linked with poverty. But while there is undoubtedly some class-based correlation here, to simply see in these figures a connection between a larger number of a wealthier 'church-attending class' in some wards and an increased level of both Conservatism and religious observance is to see only a small part of the story. Further material relating to religious observance tells us a great deal more about social and attitudinal differences between these wards, and suggests that there were a number of other factors at work. It is apparent that the differences between Protestant church-attendance levels in these areas were not predominantly due to differences in the number of those of

[70] See A. Bryman and D. Cramer, *Quantitative Data Analysis for Social Scientists*, rev. edn. (London, 1994), 170. The levels suggested there for correlations are: less than 0.19 'very low'; 0.2–0.39 'low'; 0.4–0.69 'modest'; 0.7–0.89 'high'; 0.9–1.0 'very high'.

[71] See McLeod, *Class and Religion*, 299–307 and *passim.*, and J. Cox, *The English Churches in a Secular Society: Lambeth, 1870–1930* (Oxford, 1982), 31.

[72] Appendix 4 addresses in detail concerns regarding this evidence, such as: (1) The attendance figures used were for churches and not 'charity missions'; (2) Similar trends are shown for Church of England and Nonconformist churches; (3) Irish or Jewish immigration did not distort the Protestant attendance levels between parishes; (4) It is appropriate to use Poplar and Bow and Bromley as representative of much of the East End.

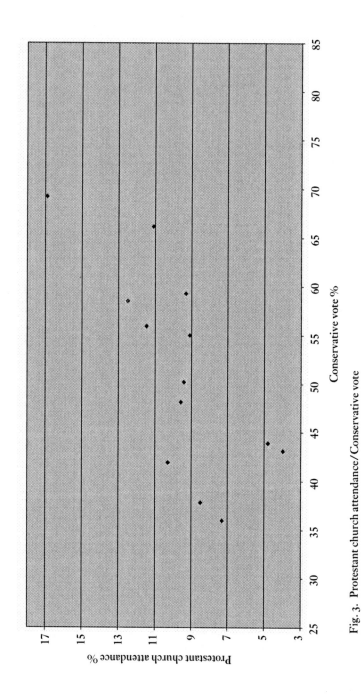

Fig. 3. Protestant church attendance/Conservative vote

the wealthier classes, or even white-collar workers, attending. The evidence suggests that the greatest difference between wards was in working-class church attendance. The highest levels of attendance were in the areas where the working class attended church much more frequently, and these indeed were the areas with the highest apparent levels of Conservative support.

Unfortunately, the class composition of congregations cannot, in most cases, be described by anything other than anecdotal evidence from the clergy interviewed in 1897–8 by Booth's workers, and the personal visits to churches by these informants. Both are clearly affected by issues of subjectivity. But they build a reasonably strong case.

We may start to examine this in detail for an area where the churches and Conservatism seem both to have been at their weakest. Bromley South West ward elected only one Conservative councillor out of fifteen in the five elections covered (with a 37.8 per cent average Conservative vote). In St Gabriel's, one of the two parishes covering this ward, which was 'very poor' and had one of the lowest overall levels of church attendance, working-class attendance was almost negligible. The vicar said that those 'who go to church are with few exceptions the fairly well-to-do, with a few old women'.[73] In the part of the adjoining All Hallows parish, covering the rest of the ward, and which contained the 'poorest streets in Bromley', the modest congregation was similarly made up mainly of 'small shopkeepers'.[74] At St Michael's and All Angels, Bromley, which covered almost exactly the Bromley Central ward, and which had a 36 per cent Conservative vote in the period, Booth's reporter found an evening congregation of '2/300 well dressed middle class women mostly young'.[75] In St Mark's, Bow, which covered one of the next-lowest Conservative voting wards—Bow North—it was said again that 'Only the well dressed and respectable came to the churches'.[76]

But in areas where the Conservatives did best, and with higher church-attendance levels, quite a different pattern emerged. In St John's, covering most of the generally Conservative Cubitt Town ward, the minister noted that the 'congregations are entirely working people'.[77] In St Matthias's in

[73] The Revd A. Wentworth Bennett, Booth MSS B175, 123.
[74] The Revd J. P. Noyes of All Hallows parish, Bromley, which had a Church of England adult attendance in 1902–3 of 2.9% of the adult population. Booth MSS B175, 7. An identifiable part of this parish was also within the Bromley North West ward, as will be noted below.
[75] Booth MSS B385, 75. Only around 40 adults attended the morning service.
[76] The Revd M. Sweetnam, Booth MSS B175, 83.
[77] The Revd D. G. Cowan, Booth MSS B169, 75.

Poplar, with the highest of all overall church-attendance levels, and which formed a large part of the apparently very Conservative Poplar West ward, the churchgoers were 'men and women about equally; mostly regular; very mixed class: watermen . . . pilots, working-men'.[78] In St Mary's, Bromley, which covered both Bromley North East and North West, with a total 56 per cent Conservative voting record, the main evening congregation of 500 or so was 'mainly artisan' and with 'a good proportion of men'.[79] Booth's reporter found an afternoon congregation there which was 'a genuine gathering of men, of whom fully half were working class'.[80] Eight out of ten councillors elected in Bow Central were Conservative in the period, and its area was coterminous with St Stephen's parish, which had the highest level of Church of England attendance of the parishes surveyed. The area was 'of varying character . . . and some parts quite poor, the population mainly working-class and lower middle-class'. The vicar said his roll of communicants—like the other parishes with relatively high levels of church attendance—was 'fairly representative of the parish, as regards occupation etc. Both sexes were represented and every age.'[81]

These examples are only from the Anglican churches, to avoid any suggestion of differences being caused by a working-class preference for particular denominations. There is little doubt that in some areas the working class as a general rule attended church in much greater numbers than in others. The churches mentioned also were not the 'charitable' organizations often argued to have attracted keen working-class attendances.[82]

But the overall church-attendance figures were still obviously quite low in nearly all of the areas. Yet if, as a rough approximation and very conservatively, we can suggest from this evidence that perhaps on average the working class made up one-quarter of congregations in the low-attendance areas, and one-half in the high-attendance areas, the significance of this can be seen. We can take the combined 'Conservative' Bromley North East and North West wards, and the 'Non-Conservative' Bow North ward, as examples. These figures would mean that one in thirteen of the 'Conservative' Bromley North wards' adult working class attended church on the *Daily News* survey day (a larger number, perhaps more than one in ten, would

---

[78] The second occupation on this list is indecipherable. The Revd J. Neil, Booth MSS B169, 51.

[79] The Revd J. Parry, Booth MSS B175, 53–5.

[80] Booth MSS B385, 93.

[81] The Revd H. A. Mason, Booth MSS B175, 19–21 and 29.

[82] Again, see Appendix 4 for evidence of this, and that Nonconformist attendances followed the same pattern. The relationship of Nonconformism to working-class politics will be discussed in a following chapter.

naturally have attended at least on a relatively regular basis), while less than one in sixty of the Bow North ward's adult working class did the same.[83] Generally also, the areas with higher overall church-attendance levels had a larger proportion of men attending. These facts can suggest a much greater social difference than merely the bald comparison of differences in the level of middle-class/lower middle-class residence between the wards. They suggest much more strongly a difference in overall working-class social structures and mores between these areas. This will be discussed in greater detail below.

Pointing out the significance of a connection between increased working-class church attendance and electoral Conservatism is certainly not to claim a causal link, but only that the strength of this correlation suggests that conditions may have existed in some areas which supported both outcomes. As part of this, a very important point to emphasize again here is that these electoral variations were more often likely to be based upon abstention by progressive voters, rather than differences in the Conservative vote. This was as apparent in borough elections as it was clear in parliamentary polls, and the reasons for it are vital in understanding much of the dynamics of East End politics.

Figure 4 shows that progressive voter turnout tended to fluctuate much more widely from one election to the next in those wards with higher levels of church attendance.[84] To refine even further what the analysis in this chapter can most clearly show us, it is not so much about levels of Conservative support, as that there was a strong apparent correlation between the level of Protestant church attendance in an area and the likelihood that its progressive voters would abstain from voting at certain points.

The uneven swings between these wards each year suggest strongly that we should also be looking much more closely at a propensity to abstain in an area, and the reasons why, rather than simply at economic structure, or the 'trigger' of political issues or discourse, in trying to understand electoral variations in the East End. As discussed earlier, abstention from voting was often an important component of Liberal defeats in the East End, as elsewhere.[85] In the Mile End election of 1905, the Liberals thought the result showed 'no extraordinary movement of the public mind, simply the usual steady Tory vote, with the Liberal vote stirring and stretching in its sleep, as it does now and then'.[86]

---

[83] For these calculations, see Appendix 4.   [84] For technical points, see Appendix 5.
[85] See Pelling, *Popular Politics*, 7–8, on abstentions by agricultural labourers.
[86] *Eastern Post*, 21 Jan. 1905, p. 5 col.e.

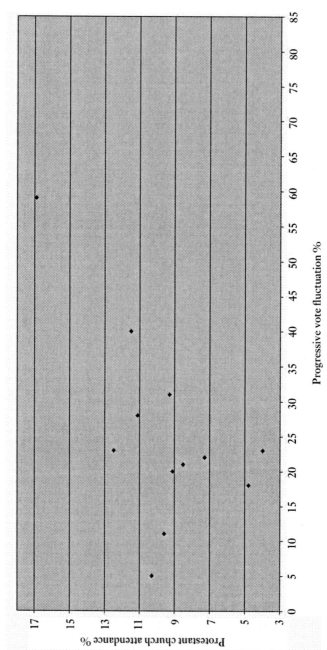

Fig. 4 Fluctuations in Progressive vote/Protestant church attendance

It is worth also looking at the specific East End response to the 'Khaki' election of 1900 in this regard. Popular imperialist support for 'British international prestige' has often been named as an important factor in Conservative victories in London working-class electorates in this period, no more so than in relation to the 1900 result, during the South African War.[87] As has been emphasized throughout this study, 'jingoism, anti-alienism, the residual protectionism of the riverside districts, and hostility to Home Rule'[88] have often been put together as the main determinants of the politics of the London poor.

But Richard Price has argued for the importance generally of 'voter apathy' across the country in the outcomes of the 1900 election,[89] and importantly, the situation was essentially no different in the East End, although the specific patterns of abstention are again significant. The Liberals had performed badly in 1895 in the East End in an election fought largely on the 'straight' political issues of the failings of their government elected in 1892, and on disunity (an important factor, which will be mentioned further below) within a Liberal party 'broken into factions, and without any common policy'.[90] These difficulties continued in part into the 1900 campaign. The party held four of the eleven East London constituencies after 1895. It lost two and recovered one in 1900.[91]

Paul Readman has recently argued for the reassertion of the centrality of war and patriotism as the determining issue in the 1900 election, against much of the analysis of Price and others. Although a useful corrective to the overall perceptions of the politics of the period, Readman's evidence does not indicate a greater level of jingoism amongst the London working class than among other groups in the nation. Amongst other things, Readman bases his views upon an argument that 'Liberal Imperialists' (defined by their parliamentary voting patterns and public comments on war-related issues)—in London working-class constituencies as well as elsewhere in Britain—did generally better in their constituency contests than those of their party that Readman defines as 'Pro-Boers'.[92]

The situation in the East End, however, provides limited evidence, if any, of the 'electorate's differentiation'[93] in this regard. Hoxton, held by a

---

[87] Tanner, *Political Change*, 165, and see other sources referred to in the Introduction.

[88] Davis, *Reforming London*, 190.

[89] R. Price, *An Imperial War and the British Working Class: Working Class Attitudes and Reactions to the Boer War 1899–1902* (1972), 105.

[90] A. Gardiner, *John Benn and the Progressive Movement* (1925), 192.

[91] Stepney had also been won by the Liberals in a by-election in 1898 (after being held by the Conservatives even in 1892), but it returned to the Conservatives in 1900.

[92] Readman, 'The Conservative Party', *passim*.   [93] Ibid. 138.

Liberal 'Pro-Boer', was indeed captured by the Conservatives. As Price noted, the 'total poll was about 400 votes down on that of 1895, the Conservative vote was about the same (2,866 to 2,862 in 1895) and the Liberal vote of 2,592 about 400 less than their vote of the previous general election (2,990), indicating that few actually changed sides but rather abstained'.[94] But the constituency adjoining Hoxton, Haggerston, was at the same time won back by the Liberals after a 1895 loss, and by the most anti-war of any of the East End candidates—Randall Cremer, 'devoted to the international peace movement, and [who] undertook a constant campaign for treaties of arbitration between states'.[95]

There is no doubt, as Readman suggests generally, that the local East End campaigns were fought largely on war issues. Yet, despite Jonathan Schneer and others' claim of special support from dockers for the imperial cause,[96] it is clear that in the riverside constituencies of Limehouse, Poplar, and Whitechapel the Liberal percentage of the vote increased, even if only slightly (although it fell in St George's, where the Liberals had lost the charismatic and controversial John Williams Benn as a candidate).

It was in the more prosperous East End constituencies of Mile End, Stepney,[97] and Bow and Bromley that the Conservatives generally did best in 1900 in terms of swings (largely caused by lower turnouts for their opponents). While Stepney was certainly lost by a 'Pro-Boer' Bill Steadman, the 'Liberal Imperialist' C. Goddard Clarke, in adjoining Mile End, suffered the third-largest drop in Liberal support in the East End, and he achieved the lowest percentage vote for any Liberal candidate in the area.[98] In Bow, comparisons are somewhat confused by the candidature of George Lansbury as a Socialist. But it is in that constituency that evidence can be found from both 1900 and also from the earlier 'abstaining' election of 1886 that provides one of the most direct indications of the likely type of Liberal voter who did not turn out to vote in these circumstances. While the Home Rule election could be thought to have been a very special case, in the general election of 1900 and also a by-election in 1899, a very similar drop in turnout again occurred in the vote in Bow and Bromley to that which

---

[94] Readman, 'The Conservative Party', 114.   [95] Pelling, *Social Geography*, 48.

[96] See Schneer, *London 1900*, ch. 3.

[97] See Appendix 1 and the final section of this chapter.

[98] It is instructive, in fact, despite Readman's argument regarding local responses to the position of candidates on the war, to see the similarity of the statements made by the Liberal candidates—with quite divergent results—to their constituents on this issue. See e.g. addresses and advertisements for Mile End, Limehouse, Poplar, and Whitechapel Liberals, *East London Advertiser*, 29 Sept. and 2 Oct. 1900.

occurred in 1886, although of course with Liberal abstentions seemingly related this time to the South African War.[99]

Where these abstentions occurred can be suggested from the voting figures for the borough elections which occurred only a few weeks after the 1900 election. In Bromley North West, with a large number of more prosperous working-class, the percentage voting was 38.4 per cent, the lowest of all wards. In the adjoining poorer Bromley North East ward, 56.2 per cent voted: the highest turnout, and 10 per cent above the average for the borough.[100] It would make little sense for this difference to vary greatly from the relative levels of enthusiasm for voting shown in the wards in an election the previous month. In addition to this, to complete a quote given earlier regarding the 1886 election, it was said about Bow and Bromley that the 'men of the North London Railway are an important factor in the situation, as they influence some 600 votes. It is alleged that their abstention from polling in 1886 placed Sir John [Colomb, Con.] in the seat.'[101] The vicar of All Hallows in Bromley described a large part of his congregation as coming from the 'better streets to the north' which adjoined the North London Railway Works, '[where] there are a good many artisans'.[102] This part of the parish was 'inhabited by railway and police men',[103] and was part of the generally 'Conservative' Bromley North West ward because, it seems, of voters easily 'put off' the Liberal party. Again, it was apparently this area of the constituency which helped to deliver a larger Conservative victory in 1900.

There are difficulties in taking these arguments too far, given the apparent relative consistency of the socio-economic position of voters across wards and constituencies, as argued in Chapter 2. But as will be seen below, even given this factor, an area's nature could strongly influence such results. The statistical and anecdotal evidence does suggest strongly that the impact of 'issues' on East End politics was hardly uniform, and that the tendency of voters in a particular area to abstain from voting could be as important electorally as the issue itself. As noted, Figure 4 indicates a connection between higher levels of church attendance and increased abstention at times. There are some exceptions to a uniform pattern in this, most notably Bromley South East ward which, despite having relatively high church-attendance figures, experienced almost no variation in progressive voter turnout in the period. There are specific, and very

---

[99] See interview with the Liberal candidate, ibid., 4 Nov. 1899, p. 2 col.f.
[100] Ibid., 10 Nov. 1900, p. 8 col.a.   [101] Ibid., 2 July 1892, p.8 col.b.
[102] The Revd J. P. Noyes, Booth MSS B175, 1. Cf. congregation from poorer part of this parish, as noted earlier.
[103] Duckworth in Booth MSS B346, 29.

significant, reasons for this exception which in fact strongly support this general argument, and which will be discussed later in this chapter.

'I CAN READ MY BIBLE JUST AS WELL AT HOME'

Church attendance by the working class in London is usually suggested to have been regulated to a large extent by the operation of social pressures within the working-class community. As Ken Inglis points out, leading church figures began to understand in the 1880s that 'it was a fashion among higher classes to go to church, but among the poorer classes "the marked men are those who go to church—not those who stay away"'.[104]

There is no doubt that the threat of 'chaff' from neighbours or workmates often discouraged working people, particularly men, from attending church. Hugh McLeod argues that, in nineteenth-century working-class London, 'Church goers were suspected of thinking they were better than they were, of a sense of superiority to their neighbours, and were thus apt to be mercilessly taunted for any act that fell short of the standards of perfection. Any sort of religion that set a man apart from his neighbours in any way or gave him distinctive habits was suspect for this reason.'[105] One East End parson noted that 'Anyone who attends communion or takes any active part in religious work is sure to be "rotted" by his friends, and even those who belong to the church are almost afraid to recognize the parson in the street if in company with others'.[106]

The issues of hypocrisy and sanctimoniousness that we saw earlier come through again here. But Booth suggested neighbourhood-related differences that altered such pressure. While in the 'pink' areas on his maps—in his code, meaning the comfortable working class—there seems to have been somewhat of a 'neutrality' regarding religion, in the class 'mixed' areas, populated by the 'upper-grade artisan and lower-grade salaried classes', Booth found there was often a feeling that it was 'rather the correct thing to attend a place of worship, and neither chaff nor ridicule ensues from so doing'.[107]

McLeod has similarly shown the importance of the specific local social makeup in determining the religious outlook and activities of an area. While middle-class churchgoing residents lived occasionally in the poor streets,

---

[104] K. S. Inglis, *Churches and the Working Classes in Victorian England* (1963), 323, quoting W. D. Maclagan, the future Archbishop of York.

[105] H. McLeod, *Class and Religion*, 51.   [106] Booth MSS B169, 67.

[107] Booth, *Life*, 3rd series, vol. 5, pp. 158–9.

their 'habits' often only 'repelled' their neighbours, according to McLeod. A man from a very poor street in Bromley said they had 'one or two church-goers' whose children went to 'private schools somewhere'. They 'never mixed in any shape or form' and were clearly resented by the working-class residents of the street. Any worker who joined them at church would have very likely found himself on the receiving end of much 'chaff'.[108] Similarly, Walter Southgate lived in a street near the Regent's Canal, in which although there were artisans and some white-collar residents, labourers, and other similar workers were in a majority. In this street, he recalled, religion was left to the few middle class who 'passed through North Street . . . in their high hats, frock coats and their womenfolk overdressed in fine clothes. A working man in his Sunday best suit hobnobbing with the gentry was unthinkable . . . none of my neighbours were churchgoers.'[109]

But, in contrast, regularly employed brewery workers who lived in a street in Mile End New Town, with policemen and similar employees as neighbours, were reported to be often keen churchgoers and to put great emphasis upon the Sunday ritual.[110] (It is interesting that Mile End New Town was also regarded as a Conservative stronghold by the Liberals, and this they ascribed to 'the Church influence'[111]). John Blake, who lived with his parents in the relatively comfortable and 'mixed' class Andrew Street, Poplar—with his father having a regular although relatively low-paid job as a plumber's mate at a ship-repairing firm—could recall 'how great a part religion played in the lives of the Poplar people'.[112]

What is most significant here is the relative absence of neighbourhood pressures against church attendance in both 'mixed' and more prosperous working-class areas. The emphasis this again places upon neighbourhood differences, and the personal relationships underlying them, are very important issues for both religion and politics in the East End.

The relationship between the working class and formal religion was complex, and the church-attendance statistics we looked at above only accounted for a small minority of the working class in most areas. But while attendance at church generally may not have been high in East London, a number of clergy noted that 'Altogether the East End is much more alive

[108] H. McLeod, 'Working-Class Religion in Late Victorian London: Booth's "Religious In-fluences" Revisited', in Englander and O'Day, *Retrieved Riches*, 279–80. The examples given by McLeod are from interviews taped by Raphael Samuel, as acknowledged by McLeod.
[109] Southgate, *That's the Way*, 39 and 76.
[110] McLeod, 'Working-Class Religion', 279–80.
[111] Samuel Montagu, MP, reported in the *East London Observer*, 20 Mar. 1886, cutting in Swaythling Papers, Hartley Library, University of Southampton, AJ1–1, 75.
[112] J. Blake, *Memories of Old Poplar* (1977), 7, and see Booth MSS B346, 41–3.

[spiritually]' than most of South London; that the people in their parish 'were the most religious in London'; that the 'influence of the church in the district is strong'; and that 'people are no more irreligious than they were but that there is a greater neglect of church-going'; or that 'Most would call themselves Christians. If asked to attend church people will say, "I can read my Bible just as well at home".' A missionary noted that 'Nearly all the working people in my district who are in comfortable circumstances are more or less under religious influence.'[113] Loane commented upon the 'strong religious faith' of her patients, although their 'views on doctrinal questions could scarcely have been considered orthodox by the instructed members of any church or sect'.[114] It was remarked on the opening of St Faith's church in Stepney in 1891 that: 'To have seen that vast, silent, and respectful crowd of all sorts and conditions of workers stand as the clergy passed in procession would carry the conviction that Mother Church has got too close a hold on people's hearts and minds to be shaken off even in a century.'[115]

Combining these beliefs with some of the feelings we saw expressed in a previous section, Lizzie Alldridge in Bow in 1894 commented that:

even among those of our working people who make no profession of religion . . . there is a feeling that Jesus Christ is the truest Friend of the Poor; that He . . . is the one real champion of their rights, in a manner they cannot explain, but of which in their heart of hearts they are deeply conscious . . . He is their ideal standard of excellence; and they are keen judges of the consistency of those who profess to be Christian.[116]

Sarah Williams has discussed in detail 'the ranks of devout working-class believers who are frequently ignored in studies of working-class religion and who existed in far greater numbers than was appreciated by observers such as Charles Booth'.[117]

It is clear that in much the same areas as displayed a high level of working-class church attendance, there existed also to a larger extent what Jose Harris has described as the 'great deal of informal and unstructured working-class religious activity which has largely escaped the eyes of

[113] The Revd W. Daniel, Coverdale Chapel, Limehouse, Booth MSS B171, 20; the Revd T. Sissons, Wycliffe Chapel, Commercial Road, B223, 15; the Revd A. E. Dalton, St Dunstan's, Stepney, B182, 45; the Revd F. H. Dinnis, St Peter's, Mile End, B182, 5; the Revd A. Chandler, Rector of Poplar, B169, 35; *London City Mission Magazine*, 51 (June 1886), 105.

[114] Loane, *Neighbours*, 203.

[115] *East London Advertiser*, 21 Nov. 1891, p. 8 col.c. See also 14 Mar. 1891, p. 8 col.a.

[116] *Biblewomen and Nurses*, 11 (Sept. 1894), 168–9.

[117] Williams, 'Religious Belief', 208 and *passim*.

historians'.[118] This was important in the politics of these areas. This 'informal' religious activity could involve much that was 'marginally' attached to the church—mothers' meetings, clubs, discussion groups, linked usually with occasional church attendance at the 'ritual' times of baptism, marriage, or funeral. Participation in such rituals, says Williams, 'could include a reaffirmation of an ideal of "right living" drawn from church-based culture. It aroused a wave of nostalgia which was signified in response to prayer, preaching and hymn singing and it involved an emotional link with the church which formed a powerful, if intangible bond with Church-based culture even among those who only attended very infrequently'.[119]

Williams has argued that this marginal attachment was to be found most amongst the 'middle stratum' of the urban working class.[120] The extent and nature of such attachment is clearly more difficult to define than simply surveyed Sunday church attendance, but it seems most likely that these attachments were stronger amongst the more prosperous, or at least more regularly employed, working class, and in 'mixed' neighbourhoods. Carl Chinn notes, regarding Manchester, that often 'the only outside interest' of many upper working-class women was in a 'religious club' or mothers' meeting.[121] 'Biblewomen' visitors throughout the East End reported that a large number of the women who attended their mothers' meetings lived amongst the 'aristocrats' of 'dock labourers . . . carmen, and policemen, and postmen' in block model workmen's dwellings, or were the wives of workers in areas of 'rather nice' homes.[122]

St Mary's, Bromley, had one of the higher levels of overall church attendance, but this was still only around 12 per cent of the adult population. But the vicar claimed that his church was 'in touch', in one way or another, with 'quite $\frac{3}{4}$ of the parish', and in addition to the normal services the church ran seventeen Bible classes and other clubs, with a total attendance of around 2,500 people—or six times the Anglican church-service attendance, with 2,000 children also attending the Sunday Schools.[123] By comparison, the vicars in two of the parishes with the lowest attendances in Bromley, St Paul's and St Gabriel's, could say 'anything that has to do with religion is languid in this parish . . . Portion touched—Two per cent', and that the

---

[118] Harris, *Private Lives*, 160.   [119] Williams, 'Religious Belief', 178.

[120] Ibid. 43.

[121] C. Chinn, *They Worked All Their Lives: Women of the Urban Poor in England, 1880–1939* (Manchester, 1988), 116.

[122] *Biblewomen and Nurses*, 15 (June 1898), 111–13, 116–18; and 6 (Dec. 1889), 223; and see 19 (Mar. 1902), 50, and *Bible Work at Home and Abroad*, 3 (Nov. 1886), 329–31. On block dwellings, see below.

[123] The Revd J. Parry, Rector of Bromley, Booth MSS B175, 53–5.

'influence of the Church on the whole is very slight . . . we are only just scratching the surface'.[124]

In St Matthias's, Poplar, which had a high attendance level, the vicar claimed the church was 'in touch with the whole parish', and that they doubled their congregation size each Sunday with outdoor services attended by men and women who did not go to church itself, but who were 'prompted to attend by a vague religious instinct'. In St Frideswide, Poplar, which had a reasonable Anglican congregation of around 500–600, and no other churches, the vicar believed that 2,000 of the 7,000 in the parish were 'under the influence of religion'.[125]

Interestingly, the prevalence of religious attachment 'outside' the parish church is also linked to major reasons why the type of analysis of church attendance and politics undertaken earlier for Poplar and Bow and Bromley becomes almost impossible for areas closer to the inner East End. First, there was the significant Jewish immigration into these inner areas, and a large number of Catholic residents from earlier Irish immigration, which means that the strength of Protestant churches cannot be estimated as precisely against the total population. Secondly, the electoral wards rarely had common boundaries with the parishes. In Limehouse and other constituencies, wards contained parts of up to four different parishes, making calculation extremely difficult. But the third and major reason was that the influence of huge preaching centres in some of these other areas greatly distorted the picture in individual parishes in a way that did not occur in Poplar and Bow and Bromley. In Limehouse, to take one example, this was apparent particularly in relation to Dr Barnardo's 'Edinburgh Castle', which was located in Rhodeswell Road, Limehouse, but which fell within the Mile End South East ward. It drew huge evening congregations of between 1,500 and 3,000 people.[126] Booth's reporter stood outside the centre one night and 'watched the people going in. They came in a continuous stream from the East, and there was evidently a large congregation . . . the quarter from which they came shows that they are dwellers in Burdett Road, and the respectable streets in its neighbourhood.[127]

The geography of the electoral wards means, from this, that the crowd was in fact mainly coming from the northern parts of the Limehouse North and Limehouse South wards into this other area. But there is no way, of course, that their attendance can be estimated and used in relation to these wards in the same way as for the other districts analysed earlier.

[124] Booth MSS B175, 147, 161, and 131.
[125] The Revd J. Neil, Booth MSS B169, 51 and the Revd W. A. Carroll, MSS B175, 113.
[126] See Booth MSS B385, 17 and B183, 237.   [127] Booth MSS B385, 45.

Such movement did occur in Poplar and Bow and Bromley, with some Nonconformist churches drawing congregations across parish boundaries, but it was the massive size of these evangelical centres in Limehouse, Mile End, Stepney, and surrounding areas which completely distorted the attendance figures. They drew crowds away from both the Nonconformist and Anglican churches, which means that it is also not possible to accurately examine the separate Anglican figures, as could be done in Poplar and Bow and Bromley. The Anglican rector of Limehouse complained that the 'most important influence now was Barnardo's "Edinburgh Castle" where large crowds were attracted—2,000 people sometimes in the large hall . . . young men and girls liked to go'.[128] Booth's summary of the effect of these centres was that they 'simply cater successfully for the religious tastes of many people of the middle and working classes. What they offer falls in with the usual habits of large numbers of the people, especially young people, on Sunday, and their audiences are drawn from a wide area.'[129] One minister said that such 'missions attract the floating Christian population: people who but for these missions would be in the churches'.[130]

The Stepney seat, as a further example, must have been unique in having on streets just outside its boundaries four extremely large places of worship, which at the turn of the century attracted perhaps 10,000 people in total regularly to their services. These were the East London Tabernacle in Mile End, 'the second largest Baptist church in England', with a membership of at least 2,000; the 'Edinburgh Castle' in Limehouse; the Wesleyan East End Mission in Commercial Road, with around 1,000 attending each Sunday; and the largest of them all, Frederick Charrington's Great Assembly Hall in Mile End Road, which regularly held 5,000 worshippers. As one Stepney Congregationalist put it, 'Charrington's swallows everything', and the severe effect of all these places was regularly mentioned by the clergy in Stepney and surrounds.[131] There is much to suggest that the attendance at these great halls has not been sufficiently noted in discussions of religion in the area. In St Philip's parish, Stepney, a London City Missionary thought that, although few people were seen at any of the churches in the parish, the quite high total of 20 per cent of the adult population attended one place of

---

[128] The Revd F. Gurdon, Booth MSS B169, 105. See also the Revd A. E. Dalton of St Dunstan's, Stepney, B182, 45.

[129] Booth, *Life*, 3rd series, vol. 1, p. 45.

[130] The Revd J. F. Fletcher, Commercial Road Baptist Church, Booth MSS B224, 45.

[131] Booth MSS B223, 27; and see the Revd Chambers, Congregational Meeting House, near Stepney Green—'Barnardo's, Charrington's and other places near has reduced the numbers'—B223, 39; Sissons at Wycliffe Chapel—'Charrington's is strong'—B223, 15; see also B171, 20, and B176, 139, and 207.

worship or another. The Great Assembly Hall 'swallows up the people', he also argued.[132]

Grace Foakes, whose father was a regularly employed wharf worker, lived in a block dwelling in Wapping, and as a child before the First World War attended the local Wesleyan Sunday School regularly. But her parents on many Sundays walked for an hour each way to attend services at the Great Assembly Hall.[133] It is difficult to tell how many others from the 're-spectable' block dwellings did likewise. Foakes noted that when church missionaries visited the area, 'Windows were flung open and people leaned out, listening to the singing. When the hymn finished, the old man prayed and men bared their heads.'[134] It is an examination of the type of social mi-lieu experienced by Grace Foakes, and very many others in the East End in this period, that can illustrate in more concrete terms some of the points made above, and the likely importance of neighbourhood relationships, and religion, in the political responses of the working class.

ISOLATED AND FRIENDLESS

Block 'model' workmen's dwellings, built by local authorities and philan-thropic trusts to replace slum areas, were increasingly common in London from the 1880s. They were one place where the habits of the more prosper-ous, and voting, working class, often in a 'mixed' social environment, could be observed. As Stedman Jones notes, the result of the strict rules of the dwelling companies regarding both the prohibition of arrears and the pay-ment of rent in advance put this accommodation 'out of the reach of the cas-ual poor. Such dwellings were in effect confined to a relatively more prosperous and more secure section of the working class.'[135] An architect and advisor to the Board of Works told the Select Committee on Artizans' and Labourers' Dwellings' Improvement that, regarding the ordinary labourer, the model 'Peabody Buildings are of no use to that class, or of very little use to that class, but only to a higher class'.[136]

It is useful to look at where there was an extremely high concentration of such block dwellings, in two districts in the Limehouse and St George's constituencies respectively—the areas of Shadwell and Wapping. In

---

[132] Mr W. B. Murray, Booth MSS B223, 105.
[133] G. Foakes, *My Part of the River*, combined edn. (1976), 38–41.
[134] Ibid. 123–4.   [135] Stedman Jones, *Outcast London*, 184–5.
[136] *SC Artizans' and Labourers' Dwellings*, P.P. 1881 VII, q. 3271. See also the evidence of the Revd John Horseley, *RC Housing*, P.P. 1884–85 XXX, qq. 2266–70; Wohl, *The Eternal Slum*, ch. 6; and id., 'The Housing of the Working Classes', 39–40.

walking through Shadwell in 1898, Duckworth noted area after area where there had been 'wholesale clearance followed by the building of high blocks of model dwellings'.[137] The vicar of St Paul's, Shadwell, said that in the area the housing was 'very good. Many blocks. Slums cleared away. Mentioned the Peabody Buildings . . . 3 blocks under the control of Col. Drew . . . the L.C.C. blocks in Bewley Street and Dellow Street; and Ashby Homes in Juniper Street.'[138] The Peabody, LCC, and Juniper Street buildings alone by 1901 housed 618 families—or around 2,500 people—approximately one-third of the whole population of the Shadwell ward.[139] With the other blocks in the area, model dwellings housed a total of between 40 and 50 per cent of the population. Duckworth, in 1898, had noted the additional 'great clearances' ready for construction.[140]

The London City Missionary who worked in the Shadwell ward defined both its dominant housing type and the character of the tenants: 'The people are rather better than those east or west of his district and there is no extreme poverty. If the people cannot pay the rent in the dwellings, they have to go.'[141] Of Wapping also, Duckworth said it 'was peculiar in that the best of its inhabitants have gone to live in Buildings rather than in the small houses'.[142] Shadwell and Wapping had easily the highest percentage of rated households of any identifiable area in the East End, and flowing from that, the highest level of enfranchisement of any wards in the Stepney borough.[143] Both of these were the result of the compounding of rates in the model dwellings. That is, the owners of the blocks paid the rates of the tenants in a lump sum (at a discount), and included this cost in the rent. This practice made the individual tenant a ratepayer, and eligible for the vote, if the landlord passed on their name to the authorities (as was discussed in Chapter 2).[144] In the block dwellings, with a direct relationship between the tenant and landlord company, more than elsewhere the names of tenants

---

[137] Booth MSS B350, 207.   [138] The Revd E. Bray, Booth MSS B222, 147.

[139] See A. Newsholme, 'The Vital Statistics of Peabody Buildings and other Artizans' and Labourers' Block Dwellings', *Journal of the Royal Statistical Society*, 54 (Mar. 1891), 88; the evidence of William Sims Horner in *RC Housing*, P.P. 1884–5 XXX, q. 12309; LCC, *Housing of the Working Classes in London, 1855–1912* (1913), 33 and 153; and Census, P.P. 1893–4 CIV, pp. 254 and 264.

[140] Booth MSS B350, 179.

[141] Mr W. J. Howell, London City Missionary of Love Lane Mission, Shadwell, Booth MSS B224, 71.

[142] Booth MSS B350, 227.

[143] See Census, P.P. 1893–4 CIV, pp. 80–1 and 253–4. The comparison excludes those areas, such as the Minories in Whitechapel, with only a handful of households. For the enfranchisement level, see *London Statistics*, vol. 23, *1912–13*, 33. Tower ward, although not covering all of Wapping, is used for this comparison.

[144] Subject to the residency and other requirements.

were properly provided to the municipal overseers for inclusion on the ratepayers' lists and then on the voters' registers.[145] In Shadwell and Wapping, as a result, 80 per cent of households were rated, up to a third higher than in other areas of the East End. It was noted in 1910 that, in comparison to other parts of St Georges, where in streets 'containing 100 houses there are not more than 20 voters', in Wapping 'the conditions are exactly the opposite'.[146] Even in 1891 around one-quarter of the electors in the relatively small Wapping polling district lived in just two blocks of dwellings, and of the flats in these blocks, 80 per cent had a registered voter.[147]

More than 3,000 people were living in the model dwellings in Shadwell at the turn of the century. It is more difficult to estimate the figure in Wapping, but clearly the numbers were high. Given that block dwellers perhaps accounted for at least 40–50 per cent of all households in these areas, then it is clear from the registration requirements that the percentage of voters on the registers who came from these dwellings would have been significantly higher than this. These block dwellers were the most important single voting group in these wards, and provided the clearest difference with other parts of the district.

Politically, the significant point is that these wards were also easily the most Conservative of the wards in the Limehouse and St George's-in-the-East constituencies. Shadwell Ward was the most electorally Conservative in Limehouse, returning 60 per cent Conservative councillors in 1900–12, with an average Conservative vote of 56 per cent. Wapping was joined for local-government elections to a part of Whitechapel around the Mint which was also 'a mass of Dwellings',[148] to become the Tower ward of Stepney. Tower ward returned only Conservatives to council in this period, and had an average Conservative vote of 60 per cent. In both the 1900 and 1903 borough elections, Shadwell, dominated by model dwellings, was the only ward in the Limehouse constituency to show a clear majority for the Conservatives. This suggests that the Tories might have struggled, even in the parliamentary contest for this seat, without the strength of this ward. Both Shadwell and Tower wards were significantly more 'Conservative' than the other, perhaps 'poverty sink-hole', riverside wards.

[145] See Davis, 'Slums and the Vote', for the clearest discussion of this complicated issue. For the compounding actions of the model-dwelling companies, see *RC Poor Laws*, P.P. 1910 XLIX, Apps. No. XXXIII–XXXVII, pp. 827–37.

[146] Feb. 1910 cutting from unnamed newspaper, Stansgate Papers, House of Lords Record Office, file ST/11, 17.

[147] New Tower and Old Tower Buildings, Wapping Polling District, St George's Division Electoral Register 1892.

[148] Booth MSS B351, 2. See also *London City Mission Magazine*, 77 (June 1912), 111.

But most importantly, if we examine the consistency of the progressive and Conservative 'core' vote for borough elections in Shadwell, we find, again, that the numbers voting for the progessives fluctuated widely, while the Conservative vote remained relatively stable. There were four contested borough votes in Shadwell in the period. The largest number of 'core' voters the progressives obtained was more than double their worst result, while for the Conservatives, their 'core' voters only varied by a tiny 14 per cent below and 6 per cent above the average number across the twelve years. The one time that the progressives were able to maximize their core vote, in 1912, they swept all positions in the ward. Significantly, however, the Conservative vote did not fall at all in that election from the previous contested poll. This suggests, again, that Conservative dominance in this model-dwelling dominated ward was the result of a general weakness in allegiance of its progressive voters, but that the 'underlying' majority was perhaps for the progressives.

The 'milieu' of the model-block dweller was in many ways very similar to that of the abstaining railway workers in Bromley North West noted earlier. Although the Peabody buildings in Shadwell had among the lowest rents of that Trust's buildings—averaging 3s. 3d. to 3s. 6d. a week for two rooms—and the lowest rents of any of the blocks in Shadwell, even in these buildings the majority of tenants were not of the poorest class. Nearly three-quarters of the tenants in 1887 had wages of at least 23s. a week, with 40 per cent earning more than 25s.[149] The vast majority were described as being in regular work. Booth calculated for one of the blocks of these buildings, that 60 per cent of tenants were within his definition of 'in comfort' (i.e. Class E or F).[150] In the thirty dwellings accommodating 240 families in Juniper Street, the lowest rent set was 5s. 9d., which was out of reach of all but the better-paid. Less than a sixth of dock workers (including the better-paid stevedores) in the adjoining area who were surveyed in 1887 were paying this much in rent. It was only amongst the machine- and instrument-makers and similar workers, and the lightermen, watermen, and seamen that perhaps a majority could afford this amount.[151] The Peabody blocks were the cheapest of all the dwellings, and while labourers and porters formed the largest single occupational groups generally in

---

[149] From an 1887 list of all tenants of this block in Booth MSS B19, 49–58.

[150] See Booth, *Life*, 1st series, vol. 3, pp. 49–50, under the pseudonym 'Lyndon Square'.

[151] See *Statements of Men*, P.P. 1887 LXXI, using the Eastern District statistics, which cover St George's-in-the-East. In the LCC buildings, most tenements were of two or three rooms, and the rents charged for these in 1912 were between 5s. 6d. and 7s. 6d. per week, LCC, *Housing of the Working Classes*, 155.

Peabody buildings[152]—of course dock workers in Shadwell and Wapping—they undoubtedly needed to be the regularly employed and certainly 'respectable'.

Interestingly, in both the Peabody and LCC dwellings, the third- or fourth-largest male employment group was police constables. Police and their families formed usually around 5 per cent of residents. The figure was even higher than this in the Shadwell Peabody blocks. As Stedman Jones notes, the model dwellings 'attracted more curates and policemen than unskilled casual labourers'.[153] It is noticeable that police-constable residents were almost a constant feature of respectable, mixed East End areas. (Also interestingly, the Liberal party did not believe that police constables were likely to support them. On more than one occasion they objected at the revision courts to the franchise of all the police in a station.[154])

Pember Reeves noted that demand for rooms in such dwellings was such that they were 'snapped up, and tend to go to the man with . . . a recognized and permanent position'.[155] Beatrice Potter's knowledge of the type of labourer who could remain in such dwellings came from her own experience in managing the Katherine Buildings further along the river in Whitechapel. The rents in these buildings were similar to the Shadwell Peabody blocks,[156] and Potter and her co-managers had been keen to house the 'lowest class of the self-supporting poor', but Ella Pycroft, the co-manager, had to admit that 'It has been much to my disappointment that the tenants of the lowest class can not be kept in the Buildings . . . & I have been obliged to turn out the rough set.' Like the Peabody and other buildings, it 'was a varied community in occupational terms', including skilled and semi-skilled workers.[157]

Octavia Hill provided an extensive description for Booth of life in model dwellings. There was a limited level of community spirit and contact. Hill noted that 'Mrs. A. has a brisk gossip on her threshold with Mrs C., the tram-conductor's wife . . . In the evening some of the men go out to the neighbouring "Club" and sing songs or talk politics, one or two drop

---

[152] See Newsholme, *Vital Statistics*, 90, and *SC Artizans' and Labourers' Dwellings*, P.P. 1881 VII, App. No. 16.

[153] Stedman Jones, *Outcast London*, 187.

[154] See *East London Advertiser*, 10 Sept. 1887, p. 3 col.a, and 8 Sept. 1888, p. 3 col.a.

[155] Pember Reeves, *Round About*, 29.

[156] See Booth MSS B19, 1–15. The Katherine Buildings were probably slightly poorer than the Peabody Buildings in Shadwell.

[157] See R. O'Day, 'Katherine Buildings', in R. Finnegan and M. Drake (eds.), *From Family Tree to Family History* (Cambridge, 1994), 144–5 and 147, and L. Alldridge, 'East of the Tower', *Biblewomen and Nurses*, 6 (June 1889), 108–9.

into the bar of the favourite "pub"', but the majority, she said, 'simply stay at home with the wife and children'.[158] Generally Hill described the 'large groups of blocks where the tenants are the quiet, respectable, working-class families, who, to use a phrase common in London, "keep themselves to themselves"'[159]—a description we will see later to be politically important. She suggested that communal laundries in some block dwellings were unpopular, due to the 'weighty objection' of the 'better class woman' to doing 'her work in a semi-public laundry. She will not: she does not like to mix up with everybody'.[160] Melanie Tebbutt, in contrast, demonstrates the importance of the washing ritual as a meeting and gossip time for those working-class areas with a strong sense of 'neighbourliness'.[161]

The 'friendlessness' of women in block dwellings, compared to those in poorer street settings, was often emphasized. This lack of mixing was often enforced by men seeking to demonstrate their family's standing. Indeed, a good deal of the 'friendlessness' suffered by women in the model dwellings was due to the desire to establish a social distance from the neighbours in order to distinguish one's family from the 'rough' working class and their habits. This was very much part of the desire to establish self-esteem through respectability and, associated with this, sexual difference, as discussed in the first section of this chapter. In the model dwellings one could find male 'respectable' residents proudly claiming they made a point of 'not mixing up with anyone—women get thick together and then there's always a row'.[162] Williams notes the existence of a 'public opinion' within poorer working-class neighbourhoods which operated to reinforce 'shared values and identities', but that in areas such as the model dwellings a 'public opinion' did not develop.[163]

Ross argues that the generally middle-class infant-welfare workers who visited working-class homes were often rejected in poorer areas in favour of 'pitiably ignorant and superstitious' advice given by older relatives and other women in the community. In sharp contrast, however, Ross points out that 'Women who were isolated from neighbours and relatives were most enthusiastic about professional infant welfare services.'[164] In a very similar way, the women from Bible societies and similar organizations who visited

---

[158] Booth, *Life*, 1st series, vol. 3, pp. 39–41.   [159] Ibid. 31.   [160] Ibid. 26.

[161] M. Tebbutt, *Women's Talk?: A Social History of 'Gossip' in Working-Class Neighbourhoods* (Aldershot, 1995), 59.

[162] Webb, MS Diary, vol. 11, p. 31, typescript 814.

[163] See Williams, 'Religious Belief', 80–4.

[164] E. Ross, 'Good and Bad Mothers: Lady Philanthropists and London Housewives Before the First World War', in K. D. McCarthy (ed.), *Lady Bountiful Revisited: Women, Philanthropy and Power* (New Brunswick, 1990), 178–9.

block dwellings, for example, could find many who were most willing to listen to them. In Mile End, one Biblewoman said of a block situated in an otherwise generally poor area, that the 'people there seem so friendless . . . Over and over again in this one block the Biblewoman had been told how glad the people are to realise that she cares enough for them to make an effort to over-come their reluctance to admit her and to manage to get on friendly terms with them.'[165] In the Katherine Buildings, Potter noted that the 'respectable tenants keep rigidly to themselves. To isolate yourself from your surround-ings seems to be here the acme of social morality . . . Do not meddle with your neighbours is perforce the burden of one's advice to newcomers.'[166]

In 1887 the Liberal MP Thorold Rogers made a comment which seemed to perceptively and accurately draw together the social structure and pol-itics of areas such as these model dwellings. Of the London voter, he said, who 'does not know who his neighbour is . . . [and who] is commendably in-different to his neighbour's private affairs', with 'comparatively few excep-tions politics have a loose hold on him. He has no alacrity in voting, a great alacrity in abstaining.'[167] As areas where neighbourhood pressures, such as in the case of 'chaff' against religious beliefs, were at their weakest, and where neighbours in fact had little contact or influence upon each other, it appears here that the motivation to vote could also be at its most tenuous.

Rogers continued, on 'political' influences upon the working-class, that 'by far the largest part of the [London] working classes, though not particu-larly sectarian, is religious. The Tory party is perfectly aware of how useful a canvasser is who can boldly state that the Radical candidate is an atheist or a freethinker.'[168] In Limehouse, with its very large number of model dwellings in Shadwell, the defeated Liberal candidate in 1895 attributed his loss in part directly to such influences—'The spread of electioneering lies, such as that I was an "Atheist" . . . [and the] hostility of the established clergy.' It is also notable that in the same context he commented bitterly upon the 'pretty general ignorance of Liberalism and Toryism in the past, and their aims in the future'.[169] There are very good reasons for suggesting that the Conservative party could spread precisely such 'electioneering lies' with much greater effect. This was at least partly because of the combin-ation, suggested by Rogers, of 'marginal' attachment to the Church with the isolating aspects of the 'respectability' of sections of the voting working class.

---

[165] *Biblewomen and Nurses*, 20 (Nov. 1903), 226.
[166] Webb, MS Diary, quoted O'Day, 'Katherine Buildings', 146.
[167] Rogers, 'Confessions', 688.   [168] Ibid. 689.
[169] *East London Advertiser*, 27 July 1895, p. 8 col.c.

Carl Chinn, to give the full context of a brief quote mentioned earlier, notes, regarding working-class communities in Manchester, that:

The houses of the poor were small, their furnishings sparse and their comfort minimal. This in itself encouraged their women to spend whatever time they could on the street, which became as much a centre for community life for wives as it was for husbands or children . . . whilst a woman of the urban poor preferred to pass any spare time she had in chat with others, open to public view and reproach, the wives of the upper working class spent their moments of relaxation indoors and thus evaded the slur of idleness . . . With the advance of the social scale . . . family life became more private, with the women left in the house all day whilst their husbands went to work. In fact, the only outside interest many wives from the upper working class had was in their membership of the Women's Co-operative Guild or of a religious club like the Mothers' Union, based at a parish church.[170]

Such a characterization is also appropriate for London. In one example, it was said, regarding a 'mixed' area, that:

The lower middle classes and some well-to-do professional people had their solid homes round the park, and as a buffer between them and our rough and ready district, there intervened streets inhabited by those who would have been offended to be termed 'working class'. It was customary here for front doors to be closed when men returned from work, and their wives were not to be seen gossiping in friendly neighbourhood fashion.[171]

Those of the working class who kept themselves 'apart' from the rest, because of such values, were clearly the most susceptible to the approaches of the visitor. Loane said that amongst those of the working class, male and female, who sought to be 'strictly exclusive',

'Not to let any one know your business,' is at once a duty, a joy, a burden, an absorbing occupation, and a consolation. It is often practiced more strictly with regard to near neighbours than with regard to educated visitors. With no further desire than to enjoy a little of human intercourse and sympathy of which they voluntarily stint themselves, men and women alike will reveal many things which they fondly hope are not even dimly suspected by the 'keerless, common sort of neighbours'.[172]

This suggests an isolation amongst both men and women in such circumstances, and little discussion or influences existing outside of the 'human intercourse' offered by the educated visitor. We saw earlier a number of such examples of isolation, as in the case of the model dwellings.

---

[170] Chinn, *They Worked*, 115–16.
[171] W. Greenwood, *There Was a Time* (1967), quoted in Tebbutt, *Women's Talk?*, 37–8.
[172] Loane, *Neighbours*, 260.

An East End Biblewoman told of her success in reaching some new mothers with advice: 'her practical guidance is of untold value to one who perhaps has no other respectable woman friend in the world, or had not until she was induced to come to the Mothers' Meeting',[173] Booth noted how influential even salesmen could be in 'better' working-class neighbourhoods, with 'Wives left at home all day'.[174] Women in this situation it seems were much more likely to listen to the 'advice' of outsiders on many issues. An insurance-society collector in the north of England:

remembered that his subscribers: 'treated you as friends when you got to know them properly. One lady I found in tears. I asked her what was the matter and she said, "I've just got this [forty pound] demand from the Income Tax"... I knew the circumstance, I knew how much she had coming in ... I said, "This is no good, it is not yours"... I said, "Just tear it up and put it on the fire".' The collector would give advice on the income tax, the Means Test, and even on whether particular employers were good or bad.[175]

Robert Roberts repeats this view almost exactly regarding the insurance collector: 'Somewhat better educated than his members, he was usually welcomed in homes as a friend and acted often as a walking citizen's advice bureau.'[176]

The political relationship of men and women within the working class, and the general role of working-class women in politics, has been somewhat downplayed by historians. This is mainly because of an assumed separateness of the male and female worlds. Ross McKibbin, in suggesting one reason why strong working-class community feeling could not be more effectively exploited by political parties, argues that a major factor was the 'sexual division of labour', in that a 'high degree of communitarian solidarity to some extent presupposes sexual solidarity: that the prime loyalties of a husband were to his family and neighbourhood. But it is doubtful if they were.'[177] Male solidarity focused upon the workplace, not the home, he says, and as 'long as the domestic and social lives of men and women were so divorced and while women remained excluded from formal political

---

[173] *Biblewomen and Nurses*, 6 (Apr. 1889), 71.

[174] Quoted Tebbutt, *Women's Talk?*, 69.

[175] Savage, *The Dynamics of Working-Class Politics*, 130, quoting an oral history transcript from Elizabeth Roberts.

[176] R. Roberts, *The Classic Slum: Salford Life in the First Quarter of the Century* (Manchester, 1971), 65.

[177] R. McKibbin, 'Why Was There No Marxism in Great Britain', in id., *The Ideologies of Class*, 9.

activity it is hard to see how a neighbourhood loyalty could override an occupational one'.[178]

Tebbutt broadly concurs with McKibbin in making her own distinction that, while 'gossip' also existed amongst males, it 'did not have the same formative effect upon local mores, since it was directed out of the neighbourhood, channelled into paid work and more organized leisure pursuits and thus dissipated. In the broader flow of talk and information which was essential to the effective functioning of neighbourhood life, male gossip was largely marginal.'[179]

But it is likely that amongst the Victorian and Edwardian working class there was perhaps less division between male and female 'worlds' than this allows, and an important aspect of working-class life has been underestimated as a result. Carl Chinn suggests, regarding the home, that there was indeed a 'hidden' relationship for men, which conflicts with McKibbin's characterization of males as 'passive members'.[180] Chinn[181] argues that:

many men helped their wives in the house, so long as it was behind closed doors and workmates and drinking partners remained unaware of such assistance . . . [there was a] 'hidden world' of many lower-working-class families, enclosed behind a facade of male dominance, separation of the sexes and female inferiority . . . Outwardly, the society of the urban poor conformed to its accepted image and indeed to the image it willingly projected. Inwardly, it was often at odds with that way of life.

Pember Reeves described a man who earned 25s. a week working for a Post Office contractor, who 'helps his wife in the housework and the cooking, and their home is one of the most spotless the visitor has seen'. Clearly, as noted earlier, it was the *demonstration* of sexual difference to the world that was important. This perception is supported by Robert Roberts, and also by evidence in parts of Tebbutt's work.[182]

The growing focus on the issues of the home, and an isolation from other influences for some men and women of the more prosperous working class, has been emphasized by Stedman Jones. He says of the skilled working man, that by the later part of the nineteenth century their:

Work-centred culture began to yield to a culture oriented towards the family and the home . . . With the shortening of the working week and the separation of living quarters from workplace, home and the family occupied a larger place in the working man's life . . . the regular pub visited would no longer be the trade pub near the workplace, but the 'local'. At the 'local' he would mingle with men of different

[178] Ibid. 11.   [179] Tebbutt, *Women's Talk?*, 49.   [180] McKibbin, 'Marxism', 9.
[181] Chinn, *They Worked*, 16.
[182] Pember Reeves, *Round About*, 171. See also Tebbutt, *Women's Talk?*, 117.

trades and occupation. Conversation was less likely to concern trade matters, more likely to reflect common interests, politics to a certain extent, but more often, sport and entertainment.[183]

Stedman Jones's conclusions about the effect of this upon politics have been questioned by historians.[184] However, his comments that the growing influence of the home, and the fact that 'wives had generally little contact with the traditional centres of political discussion', acted to help 'depoliticize' the working man may have elements of truth,[185] but in a much more complex way than he suggests.

The visiting Biblewomen and others found a close and reciprocal exchange of more than just domestic information between husbands and wives in a number of the working-class houses they visited. One woman in Bethnal Green told the visitor about the Bible stories she had been told at that week's Mothers' Meeting: 'I thought it was the most interesting story I had ever heard. I told my husband about it as soon as ever I got home.' Another Biblewoman told of the wife in rooms worth 6s. or 6s. 6d. a week: 'Her husband—a walking stick maker . . . Sunday afternoons when the little ones have gone to school . . . He always sat with her then, very often reading aloud.'[186] Tebbutt gives examples of where working-class men knew all the 'foibles' or 'troubles' of their neighbours, with this information clearly only having come via the home.[187] The wife of a carman for an LCC contractor described the end of her day:

7.30—Husband returns; get his supper.
8.00—Sit down and have supper with him.
8.30—Clear away and wash up. Sew while husband goes to bed. 'Talk wile 'e's doing it.'[188]

George Acorn in Bethnal Green remembered that in his working-class family, attitudes towards religion and God were 'the subjects of casual conversation' between his parents.[189]

At least one topic of conversation in any of these homes would undoubtedly have been any visitor coming to the house or other unusual outside contact that day, and any information of interest that this imparted, just as we saw amongst the 'strictly exclusive' couples spoken to by Loane. The

[183] Stedman Jones, 'Working-Class Culture', 217 and 220.
[184] See Davis, 'Radical Clubs'.   [185] Stedman Jones, 'Working-Class Culture', 220.
[186] *Bible Work at Home and Abroad*, 3 (Dec. 1886), 401, and *Biblewomen and Nurses*, 22 (Sept. 1905), 22–3.
[187] Tebbutt, *Womens' Talk?*, 15 and 164.   [188] Pember Reeves, *Round About*, 166.
[189] Acorn, *Multitude*, 50–1.

Conservative party's Primrose League of election campaigners argued, towards the end of the century, that in working-class areas women were politically 'the best canvassers, in as much as they are used to district visiting', and that 'advice or opinion given concerning the social or parochial matters . . . often have a greater influence than political considerations in deciding votes'.[190] A woman told one Liberal canvasser in a London working-class street of 'little cottages' during the 1885 general election that: 'if she had ten thousand votes she would give them to Mr. ——, naming the Conservative candidate. I told her his party wanted to tax the tea . . . "Well, he ought not to do that; but you know he is such a good man, he attends church regularly, and helps the poor. I couldn't help voting for such a man as he".'[191] It is possible that she had obtained such information about the activities of the candidate from attending a mothers' meeting or from a friendly visit by a worker from the 'good man's' church. Home visitors, usually female, were a common feature of many of the religious institutions in the East End and elsewhere. The political awareness of some of the 'lady visitors' was suggested by the fact that the St George's Liberal party objected in 1899 to the municipal franchise registration claims of 'four philanthropic ladies working for a mission' who 'devoted most of their time to visiting'.[192]

During the 1894 School Board elections, the Social Democratic Federation candidate in Hackney (covering Bethnal Green and Shoreditch), Rose Jarvis, complained that 'One woman whom I asked to vote for me replied that the "lady" [visitor] had not yet told her which way to vote. So you see . . . the mothers' meetings are a factor in the election.'[193] School Board elections were indeed usually more sectarian in their conflicts, but generally the influence of marginal religious attachment and morality upon the decisions of at least the female voter, as asserted by historians such as Patricia Hollis, is apparent here. Hollis says that women who did have the vote in local elections 'were known to show more independence than men by preferring moral character over party loyalty in their candidates'.[194] But politicians, such as Rogers above, evidently believed that a canvasser (who was perhaps also a local church visitor) could influence the votes of both men and women, even if only indirectly. This is clearly suggested by the

---

[190] Meresia Nevill in the *Primrose League Gazette*, 1 Oct. 1898, and *Primrose League Gazette*, 19 Nov. 1887, both quoted in Pugh, *The Tories*, 53.
[191] A Working Man, 'A Week of Canvassing', *Daily News*, 29 Sept. 1885, p. 3 col.c.
[192] *East London Advertiser*, 16 Sept. 1899, p. 8 col.f.
[193] *North Eastern Leader*, 27 Oct. 1894, p. 3 col.a.
[194] Hollis, *Ladies Elect*, 37. See also Tebbutt, *Women's Talk?*, 4.

fact that candidates from both sides used mission workers and other female canvassers even in parliamentary elections when no women had the vote.[195] This occurred regardless of Stedman Jones's argument that it was common for working-class men to hide rather than greet a church- or similar visitor in their home.[196] The role of working-class wives in transmitting political messages to their husbands, and the influence of women generally in such circumstances, is clearly a significant, but difficult, issue to study.

Vernon notes that in mid-century elections 'Candidates' wives were often used as canvassers, while the candidates themselves were always appealing to women to use their influence as wives, sisters, or daughters over the male voters'.[197] The wife of the Liberal candidate in the 1908 Haggerston parliamentary by-election made a point of making 'friends . . . among the working women' as she went from street to street on foot.[198] The Primrose League, probably with some hint of a vested interest, believed that 'the influence of the wives of the working men with their husbands is unbounded'.[199] In a less serious vein, in Whitechapel, Samuel, the Liberal candidate in 1910, issued a leaflet telling workmen they must vote against tariff reform because, 'Even if you wanted to vote for it your wife won't let you'.[200]

The influence visitors might have was directly suggested by Mrs Buckingham, who in 1910 visited a street of houses in Bethnal Green all making at least some attempt at 'respectability'. She commented upon her meeting with the resident of one house that: 'She was expecting me to call—she had "'eard up at the Church that someone was coming." She began to consult me about her children and everything else under the sun, and finished up by asking me how her husband was to vote.'[201] It was most likely in such circumstances that it would be the moral worth, or failings, of a candidate that would be commented upon, as we saw in the examples above.

They were perhaps not the typical relationships, even between more prosperous and home-focused working-class man and wife, where such information was easily discussed and passed on, or had any effect on the husband's vote. But just as important a possibility is that it did not need every wife to be communicating information to every husband for occasionally

[195] *Eastern Post*, 13 July 1895, p. 7 col.b. See also ibid., 13 Feb. 1895, p. 2 col.e, and *East London Observer*, 13 July 1895, p. 7 col.d.

[196] Stedman Jones, 'Working-Class Culture', 197.

[197] Vernon, *Politics and the People*, 92.

[198] *Daily News*, 29 July 1908, Shoreditch Cuttings Collection, Hackney Archives Department, Rose Lipman Library.

[199] *Primrose League Gazette*, 14 July 1888, quoted in Pugh, *The Tories*, 53.

[200] *Daily News*, 13 Jan. 1910, p. 9 col.d.

[201] *Oxford House Magazine*, 2: 7 (July 1910), 34.

some of these ideas to be 'channelled', as Tebbutt put it, generally into the 'male world'. A barber, quoted by Tebbutt, noted about men in Sheffield that: 'Gossip would spread in the street like wild fire, via the barber's shop, because they always used to tell me any scandal that was going on, whilst they were having their hair cut.'[202]

The connection here is emphasized by research, which suggests that while male and female gossip is different, the difference relates to its subjects and the direction in which it is 'channelled', rather than to its nature. Levin and Arluke found that:

Although male and female gossip did not differ with respect to tone, significant sex differences were uncovered for characteristics of their targets of gossip. Women were much more likely than men to gossip about close friends and family members . . . In contrast, men (46%) were more likely than women (16%) to talk about celebrities including sports figures . . . These sex differences in characteristics of targets seem to reflect traditional sex-role divisions, whereby women's activities were confined to family and friendship networks, while men's activities involved instrumental, usually distant, relationships . . . [If] gossip is regarded as only derogatory talk about others, then no significant differences in gossiping between men and women can be said to have occurred.[203]

Derogatory talk about 'celebrities'—if we can define politicians as such in the early twentieth century—is likely to have been as much a talking point amongst males, perhaps at the 'local' as Stedman Jones suggests, as personal, neighbourhood gossip was amongst poorer females. Vernon urges us to remember 'the immense significance of political leaders in nineteenth-century England. In a world devoid of the "stars" of mass entertainment and organized sport, they occupied a (possibly the) central place in popular culture, at once revered and reviled, loved and loathed. Indeed, when football and the music-hall eclipsed politics in the hierarchy of popular interests during the late nineteenth century, politicians were well represented in the supporting casts'[204]—perhaps like the 'marionettes' performing for working-class amusement, as mentioned earlier.

In a modern analysis, Robert Huckfeldt, in discussing the importance of neighbourhood, or 'contextual' influence on voting, has argued that:

superficial opinions are more likely to be affected than deeply embedded elements of the political psyche. Opinions toward political figures and personalities are

[202] T. Furniss, *The Walls of Jericho: Slum Life in Sheffield Between the Wars* (Sheffield, 1979), 27, quoted in Tebbutt, *Women's Talk?*, 49.

[203] J. Levin and A. Arluke, 'An Exploratory Analysis of Sex Differences in Gossip', *Sex Roles*, 12: 3/4 (1985), 284–5.

[204] Vernon, *Politics and the People*, 251.

certainly more transitory and peripheral than party identification . . . candidate preference during the latter stages of an election campaign is highly salient and frequently discussed and thus is especially susceptible to contextual influence.[205]

Perhaps the most important political role of working-class women, in relation to parliamentary elections at least, was as a 'conduit' of information, especially regarding the morals and 'worth' of politicians, and particularly local ones. Advice or information on such matters from visitors to the home, or from clubs or meetings, could either be directly influential upon husbands who may have similarly felt a moral, or 'marginal' attachment to the church, or it may have needed few entry points from women to men for it to be channelled out of the home environment. While Huckfeldt is talking of the direct neighbourhood and social effects of an area, such information, coming into the male 'gossip networks' communities through female contact with 'outsiders', could add much to the 'contextual influence' acting upon male political decision-making.

But an interest by the working class in such 'electioneering lies' should not necessarily have even indirectly favoured the Conservatives any more than the Liberals. Perhaps the reverse should have been the case, if one follows the normal models presented for politics in the poor urban areas. Duncan Tanner writes of the number of East End Liberal MPs involved in 'good works', and that generally Liberal policies were in fact often a 'shade too moral' for London constituencies. Jon Lawrence has discussed this last point broadly in regard to what he sees as the success of 'popular Toryism' against the 'faddist' Liberals. Susan Pennybacker has argued comprehensively, in fact, that Progressive 'moralizing' became very unpopular with London voters.[206]

But one central reason why any such generalized religious discourse amongst the working class seems not to have assisted the progressive side of politics was the fact that most of the 'marginal' attachment to religion discussed earlier was to Anglican rather than Nonconformist churches. This meant that most contact that these people had with religious issues, and the social activities associated with them, was through the perspective of this denomination and its activists. Most importantly in relation to this, the

---

[205] R. Huckfeldt, *Politics in Context: Assimilation and Conflict in Urban Neighbourhoods* (New York, 1986), 53–4 and 56.

[206] Tanner, *Political Change*, 166 and 171; J. Lawrence, 'Class and Gender in the Making of Urban Toryism, 1880–1914', *English Historical Review*, 108: 428 (July 1993), 635 ff.; S. Pennybacker, '"The Millennium by Return of Post": Reconsidering London Progressivism, 1889–1907', in Feldman and Stedman Jones, *Metropolis*, 155, and her *A Vision for London 1887–1914: Labour, Everyday Life and the LCC Experiment* (1995). See also Vernon, *Politics and the People*, 207.

general association of Conservative candidates with Anglicanism and Liberal candidates with Nonconformity seems to have been as strong in the East End as studies have shown it to have been elsewhere.[207]

Attachment to a Nonconformist church tended to be a more 'serious' commitment, with less scope for tenuous connections. Marginal attachment was also held to some extent by the ritual attendances of post-birth 'churching', baptism, funerals, and weddings, and the last in particular was very much concentrated in the parish church, partly for financial reasons.[208] As Booth noted, the Church of England 'fills a definite place in a definite area which the Nonconformists do not and cannot occupy'.[209]

The Anglican rector of Poplar said that the 'weakness of the Dissenters generally is that they do little or no visiting. They lay too much stress on preaching, and the Church is certainly in much closer touch with the people.'[210] This did vary to some extent between areas, depending upon the capability and approach of the individual minister, but generally the Established Church played a greater role in the 'social' and community activities which maintained some connection to the church. In St Dunstan's, Stepney, where the influence of the church was 'strong', the parish was 'thoroughly visited from house to house . . . by the clergy, the scripture reader, and the 13 lady workers'.[211]

In the Bible classes, mothers' meetings, and home visits and other activities associated with marginal attachment to the Church of England, it was in the interests of the activist, or the group, to emphasize any 'scandal' or atheism or other individual moral limitations, particularly in public life. As was said regarding a young wives' club run by the church, the 'club is not primarily a place to exchange gossip, but a centre where it can be judged against a set of standards which the members feel to be superior'.[212]

---

[207] See McLeod, *Class and Religion*, 172–3; Wald, *Crosses*, 196–7; and e.g. *Eastern Post*, 29 Sept. 1900, Supplement, p. 4 col.f; *East London Advertiser*, 6 Aug. 1892, p. 8 col.b, 26 Jan. 1907, p. 3 col.f, and 17 Nov. 1900, p. 8 col.f; and see also Thompson, *Socialists, Liberals and Labour*, 20.

[208] See the Revd W. Knight Chaplin, Poplar and Bromley Baptist Tabernacle, Booth MSS B176, 57–9, the Revd T. P. Lansdowne, Brunswick Congregational Church, B223, 29; and McLeod, *Class and Religion*, 32.

[209] Booth, *Life*, 3rd series, vol. 2, 85.

[210] The Revd A. Chandler, Booth MSS B169, 29.

[211] Booth MSS B182, 41. See also the Revd R. Free of St Cuthbert's, Millwall, B170, 7.

[212] J. Mogey, *Family and Neighbourhood* (1956), 107–8, quoted in Tebbutt, *Women's Talk?*, 63.

THE LOCAL ARISTOCRACY

It is clear that the areas which, at least in Poplar and Bow and Bromley, exhibited higher levels of church attendance, and as we saw were also linked
to greater apparent Conservatism, were those in which the more prosperous working class lived, or were, more likely, 'mixed' class areas. In combination with St George's and Limehouse (which included the Wapping
and Shadwell block-dwelling areas discussed earlier), the seats of Mile End
and Stepney formed the group of four 'classically' Conservative seats in the
East End in this period. The district of Mile End Old Town, which covered
the latter two constituencies, was clearly the wealthiest of the areas in East
London. As noted in Appendix 1, nearly 75 per cent of the residents of that
district were deemed to be 'in comfort' by Booth, far higher than any other
local area.

The Times described the comfortable nature of much of the Mile End seat
in 1905. It called this seat the 'principal residential district of East London',
citing this as the reason it had 'hitherto remained impervious to Liberal attacks'.[213] The East London Observer reported in 1895 that, at polling booths
in the constituency: 'Between six and eight the greatest rush was experienced as the residents returned from the City. For this important period
every preparation was made, and not a little of the [Conservative] success is
due to this cause.'[214]

The Stepney seat also included a similar central core of more prosperous
voters. Of the major areas of the Stepney Centre and South wards, Booth
said, respectively, that the 'majority of these people belong to a fairly comfortable class of artisans, shopmen and clerks' and the 'majority of the
people are in regular steady work: artisans, postmen, policemen, clerks,
shop assistants'.[215]

Much of this evidence can be seen to reverse the general argument, particularly seen in the quotes from Duncan Tanner and others noted in the
Introduction, as to the likely class geography of Conservative success in
London. There is also little doubt that a common response amongst a section of the more prosperous East End working class was to abstain at times
from voting. The evidence shown earlier has suggested that it was this, and
certainly not poverty and its effects, that was a major cause of the apparent
Conservatism of the East End. One reason suggested for this is that any

---

[213] 3 Jan. 1905, quoted *East London Observer*, 7 Jan. 1905, p. 7 col.c.
[214] *East London Observer*, 20 July 1895, p. 6 col.d.
[215] Booth, *Life*, 1st series, vol. II, App., areas 75B and 77B.

political influences in favour of progressivism were often weakened by specific social factors amongst parts of the more prosperous working class. A relatively widespread marginal attachment to the Church of England, and a greater isolation from the surrounding community, may have led to a much greater effectiveness of 'electioneering lies' and similar messages in favour of the church and Conservatives amongst this group. When such moral/religious comments were in conflict with their political leanings—again as Rogers stated, directly on this point—'it does not follow that electors to whom these statements are made and reiterated are made hostile to a candidate, but they are rendered indifferent, and think that, after all, they had better abstain from voting.'

By itself, this might have caused relatively few voters to neglect to vote, but Rogers also noted how influences could compound the effect. It was this type of voter, he said, who, when faced also with perhaps 'a schism in the party to which he has previously given his support', could become 'entirely neutral' in his politics.[216] It was a combination of such factors which could have the greatest impact on the political responses of the working class. The Liberal party had its very public 'schisms' around the time of the disastrous elections of 1886, 1895, and 1900. Yet it may not have lost its support so quickly amongst these groups of voters if their political allegiances had not been already weakened by the type of influences suggested above.

Yet it is very important to note that the simple strength of the church in any area did not automatically lead to this influence and response amongst the working class. This is an essential point in seeing the significance of personal and local dynamics. As noted earlier, the Bromley South East ward stood out as having an extremely low level of change between elections in its progressive turnout. The progressive vote in that ward was extremely stable. The ward covered an area of working-class comfort in Poplar, around the Abbott and Macintosh estates, which were described as 'occupied by a very respectable class . . . employed in the Docks, or as lightermen, or foremen in the factories and about'[217]—relatively prosperous workers. As also noted earlier, Bromley South East, partly as a result of this stability of the progressive vote, had a very much lower average Conservative vote (41.9 per cent) than its high Church of England attendance (9.7 per cent—one of the highest) would suggest. The parish church for Bromley South East was All Hallows, Poplar.[218] The Revd Dalton, who had moved from All Hallows

---

[216] Rogers, 'Confessions', 691 and 688.   [217] Booth MSS B346, 43.

[218] Confusingly, not the same as All Hallows, Bromley, which covered part of the Bromley South *West* ward.

to St Dunstan's, Stepney, said in 1897 that while the church had significant influence in his new parish, it was 'not so strong as at All Hallows, Poplar: there the working man while sticking to his opinion that the clergy were generally knaves and fools made an exception in favour of the clergy of All Hallows. Here [in Stepney] the influence of the church among working men is confined almost entirely to conservatives: further east they got hold of radicals and socialists.'[219]

Dalton was suggesting here that those involved with the church in St Dunstan's in Stepney were likely to be Conservative in attitude. This could be important in the overall milieu and political influences acting upon those workers who came into marginal contact with the church, as we saw above. In All Hallows, Poplar, by contrast, there were radicals and socialists involved heavily with the church, and they formed at least part of the social contact for those who were attached to the church. Conservatives complained that in parts of Poplar, of their supporters, 'more than half of them never attend church, because the sermons have become eulogies of Socialism and local Socialists'. The nature of the sermons at All Hallows is an important point in an examination of the strength and influence of socialism within general progressivism in Poplar. But for this study the most significant comment by local Conservatives in this period was their outcry at the clearly unusual situation that 'a great obstruction in the path of a Unionist candidate' was the attitude of Anglican clergymen in Poplar.[220]

The Anglican church milieu was quite different in this part of Poplar. Known widely for its radicalism, All Hallows seems to have greatly improved its reputation amongst working people by offering free marriage services at certain times of the year, a practice greatly resented by other churchmen in the area.[221] John Blake, who lived on the border of All Hallows, as we saw earlier suggested the 'great part' religion played in the lives of local people.[222] At the same time, the deacon of the nearby Congregational Church in Poplar complained that:

On Sundays parties of T[rade].U[nions].'s are marching about the district with bands and banners. Have had as many as twenty bands pass Trinity Church with their bands playing and banners waving, quite disturbing the congregation. Began about the time of the Great Dock Strike [eight years before] and has gone on since. Seldom a Sunday without something of the sort.[223]

[219] Booth MSS B182, 45.
[220] *Standard*, 29 Jan. 1909, cutting in Tower Hamlets Local History Collection, file 320.7.
[221] See interview with Father Thompson, Presbytery, Bow Common Lane, Booth MSS B180, 29.   [222] Blake, *Memories*, 7.
[223] John Gretton, Trinity Congregational Church, East India Dock Road, Booth MSS B171, 53.

This would clearly be thought to represent a much more important political influence on the local working class.

But the unions also marched through All Saints, the parish adjoining All Hallows in Poplar, which had a very similar population makeup and where the overall activity of trade unions was undoubtedly as strong. Indeed, the parish vicar of All Saints was the rector of Poplar, Dr Chandler, who was also Treasurer of the Poplar Labour League. Paul Thompson argues that Chandler was 'important as an early Labour supporter . . . It was acknowledging rather than leading local political feeling: but the support . . . in Woolwich and Poplar of the clergy, help to explain why these were the first areas in London to maintain successful independent Labour Parties.'[224] But, unlike All Hallows, Chandler's All Saints parish (Poplar East ward) returned thirteen out of fifteen Conservatives in the borough elections, and showed an average Conservative share of the vote of at least 60 per cent.

The generally progressive clergy in All Hallows undertook 'Systematic house to house visiting . . . [and] can thus give a very fair account of nearly all the houses in the parish'.[225] By contrast, the church in All Saints was quite different in this regard. Chandler noted that the clergy in his parish had little time for visiting in the area, which was done mainly by fourteen voluntary district visitors, who also attended the mothers' meetings. Significantly, Chandler said that of these visitors: '5 are residents who belong to the local aristocracy, daughters or wives of doctors etc. The remaining 9 are ladies from other parts of London.'[226] This, it seems, is much more likely to have been the 'face', and the influence, of the church met by working people in that parish.

There was a strong union involvement and presence in All Saints and All Hallows. But contact with the church in All Hallows with its radical visiting clergy, unlike All Saints, possibly did not act to weaken the milieu and ideas of working-class politics in the parish. To reinforce again the point of the importance of abstention, in Poplar East (the ward covered by All Saints), the number of Progressive voters in the party's worst borough elections dropped to nearly half that in its best year, while in Bromley South East (All Hallows) the number of Progressive/Labour voters, as we saw, varied by only an average of a tiny 5 per cent across the period. Bromley South East exhibited probably the most consistent overall turnout of voters in borough elections from 1900 to 1912 of any of the Poplar wards.[227]

---

[224] Thompson, *Socialists, Liberals and Labour*, 22 and 24–5.
[225] Booth MSS B169, 177–9.   [226] Ibid. 5–9.
[227] See *London Statistics*, vol. 23, *1912–13*, 32.

Again, in All Saints/Poplar East, where 'reinforcement' of progressive political ideas seems less likely to have occurred through overlapping milieus, or indeed where loyalties clashed, the commitment to progressive politics may have been weakened. Michael Savage suggests something of a similar pattern in his work on Preston. Between the 1890s and the First World War, he says, as church institutions were 'taken over' by the working class, they changed from being bodies which worked to 'pacify' the working class, to become 'sites of neighbourhood-based capacities leading to political mobilisation'.[228]

This chapter has concentrated upon explanations of the apparent Conservatism amongst the East End working class, in line with the key focus of this study. In many ways this has meant a simplified emphasis upon factors possibly acting to dilute the expression of the 'existing' political tendencies of the working class. But clearly the evidence does show, on a number of occasions, that voting abstention seems to have distorted an underlying majority progressivism amongst the more prosperous working class in some areas. The smaller number of poorer working-class voters, as we saw earlier in the chapter, instead seem on occasion to have seized upon 'scandal' to randomly, but actively, reject middle-class candidates of whatever party, with political results that are difficult to measure. So a range of potentially 'progressive' belief systems, and some broad 'class' understandings, seem likely to have formed the underlying foundation of the politics of the East End working class. This will be discussed in the following chapter. But it will also be suggested that these beliefs again acted to emphasize the personal in politics in a way which also reduced their own ideological impact.

---

[228] Savage, *The Dynamics of Working-Class Politics*, 108 and 117.

4

Small-Scale Radicalism

The progressive vote in some areas of the East End often fell well short of its potential. But of course voter abstention by itself could not deliver a seat to an opponent. The Conservatives still collected a large number of votes in these areas. The arguments above do not deny that factors such as an interest in 'sectional' benefits, and the impact of a range of political issues, could gather working-class support for Conservatives in the East End. As noted earlier, it is difficult to determine the precise effect of any such individual concerns. But this chapter will suggest that it remains more important to look at the overall milieu of voters in understanding their motivations, and that the 'occupational' assumptions made by many historians regarding politics in the East End have been much too simple.

Having said that, it still needs to be remembered that much of the Conservative vote in the East End potentially came from other than the working class. For example, even in the very poor St George's North ward examined in Chapter 2, around 20 per cent of those on the electoral register were of the middle class, shopkeepers and workers, or white-collar employees. In a wealthier area, such as the section analysed of Mile End East, such residents comprised at least 30 per cent of the register. Given the fact that they may have been slightly more likely to vote at all than many of the working-class voters (as discussed at the end of Chapter 2), and the fluctuations in voter turnout levels, these voters may have accounted for up to 50 per cent of votes in some elections in an area such as Mile End East.[1] But this is not to assume that all, or even a majority, of such voters supported the Conservatives on a 'class' basis. A number of indications suggest, however, that support for the Liberals was fading amongst many wealthier residents from the 1880s onwards, as politics did indeed tend towards some degree of class polarization. David Bebbington suggests that it was in London that 'the process whereby the middle classes were swinging towards solidarity

---

[1] This assumes an average voter turnout of around 65% in those parliamentary elections in which the Conservatives did best. But Mile End had a lower average voter turnout than, say, St George's.

against Liberalism was more advanced than anywhere else in Britain', even amongst those who formed the core of Nonconformism in the city.[2] This specific point will be discussed in relation to the East End in the next chapter. As Blewett notes, the 'middle-class exodus from the Liberal Party', which was 'most noticeable' in London, reached a 'new peak' in 1886, with Liberal Unionism being used as a 'stepping stone' to Conservatism.[3] With a number of notable exceptions, the 'trading element', as was said of Mile End, was perhaps by the end of the century 'mostly Moderate' (the name commonly used by Conservatives in local-government elections).[4] But, again, this study does not argue that electoral results should be looked at in such relatively simple class or occupational terms. It is probable that the currency of a range of social and political understandings amongst the working class in the East End created the *potential* for a majority progressive vote before the First World War. But there was a great complexity in the issues which acted to reduce and distort the impact of these beliefs, and indeed acted to build at least some level of working-class Conservative support upon them.

A key point underlying much of the previous chapter was the importance of the complex interrelationship between the two forms of the 'personal' affecting politics in the East End; for example, the particular connection between an interest in the importance of moral or individual character and the very specific local, personal circumstances that could foster and 'translate' this interest into politics. It was the multifarious relationship between convictions and social milieu that greatly influenced how politics would be responded to by the East End working class. More of this will be seen below.

The importance of a working-class desire for self-esteem has also been looked at. From this, the significance was suggested of a resultant 'outward' resentful response against the middle and upper classes within the political attitudes of, particularly, the poorer working class. This clearly indicated at least elements of a partial class divide in politics. But this is certainly not the way such desires have usually been seen to have impacted upon East End politics. Seen as much more important has been an 'inward-looking' response to this desire for self-esteem, causing an obsession with what Johnson says generally was the 'minutiae of keeping up appearances for the sake of neighbours, and of outdoing them if possible'.[5]

There is little doubt that competition regarding displays of status was keen in all neighbourhoods. It was discussed above how such concerns

---

[2] D. W. Bebbington, 'Nonconformity and Electoral Sociology, 1867–1918', *Historical Journal*, 27: 3 (1984), 645, and see 646–54.
[3] Blewett, *The Peers*, 6 and 15. [4] *East London Advertiser*, 29 Mar. 1902, p. 5 col.g.
[5] Johnson, *Saving and Spending*, 231–2.

could lead to isolation, and with quite specific political effects. But there is little reason to suggest that such competition was an overriding influence on working-class political attitudes, or in fact, as is usually argued, was far more extreme in the East End and a major cause of a lack of 'solidarity' and a fragmented approach towards politics by the East London working class.

As another aspect of this, Stedman Jones argues that in 'the docks, ship workers looked down upon shore workers and permanent labourers despised casuals. A bricklayer's labourer looked down upon the navvy. English costers despised Irish costers, and all unskilled labourers . . . felt entitled to look down upon the sweep.'[6] The 'classic' and often-used statement of these distinctions is that of Harry Gosling, the lightermen's union leader, who said that: 'The wife of a lighterman felt that she was with her equals when she went out shopping with the wife of a stevedore or the wife of a shipwright, but never with the wife of a docker or an unskilled labourer.'[7] Bush describes the East End as having 'a workforce so unstable, and so divided against itself', with 'endless rivalries and divisions of status'.[8] McKibbin notes that, while poor working-class communities 'were notoriously characterized by extraordinary mutuality they were also marked by backbiting, gossip, and a jockeying for social superiority'.[9]

Gosling's statement about the keen status awareness of the lighterman and his wife has often been cited by historians. Indeed lightermen, who sailed the barges on the Thames, have in particular often been credited with a strong Conservatism in the East End. Henry Pelling, Stedman Jones, and others have argued that, with a general dominance of status and fragmentation and a resulting absence of any general working-class consciousness or the conditions for strong trade unionism, it was understandable that 'sectional interests' motivated such relatively skilled workers in London to support the Conservatives. So did:

watch-makers and sugar refiners . . . because they thought tariff reform would arrest the decline of their trades. Lightermen . . . because they [the Conservatives] promised to defend their traditional corporate privileges; munitions workers and engineers in the Arsenal, because they believed that an aggressive foreign policy would mean fuller employment and higher wages; [and] brewery workers, because a Liberal government would mean the threat of temperance legislation.[10]

[6] Stedman Jones, *Outcast*, 338.

[7] Gosling, *Up and Down Stream*, 144–5, quoted Stedman Jones, *Outcast*, 338.

[8] Bush, *Behind the Lines*, 2–4.   [9] McKibbin, 'Marxism', 11.

[10] Stedman Jones, 'Working-Class Culture', 213, paraphrasing Pelling, *Social Geography*. See also Pugh, *The Tories*, 107.

But while such issues were naturally of significance in the politics of workers, this characterization is far too simple.

Regularly employed brewery workers living in a street in Mile End New Town, who Stedman Jones would have said feared Liberal temperance, were, as we saw, reported to be often keen churchgoers. Conservatism in their area was put down to 'the Church influence'. A conflict between the implied sectional and cultural interests is apparent here. Lightermen, again, although they lived in some numbers in the model dwellings, could not by themselves have determined the Conservative success in Shadwell and Tower wards. Voters in a wide range of relatively prosperous and regular positions—and importantly, in a somewhat socially 'mixed' environment—generally dominated these wards, and, as we saw, abstention amongst progressive voters, not direct Conservatism, was perhaps most important here. These were also not simple, economically determined cases of a working-class 'aristocracy' perhaps exhibiting its sectionalism and status and failing to support its 'class'. In different circumstances and milieus, as we saw in Bromley South East, similar workers, even including the lightermen, did support progressive politics.

Johnson, like McKibbin, seeks to qualify perceptions of the 'neighbourliness' and culture of sharing within working-class communities. Despite 'the charity, the gossip, the strong sense of community', he says, one could also find in such areas that (and here he quotes Maud Pember Reeves regarding South London), 'the inhabitants keep themselves to themselves, and watch the doings of the other people from behind window curtains'. 'Within each street', Johnson says, 'there was a curious mixture of neighbourliness and isolation.' This isolation came from the fact that the working-class was 'decomposed into many strata with slightly different value systems, aspirations, interests, and incomes'.[11] Working-class solidarity, according to Johnson, failed again because of this 'decomposition'.

But such explanations are essentially as one-dimensional as the idea that there existed a 'monolithic' class consciousness in the late nineteenth century 'which united workers of all strata and sections', a concept that Johnson is keen to disclaim.[12] In a similar way, analyses such as Johnson's also tend to portray the working class as one conglomerate group, but consistently riven everywhere by the 'minutiae' of minor status differences. Johnson neglects to make clear that Pember Reeves's quote above concerned a specific area whose inhabitants were 'not the poorest people in the district. Far from it!' While many may have been manual workers, they were

---

[11] Johnson, *Saving and Spending*, 227 and 231.   [12] Ibid. 231–2.

'respectable men in full work, at a more or less top wage'.[13] It is clear from a number of studies, as examined in Chapter 3, that personal isolation was much more a function of the lifestyles of more prosperous workers. Communal sharing, and the charity and the gossip, can be much more closely associated with poorer communities and individuals.[14] The differences between the mores of working-class areas and groups needs to be acknowledged and studied, as does the fact that it was possible for there to be a wide range of not mutually exclusive, concurrent responses to social circumstances, as this study has attempted to show.

Neville Kirk, in a critique of Johnson's work, suggests that even 'in the course of pursuing a variety of aims (personal and, for example, family-based) within circumstances largely not of their own choosing people can . . . identify common points of interest and come to act, and even struggle, around these common points of identity both as individuals and as members of wider collectivities'.[15] In political terms, one aspect which was most important in the East End was not simply individualist working-class responses leading to status division and fragmentation, but instead an acceptance of the closely related and concurrent view that there also existed 'common points of identity' based upon the *moral* division of society. This was an approach that was also clearly encouraged, as we will see, by a number of aspects of progressive and labour politics.

Of the All Hallows/Bromley South East area discussed earlier, it was said that: 'working men are generally under the influence of trade unionism. Their teaching if anything is social and ethical. Not that socialism proper is strong here . . . It is really a modified socialism, reflecting the influence of Mr Crooks who is the leading spirit here and holds meetings outside the Dock gates on Sunday. One good thing about it is a strong opposition to drink and gambling.'[16] Patrick Joyce and Jon Lawrence have drawn parallels between the ideals of such 'modified', moral, ethical, or religiously based socialism, and the strong traditions of popular radicalism.[17]

---

[13] Pember Reeves, *Round About*, 2–3. Johnson's quote is from 3–4.

[14] See Tebbutt, *Women's Talk?*, 2, and E. Roberts, *A Woman's Place: An Oral History of Working-Class Women 1890–1940* (Oxford, 1984), 195. Clearly this line cannot be drawn too sharply, and undoubtedly individual exceptions were not uncommon, but the general point holds. See Ross, 'Not the Sort', 51 and *passim*.

[15] N. Kirk, '"Traditional" Working-Class Culture and "the Rise of Labour": Some Preliminary Questions and Observations', *Social History*, 16: 2 (May 1991), 206.

[16] Robert Brown, Poor Steward of Poplar Wesleyan Methodist Church, Booth MSS B171, 11.

[17] See Joyce, *Visions*, 75–84, and Lawrence, 'Popular Radicalism'. For the continuing significance of popular radicalism generally, see the important contributions in Biagini and Reid, *Currents of Radicalism*, and Joyce, *Visions*, *passim*.

Bedarida's description specifically of nineteenth-century Poplar politics
also emphasizes the fundamental importance there of this combination of
old and new beliefs in the basic political understandings of the working
class. Although Bedarida says that there was a good deal of 'political indif-
ference' in Poplar, he also identifies two clear types of working-class political consciousness. First there was the:

democratic or *popular*: here the accent is not on class, but on the common fate of the
working people, or more exactly 'the small people' (including self-employed artisans and small businessmen), who are all victims of the selfish interests of the
wealthy and the idle. Such a notion of the *common people*, deeply rooted as it is in the
East End . . . was characterised by Will Crooks, the first labour man to be elected in
Poplar, himself a working man living amidst working men, and a doughty champion
of the Lib-Lab alliance.[18]

But there was also a '*class consciousness* which might also be called *social-
democratic*. Here the emphasis is on class opposition, specifically opposition
to an alliance with the middle-class. Based on the workers' own claims, this
attitude rebelled against radicalism. It developed only in the closing years
of the century, finding its haven in Bow and Bromley and centring on the
person of Lansbury.' But most importantly, Bedarida concludes that 'despite theoretical opposition between advocates of the class struggle and
those of the Lib-Lab alliance, there were incessant shifts among the rank
and file from one form of consciousness to another. This was entirely in
tune with the heterogeneous and ambiguous nature of the Labour movement in Poplar and its older radical tradition.'[19]

It is clear that the moral, ethical beliefs described above in All Hallows
were important in the ideologies of a number of influential labour leaders
across the East End—and with much of the political 'ambiguity' suggested
by Bedarida. The usually ignored religious basis to the thought of many
such leaders has been commented upon by McLeod, who has grouped
them generally as 'unitarians'.[20] Crooks was mentioned above, and
McLeod also describes his involvement with the marginal church organization the 'Brotherhood Movement'. In 1891 Ben Tillett suggested that the
impulse for all he had done or said 'had come from the Bible and from the
personality of Christ', and that the 'emancipation of the people from vile
conditions, from ignoble life' would not be achieved by parliament, but lay
'at the door of the churches'. He emphasized to his members, as Thompson

---

[18] F. Bedarida, 'Urban Growth and Social Structure in Nineteenth Century Poplar',
London Journal, 1: 2 (Nov. 1975), 187–8.
[19] Ibid. 188.   [20] McLeod, *Class and Religion*, 62–5.

points out, 'the ethical conception of duty', and the need for trade unionism to be 'not limited to the mere sordid sphere'.[21] Tom Mann often turned to religion.[22] In 1895 Bill Steadman, leader of the bargebuilders' union and the Stepney Labour League, and MP for the Stepney constituency for a short period, preached at the Lycett Chapel, on the theme 'Christianity in its relation to labour', and pointed out that 'the Trade Unions had done much in assisting the furtherance of Christianity'.[23] George Lansbury appealed, as a socialist, to electors in 1906 by stating that 'the flag we march under is the flag which means we are all members one of another, that the highest thing in life is giving and not receiving, and that human life and human happiness is of more importance than money'.[24] Frank Brien, undoubtedly the most politically active and influential of the dockers' union officials in the East End, thought of the unjust employer that 'it may be fairly presumed that nothing in this world can reclaim him, and that, in the next, every curse awaits him that God has declared shall be the reward of the oppressor'.[25]

The 'moralizing' tone taken by some of these leaders (as we saw with the 'strong opposition to drink and gambling') could create some conflict with their members. Tillett and others gave their support to temperance movements, which on occasion led to their being met with verbal abuse.[26] But in relation to some other aspects of the moral 'crusade', these leaders seemed closer to the rank and file. It was said by the missionary to the Gasworks in Poplar and Bromley that the 'men in my district who claim to be Socialists are in the majority, and they are influencing each other to a very large extent. The social side of Jesus Christ's teaching they hold to the front, and claim him to be their leader, but the spiritual claims put upon them by Christ they try to put aside.'[27] Importantly, we have seen that such beliefs could be closely linked to a working-class condemnation of the moral failings of rich and hypocritical employers and politicians. In many ways this both reflected, and could very easily turn into, a classic popular radical attack upon those, such as the 'corrupt parasites' in power, who were at the

---

[21] *East London Advertiser,* 29 Aug. 1891, p. 8 col.c, and 24 Oct. 1891, 8 col.d; and Thompson, *Socialists, Liberals and Labour,* 53.

[22] See Thompson, *Socialists, Liberals and Labour,* 52.

[23] *East London Advertiser,* 23 Nov. 1895, p. 8 col.f.

[24] Borough Council election manifesto 1906, quoted Thompson, *Socialists, Liberals and Labour,* 229.

[25] See F. Brien, 'The Bible and the Poor: A Labour Leader's View', *East London Advertiser,* 24 Apr. 1897, p. 8 col.d, and 1 May 1897, p. 8 col.e.

[26] See *East London Advertiser,* 14 May 1892, p. 6 col.e.

[27] *London City Mission Magazine,* 75 (Mar. 1910), 46–7.

base of society's problems. So, too, could the religious themes underpinning the thoughts of the labour activists.[28]

The dockers' union's Brien, in his exposition on 'The Bible and the Poor', argued that the principal cause of poverty in society was 'some vicious institution, some course of misrule, which enables the rich to rob, degrade and oppress the labouring classes'. Under this misrule, Brien implied, the blame should be squarely placed upon the 'fraud', 'dishonesty', and 'cheating' committed by employers and others of the rich[29]—a classically radical statement of social ills, and their cause. There is little doubt that many of Brien's members similarly accepted that social and economic corruption had a central role in their troubles.

Smith and Nash described the 'deeply rooted' general idea of the docker 'that he is being cheated at every turn'; but, very significantly, they argued, 'he knows not by whom'.[30] Encouraged by union and political leaders, and by underlying popular beliefs in a basic division of Good and Evil—of honest labour and corruption—many workers in East London sought to understand their plight in these terms of fraud, robbery, and 'parasites' feeding upon the rewards of their labour. But the specific workplace structure and social history of much of East London meant that the focus of their suspicion often fell upon the corrupting influences which they could most easily see and directly feel, and radical ideas of social and political corruption as the cause of the people's problems became stalled at a much lower, and localized, level of society, with significant political effects.

Keith McClelland has described much of the self-perceived role of trade unions in the mid-nineteenth century as being 'a kind of morally purifying agency which would dissolve the bad and the corrupt', removing moral unworthiness amongst the workers as well as the superiors in the trade.[31] Smith and Nash made the point that during the great 1889 strike, over and over again the 'docker heard the plain, unvarnished truth about himself, that this strike was being fought that he might have some chance of becoming less of a brute and more of a man'.[32] But most of these men believed they knew quite well who were the 'brutes' with whom they were associating, and what was needed to drag themselves up from this level.

---

[28] See Joyce, *Visions*, 33 and 51, on this.
[29] Brien, 'The Bible and the Poor'. See Biagini and Reid, Introduction to *Currents of Radicalism*, 19, and other contributions there, for the continuing place of such ideas in the views and statements of other labour leaders.
[30] H. L. Smith and V. Nash, *The Story of the Dockers' Strike* ([1890]), 42.
[31] K. McClelland, 'Time to Work, Time to Live: Some Aspects of Work and the Reformation of Class in Britain, 1850–1880', in Joyce, *Historical Meanings*, 196.
[32] Smith and Nash, *Dockers' Strike*, 81.

Tillett said at the end of the century, of the poorer parts of London, that 'many of those who lived in the black spots of misery had been so demoralized by want that they no longer had any desire for anything better . . . it was from these quagmires of degeneration that the hyenas of the revolution emerged. A Socialist Government would therefore have to think of ways and means to get rid of this scum.'[33] Industrially, the dockers' union was similarly desperate to remove from the docks those workers who were felt 'unworthy' of a permanent, regularly employed workforce, the creation of which was one of the union's major aims.

A docker echoed Tillett's characterization: 'All the scum of London come to the Docks, and an honest man has no chance.' Union members during the 1889 strike said of the most casual, poorest labourers who competed for work on the docks (those often recruited from the common lodging houses, as seen in Chapter 1) that: 'They don't belong to us. It's them that's given us a bad name. When we get this tanner and go in we'll take good care that the loafer doesn't interfere with us.' Margaret Harkness argued that an aim of the strike was to 'emancipate' dock labour from the 'pernicious influence' of these 'loafers, incapables and parasites'.[34]

The docker quoted in Chapter 3, who complained of being known only as a 'dock-rat', also lamented being confused with the 'miserable rabble that infests the East End'.[35] As was discussed in that chapter, he could respond in a number of ways to this characterization. He might seek to reinforce self-esteem by showing the failings of his 'betters'; or he could seek to distinguish himself from those he thought gave him a 'bad name' by exhibiting special skills or social 'respectability'; or he could seek to eliminate these inferiors from his trade. Part of the argument of this study has been that it was quite possible for the worker to try to do all at once. All of these approaches had quite definite, but complex, political impacts. The key point in understanding the underlying politics, particularly of the unskilled, in the East End, is that their desire to differentiate themselves from the 'rabble' was part of their broader and coherent view of the structure of social life, and that this could also be expressed in a number of ways. The specific result depended, again, upon particular social circumstances.

In any attempt to 'moralize' the workplace, as discussed above, and to show dockers as 'men' instead of 'brutes', the interests of the union and the employer clearly could coincide. When, after the 1889 dock strike had

---

[33] See R. Rocker, *The London Years* (1956), 80.

[34] John Law [Margaret Harkness], 'The Loafer: What Shall We Do With Him', *Labour Elector*, 21 Sept. 1889, p. 180.

[35] Ibid.

concluded, some workers were accused of not doing a fair day's work under the new system of an elected 'overlooker', Tom Mann urged them to 'act straight' and 'watch earnestly that none of their number injured and weakened the Union by skulking and shirking'. It was said that 'the better men all through the Docks' wanted to 'prove that the Union is determined to act fairly to all parties concerned', after warnings had been made that trade could suffer if productivity was not improved.[36] During the strike, John Burns had told workers that 'He pledged himself that the dock companies should adhere to the agreement, but he plainly told them that he was not going to have "any loafers on the job".'[37] But, importantly, all this moral tone could also only help to reinforce amongst workers other existing views regarding their workplace.

In complaints to the Sweating Select Committee in 1888, workers and unionists regularly decried the behaviour of one particular section of the workplace hierarchy, the 'middlemen'. Middlemen were indeed a central focus of the investigation of 'sweating' as, in many trades, particularly clothing and footwear, outwork was the key to the worsening of working conditions. In such trades a subcontracting middleman usually became the employing intermediary between worker and the manufacturer, and these contractors were often blamed for squeezing down wages and forcing excessive working hours. But amongst the middlemen class were also contractors who employed workers on the docks, foremen in a range of trades, or a number of other intermediaries between the ultimate employer and the worker. Such structures were a central part of much work in the East End.[38]

The chairman of the Sweating Committee noted with interest that complaints concerning middlemen on the docks suggested that 'the hardships the men endured . . . are more due to the individual contractor than to the system itself'.[39] James Welsh, an activist labourer quoted earlier, argued strongly that on the docks the middlemen were clearly acting against the interests of both workers and employers: 'I accuse the contractors of not being the most desirable men for the dock company. I believe there are men who are more capable and more humane, more qualified for the post, who could be obtained . . . a body of men who really would occupy the position better, be more humane to their fellows, and deal more fairly with the directors of the dock company.'[40]

[36] *Labour Elector*, 7 Dec. 1889, p. 365 and 30 Nov. 1889, p. 351; and see Lovell, *Stevedores*, 125–6.
[37] *East London Advertiser*, 21 Sept. 1889, p. 6 col.b. See also p. 5 col.d.
[38] See e.g. Schmiechen, *Sweated Industries*, and Stedman Jones, *Outcast*, Part I.
[39] *SC Sweating*, P.P. 1888 XXI, q. 13240.   [40] Ibid., q. 13063.

Resentment against those interfering with the direct relationship of employer and worker had been at the heart of the development of the first incarnation of the dockers' union—as the Tea Operatives and General Labourers' Association—who marched and protested in 1888 'against the sweating system of contract and sub-contract, and to demand the right to expose the pernicious evil of the system before the Lords Sweating Inquiry Commission'.[41] The removal of the ganger contractor (who recruited a gang of dockers and then contracted with the company) was a key demand in the 1889 dock strike. Smith and Nash suggested that most 'galling' to the men of all their grievances were 'the petty abuses consequent on the method of labour organization at the docks'.[42] A major victory in the strike was the replacement of the ganger contractor by an elected, usually union-endorsed, gang leader, who supervised hiring and the distribution of bonuses. This new system, however, was abolished under employer pressure in late 1890.[43]

Such attitudes, blaming the intermediary for many of the problems faced in the workplace, were common amongst East End workers. H. H. Champion's *Labour Elector*, organ of the dockers' and gasworkers' unions, was at the forefront in emphasizing this theme, particularly in regard to the gas employees, at Stepney, Poplar, and elsewhere. For example:

We should like to draw the attention of the Directors of the Company to the fact that the foremen are doing their level best to break up the Union. The men's spokesmen are bullied, and find it impossible to give satisfaction. If this continues the Directors will find themselves in the uncomfortable position of having to choose whether they will discharge the whole of the workmen, or get foremen who will be less bullies and more of men.

A 'tyrannical' foreman was warned that it was fairly clear which of the 'two courses the Directors are likely to pursue', if they were forced to 'choose between losing his services or those of all the men who work under him'. At the gasworks in Bromley: 'It is said that the foreman here . . . is lending himself to the worst kind of slave-driving . . . This foreman tells them that if they don't like it they can leave it, as there are plenty of men ready to do the work. Do the Directors know that this fellow is trying to incite the men to commence a strike, which would cost them thousands of pounds?' The attitude of the men themselves was summed up in a letter to the editor from 'A Union Man', who complained again of such actions by

[41] *East London Advertiser*, 1 Sept. 1888, p. 6 col.d.
[42] Smith and Nash, *Dockers' Strike*, 50, and see 54.
[43] See Thompson, *Socialists, Liberals and Labour*, 51–2, and Lovell, *Stevedores*, 134–5.

supervisors and demanded that: 'It is high time that some of these foremen were called before the manager, for I am sure that he would not allow it to be done.' A railway shunter made precisely the same point, that in that industry the foremen 'follow the men about when on duty, swearing and driving them', but 'in due respect to our General Manager . . . if he were to know how the men are treated by these petty officers . . . he would soon alter their tones, and likewise their position'.[44]

Patrick Joyce has discussed the role of the foreman and those in similar positions in the cotton factories, and found that they became the centre of 'the displacement of authority, and hence often of blame', by 'intensifying the focus of industrial conflict on the foreman, and thus exculpating the employer who might be seen as the disinterested arbitrator'.[45] But this 'displacement' of blame for social and economic ills onto the corrupt middlemen in particular, could be even broader and more intense in the East End. This was largely due to specific London factors.

The presentation of struggles of any sort in moral, melodramatic terms was a format with which the London working class was clearly comfortable. The battle between Good and Evil, between the Fair and the Unfair, was generally a staple of popular culture and thought throughout the nineteenth century, as has been well discussed by historians.[46] But in London, aspects of this took on an ever-more pervasive nature. Joyce has described the common image in popular culture of a rural idyll.[47] But as migrants from the countryside came to London in increasing numbers through the early and mid-nineteenth century, they had the opportunity to compare their situation in the metropolis to their memories of what they had left—and London did not stand up well. This could be seen in representations developed in popular forms of entertainment. Michael Booth suggests that:

> two of the particular characteristics of Victorian melodrama were its idealization of the village home and its denigration of London. The former was symbolically equated with the state of man before the Fall and represented virtue, innocence, beauty, peace, and a known place in God's world, while the latter stood for vice, the loss of innocence, squalor, degradation, bitter suffering, and helpless anonymity.[48]

---

[44] For the above, *Labour Elector*, 14 Sept. 1889, p. 173; 17 Aug. 1889, p. 102; 2 Nov. 1889, p. 278; 14 Sept. 1889, p. 175; 15 Dec. 1889, p. 378.

[45] Joyce, *Visions*, 119, and *Work, Society*, 100, and see his chapter 'Work' in F. M. L. Thompson (ed.), *The Cambridge Social History of Britain, Vol. 2: People and their Environment* (Cambridge, 1990), 164–5.

[46] See e.g. Vernon, *Politics and the People*, and Joyce, *Visions*, 32 ff.

[47] Joyce, *Visions*, 247.

[48] M. R. Booth, 'The Metropolis on Stage', in H. J. Dyos and M. Wolff (eds.), *The Victorian City: Images and Realities*, vol. 1 (1973), 213.

Vernon has emphasized the importance in mid-century of 'melodramatic' modes of thought, which provided 'their subjects with a sense of agency and a coherent moral purpose, of rightness in an evil world populated by tyrants'.[49] In London this view was essentially that, within the town, corruption or evil surrounded one wherever one turned. Although this view could at times have a 'class' sense, comparing the virtues of the poor with the vices of the rich, the circumstances of the metropolis made this dichotomy less clear. James Greenwood described those in London who 'had no faith in the sincerity, honesty, or goodness of human nature . . . [They thought that] most people will do a wrong thing if it serves their purpose.' Gertrude Himmelfarb notes the depiction in popular literature of all classes in the metropolitan setting as corrupt or 'dangerous, degraded, brutalized'.[50] The fear of the corrupting nature of the city, and the emphasis on character as a dividing-line, was diminished very little at the end of the century. For many East End workers, such ideas were directly reinforced by their experiences of the workplace and the various struggles taking place there.

The strength of the feeling amongst workers, circulating perhaps in mythical form, of one type of corruption—the misuse of the power of middlemen to hire labour—is seen in the story told to Booth's reporter: 'As an example of favouritism on the part of foremen in taking on at London and St. Katherine's a man named Donovan is said to have taken on 57 Donovans one day, until the men threatened him with violence if he took on any more relations!'[51] Allegations of corruption amongst foremen and other middlemen in a vast range of industries were common in London, well into the Edwardian period. Asked why a number of immigrants were employed by a particular gas company, a labourer's view was that, rather than a desire by the company to get a cheaper workforce, it was purely the result of a foreman accepting bribes from the new workers.[52] The allegation that dock gangers were 'extensively bribed', as Potter was told in 1887,[53] was still in place twenty years later. In 1907 the 'bonus' system which operated on the London docks was being criticized by dock union leaders for the same reasons:

the bonus system [. . .] has a most demoralising effect upon the men. Q.84338. It simply leads to driving?—Not only to driving, but to bribery and corruption . . .

[49] Vernon, *Politics and the People*, 328–9.
[50] J. Greenwood, *The Seven Curses of London* (1869; repr. 1981), 67–8, and G. Himmelfarb, *The Idea of Poverty: England in the Early Industrial Age* (New York, 1984), 452.
[51] Interview with Costello and Driscoll, Dockers Union District No. 2, Booth MSS B141, 103.   [52] *RC Alien*, P.P. 1903 IX, qq. 1764–6.
[53] Webb, MS Diary, vol. 11, p. 43, typescript 822.

. . . the man who is physically capable of doing the largest amount of work is given, by the man who has got charge of the gang, an opportunity of coming into the bonus gang for a consideration, and at the end of the week if has any kind of bonus at all, part of that bonus goes to the man who runs the gang.[54]

Similar complaints against foremen, or other contracting middlemen, were widespread amongst building workers, sandwich-board men, watchmen, carmen, and in many other industries, again well into the Edwardian period.[55]

Potter suggested that there was a 'very large extent' of bribery of foremen in the tailoring trade. She said she knew of one firm which had 'dismissed seven foremen running for taking bribes', and she accepted the belief that bribery was 'done without the knowledge and against the wishes of the manufacturer'.[56] Arnold White confirmed similar dishonesty amongst foremen in the cabinet trade.[57] The complaints were so common that it is clear that the despair amongst East End workers, described by Henry Mayhew in the middle of the century, about the necessity of bribing foremen and other supervisors had not abated.[58] Free said at the end of the century that, in the East End generally, 'the foreman holds the lives of the workers in his hands, and sells to the highest bidder. Even when a man has secured a job, he must bribe his foreman if he would keep it . . . "plush profits", as they are called, are regarded by the foreman as his "perks" . . . and to all intents and purposes are a tax on the men under him'.[59]

The economic concerns of a very large number of workers were essentially still as summed up by the words of a ballast-heaver to Mayhew: 'I don't complain of what is paid for the work; the price is fair enough, but we don't get a quarter of what we earn . . . We are robbed of all we get by the foremen and publicans [who also acted as contractors, and forced men to

---

[54] Evidence of James Sexton, General Secretary of the National Union of Dock Labourers in Great Britain and Ireland, *R.C. Poor Laws*, P.P. 1910 XLVIII, qq. 84337–9. See also Stedman Jones, *Outcast London*, 82.

[55] See Dearle, *Problems of Unemployment*, 87; *East London Advertiser*, 6 Sept. 1890, p. 6 col.e; Free, *Seven Years*, 168; Addison Papers, Box 103, File 56.1, Newspaper Cuttings 1909–13, 20, leaflet headed 'Dr Addison and the Mail Drivers: Extract from the "Star", June 24th, 1910'; B. Dix and S. Williams, *Serving the Public, Building the Union: The History of the National Union of Public Employees. Volume 1: The Forerunners 1889–1928* (1987), 40–1.

[56] *SC Sweating*, P.P. 1888 XX, qq. 3404–5. See also the evidence of James Ball Lakeman, factory inspector, P.P. 1888 XXI, qq. 16683–4.

[57] *SC Sweating*, P.P. 1888 XX, q. 2203.

[58] See H. Mayhew, *The Morning Chronicle Survey of Labour and the Poor: The Metropolitan Districts*, 6 vols. (Firle, Sussex, 1981), i. 138; ii. 232–81; v. 57–9.

[59] Free, *Seven Years*, 168–9.

take some of their wages in drink].'[60] In 1897 the method of payment of riverside workers in Poplar was said to be: 'Money paid by gangs. Always paid at the public house. Men turned out if they won't accept those conditions.'[61] Market porters who joined the dock strikers in 1889 'positively refused' to return to work without the dismissal of a contractor who 'takes more than 50 per cent of the wages which ought to go to them . . . They are also compelled to purchase from him, and in other ways are exploited.'[62] The unemployed dockers interviewed by Krausse in 1886 said they had only one real message for the government if it wished to assist the conditions in their industry—to ensure direct employment by the dock companies: 'Let them do away with contract in the docks; let them do away with the gangers.'[63]

The aim of the 'new' unions, then, was partly expressed as seeking to create such a direct relationship between employer and worker; as McClelland says, 'a world of "reciprocity" pivoted on a morally regulated exchange of labour and capital'.[64] In many ways it was part of the moral role of the union to achieve this. For the gas workers it was said that: 'Some of the foremen do not seem to understand the difference which the formation of the Union makes in the position of the men . . . [the foreman] is apparently inclined to forget that he must now be on his good behaviour.' In the railways, it was hoped that 'the time is coming when they won't dare to do as they have done; they have got to learn they are only servants, not masters'.[65] But unfortunately, the role of the unions in this reform, in London, could sometimes be undermined by actions as suspect as those they condemned.

Remembering the type of bogus working-class bodies of the 1880s mentioned in Chapter 1, such as the London United Workmen's Committee, Lovell has suggested, regarding Tillett's new dockers' union, that: 'The dockers themselves must have distrusted the intentions of the new body, accustomed as they were to the activities of Kelly and Peters in the "working class movement". Trust is an essential ingredient in working-class organisations, and after a decade of Kelly and Peters trust in the integrity of union officers did not come easily on the London waterfront.'[66] Despite the enthusiasm for the dockers' union during the Great Strike, such underlying

---

[60] Mayhew, Letter XXIII, *Morning Chronicle Survey*, ii. 255.

[61] Interview with Father Gordon Thompson, Bow Common Lane, Booth MSS B180, 19.

[62] *Labour Elector*, 14 Sept. 1889, p. 172.

[63] Krausse, *Starving*, 15.   [64] McClelland, 'Time to Work', 196.

[65] *Labour Elector*, 17 Aug. 1889, p. 102 and 14 Dec. 1889, p. 378. See Joyce, *Visions*, 122, for a comment on the implications of the continuing use of the word 'master'.

[66] Lovell, *Stevedores*, 98.

suspicion seems to have re-emerged strongly, with justification, in the years following. Union officials 'decamping' with funds was a relatively common experience. Booth's investigators' reports on the union in 1891 are full of the opinions of dock workers who felt that, precisely because of this dishonesty, they were 'better away from the union'. Branches collapsed because of defaulting secretaries, and union officials admitted that the 'wrong doing caused a feeling of distrust'.[67] Even the blatant corruption and favouritism exhibited by foremen on the docks was felt by workers 'to be not confined to Dock officials but crops up equally in the "Co-operative" work done for some of the shipowners when the men elect their own foremen'.[68]

Bringing together the overarching view of corruption as central to the worker's life, and echoing the comment of Smith and Nash quoted earlier, the *East London Advertiser* noted in 1892 that

East Enders . . . are much concerned to hear of all these defalcations and embezzlements of Dockers' Union officials, district secretaries, and office boys . . . such continually recurring episodes must quickly arouse the slumbering suspicion of the humble docker . . . This important person has an inherent idea that everyone wants to cheat him of his tanner, and the officials of the Union who got it for him are not exempt.[69]

Such attitudes were very clearly not confined to the docks. Local-government employees, who often suffered from dishonest and unfair supervisors, found in the late 1890s that their union had suffered a 'serious set back by the defalcations of a former secretary'. In fact, within the space of a few years three secretaries of this union stole large amounts of their members' money. Bernard Dix and Stephen Williams comment that, 'it must be remembered that the embezzlement of funds was not uncommon in the formative years of the trade union movement, and municipal workers' unions would not have been exceptions'. This particular dishonesty led to the breakaway of branches, and ultimately to the death of the union.[70] The gas workers, stevedores, and steamship workers also all suffered from embezzlement by their officials.[71] In 1903 the secretary of the Poplar Trade and

---

[67] Booth MSS A24 13, 39, 105, B140 37–8, and B141 98. See also *East London Advertiser*, 10 Dec. 1892, p. 7 col.b, and 6 Jan. 1894, p. 5 col.f; and Lovell, *Stevedores*, 115.

[68] Interview with Thomas Sutton, dock unionist in Limehouse, Booth MSS A24, 10–11. See also interview with R. G. S. Self, ibid. 18, and evidence of Colonel Birt, *RC Labour*, Group B, Vol. 1, P.P. 1892 XXXV, qq. 6933–4.

[69] *East London Advertiser*, 6 Aug. 1892, p. 8 col.a.

[70] *London*, 4 Mar. 1897, quoted in Dix and Williams, *Serving*, 67–8 and 89–90.

[71] *East London Advertiser*, 9 Mar. 1895, p. 7 col.a; 14 Sept. 1895, p. 3 col.d; 22 Aug. 1903, p. 6 col.b.

District Labour Council was charged with fraudulently converting branch funds for his own use.[72]

An inference of union leaders lining their pockets seemed to form part of the opinion of some men that 'they can spend 3*d*. better than paying Tom Mann and Ben Tillett'.[73] The distrust was clear when a dockers' union branch secretary noted that the men 'always want Mann and Tillett to come down here, though of course they can't be everywhere. Men are suspicious. They are dissatisfied with having polling papers counted at Central office.'[74] White notes the survival of such views amongst casual workers in Campbell Bunk after the First World War, with a 'resentment of the power wielded by trade union officials who seemed to wax fat on members' contributions'.[75]

Joyce has argued that such distrust of union leaders, or belief in their dishonesty, was merely a somewhat paranoid reflection of an underlying 'fatalism' resulting from workers' dependency upon the employers.[76] However, it is quite clear, in the East End at least, that there were rational and well-founded reasons for what may have been a growing atmosphere of mistrust of union activity—developed within the traditional London feeling of a strong sense of all-pervading corruption.

Outside the workplace such attitudes were also obvious and reinforced. David Englander argues generally that in working-class districts all authority was 'suspect', because the 'jobbery and corruption attendant upon local administration for much of the nineteenth century left a sour taste, an uncertain feeling that moneys paid went straight into the rate-collector's pocket'.[77] Ideas of corruption were also reinforced outside the formal workplace by the experience of the large percentage of married women in East London who were outworkers for various manufacturing trades—most usually clothing or footwear, matchbox making, or brush-, basket-, or sackmaking. We have seen how corruption and unfair dealing was a widespread complaint against the subcontracting middlemen in these trades. Any suggestion of being deprived of 'fair' wages would clearly have been a topic of heated conversation within the home. Other examples of the general working-class belief that they were being cheated of their pennies are not hard to find.[78]

There is little doubt as to the strength of the belief that 'corruption' was

---

[72] Ibid., 7 Nov. 1903, p. 7 col.a.   [73] Booth MSS B141, 34.   [74] Ibid. 3.
[75] White, *Worst Street*, 108.   [76] Joyce, *Visions*, 127.
[77] Englander, *Landlord and Tenant*, 89.
[78] See e.g. Free, *Seven Years*, 85, and Samuel, *East End Underworld*, 25.

central to many of the problems faced by the working class in the East End. The nature of many workplace structures, and the actions of workers' organizations, however, tended to mean that this belief did not show itself in an acceptance of the radical or ethical socialist ideas of the type put forward by Brien and other labour leaders. Instead, it led to a much more localized, small-scale 'radicalism', where the 'idle, corrupt parasite' became one's immediate supervisor rather than a member of a distant aristocracy or government.[79] This focus, particularly amongst poorer workers, could only help to emphasize to them the importance of personal, moral character in determining the treatment they received in society. Amongst this group, again, this attitude probably only reinforced their interest in the individual hypocrisy of politicians or others who sought to represent them. But it is possible that, in some areas, it could also assist in the development of a more active working-class Conservatism.

THE PATERNALIST IN THE EAST END

Both John Davis and Pat Thane have demonstrated the fundamental popular radical ideology underpinning much of the Liberal (and Labour) activism amongst more prosperous workers in London.[80] Davis has convincingly demonstrated the important political socialization role of the London Radical working-men's clubs frequented by many artisans and similar workers, and the key part they played, particularly in the 1890s, in creating feelings of loyalty and consequent support, especially, for club-sponsored candidates. Davis shows that the leadership groups in the clubs were attempting to 'sell the totems of traditional Radicalism' until the end of the century at least.[81] But in making this point, Davis also emphasizes the role of the 'personal' in politics. He suggests generally that ideological commitment, and party allegiance, were weakening in this period for many in the previously activist skilled-worker groups. Political support, in many instances, began to grow instead mainly out of the force of personal contact. Davis quotes the contemporary opinion that: 'Better than any threats or wheedling from the candidate, his agent or his committee is the public

---

[79] See *SC Sweating*, P.P. 1888 XXI, q. 13450, on the view of workers that such supervisors were 'idlers' and 'that a lot of money goes to pay men who are practically not required ... [who] only stand with their hands in their pockets'.

[80] Davis, 'Radical Clubs' and P. Thane, 'Labour and Local Politics', in Biagini and Reid, *Currents of Radicalism*, 245–4.

[81] Davis, 'Radical Clubs', 113.

feeling in a good club', where 'the earnest thinker and the indifferent voter could be brought into direct and constant personal contact'.[82]

This ability to mobilize personal support could certainly bring results. Davis notes that in the East End, one of the strongest clubs, the Borough of Bethnal Green Club, in 1899 claimed to have a total of eighteen of its members on local elected boards, with a similar number claimed by its counterpart in Shoreditch. The St George's and Wapping Reform Club claimed to have been instrumental in the election of most of the area's vestrymen and guardians that year.[83] A small selection of descriptions of Progressive candidates for one vestry election in Bethnal Green, in 1894, can illustrate this important connection:

Mr. A. J. Allord is one of the working men candidates . . . he is a large shareholder in the Borough of Bethnal Green Working Men's Club Association, Limited . . . Mr. O. R. Hales is well known as the Vice-President of the Borough of Bethnal Green Club, of which he was previously the able President . . . Mr. Geo. Copsey . . . is . . . intimately connected with the work of the United Radical Club . . . Mr. J. Hall . . . was mainly responsible for the establishment of a Temperance and Working Men's Club in Hoxton.[84]

The London City Missionary for the Virginia Row district of Bethnal Green said that the area in 1890 was inhabited mainly by artisans, most commonly furniture makers. The 'greater part of them belong to the Radical clubs, which do not improve them, but tend to make them discontented'.[85]

Davis's argument is that a great deal of influence was exerted by the Radical clubs to convince their working-men members to work and vote for candidates out of loyalty to the club and its leadership. This in turn suggests a further point in regard to the issue mentioned in the Introduction, of the differing levels of success of the progressives in local and parliamentary elections. The much greater importance for some progressive voters of personal influences in motivating them to actually turn out to vote, can suggest one reason why the Progressive turnout in local elections was closer to that achieved by the Liberals in parliamentary elections than was the case for the Moderates and the Conservative party. The 'personal touch' that was important for the Liberals would be most effective in local elections, when

---

[82] *Weekly Dispatch*, 4 Apr. 1886, and the 1889–90 Annual Report of the West Newington Liberal and Radical Association, both quoted ibid. 108.

[83] See Davis, 'Radical Clubs', 116.

[84] *North-Eastern Leader*, 15 Dec. 1894, p. 3 col.a.

[85] *London City Mission Magazine*, 55 (Aug. 1890), 200; see also 'Christian Effort Amongst Navvies and Builders', ibid. 56 (Apr. 1891), 67.

club members could be encouraged by 'clubability' to vote for fellow members. For the Conservatives, this personal factor seems to have been less important, and so their local-government vote tended to drop away more dramatically from their parliamentary support, whereas for the Liberals this particular 'personal' effect seems to have faded as the election became more distant from the local. It still seemed to apply in County Council elections, as the figures cited in the Introduction show, and this may have been due to the fact that candidates for the LCC tended to be more 'local' in character.

But the calls made to working-men's club members to mobilize their votes for the good of the club were still underpinned, at least to some extent, by the connections made to the vaguer, perhaps less party-aligned, concepts underlying the Radical appeal. Thane agrees that the policies 'most acceptable' to the London Liberal activist were those which placed 'equal stress . . . on the assault upon privilege and monopoly' as well as social reform.[86] Tanner suggests that the combination of '"morality" tied to an attack on the rich' was the most popular of progressive messages in London.[87]

Joyce has said that *Reynolds's Weekly Newspaper*, the 'massively popular' radical Sunday newspaper produced by G. W. M. Reynolds from 1850, was 'the special favourite of the "old", often London-based, artisan trades'.[88] The paper was widely read by skilled workers in the mid-century, and little had changed by the century's end.[89] Joyce suggests that this was due to the paper promulgating 'a particular vision of society' which 'corroborated the deep-seated predilections of its readership'.[90] David Vincent says of the content of *Reynolds's Weekly Newspaper* that:

Whilst the substance of the news often involved crucial developments in industrial and later political conflict, the conceptual framework of the accounts and the language in which they were conveyed remained locked in a theatrical analysis of Old Corruption . . . Rather than the reporting of class conflict informing the other categories of news and entertainment in the paper, the style and preoccupations of popular melodrama inherited from street literature invaded the presentation of organised struggle . . . The account of the latest strike was connected to the report of a murder or review of a play by little more than an appeal to the reader's pleasure in the sensational, and to his confidence in the moral worth of himself and his class as a whole.[91]

---

[86] Thane, 'Labour and Local Politics', 246.
[87] Tanner, *Political Change*, 168–9.   [88] Joyce, *Visions*, 66.
[89] See V. Berridge, 'Popular Sunday Papers and Mid-Victorian Society', in G. Boyce, J. Curran and P. Wingate (eds.), *Newspaper History from the Seventeenth Century to the Present Day* (1978).   [90] Joyce, *Visions*, 67.
[91] D. Vincent, *Literacy and Popular Culture: England 1750–1914* (Cambridge, 1989), 254–5.

In *Reynolds*, Joyce says, well into the Edwardian period, 'Class terms were in fact chiefly remarkable by their absence, and hostility to the state was unabated, government frequently being associated with scandal and corruption.'[92] *Reynolds* was not the only popular newspaper to continue this tradition. In 'all papers of this type', says Virginia Berridge, particularly *Lloyd's Weekly Newspaper* and the *Weekly Times*, both also Sunday papers, there was a regular use of 'sensationalism in an explicitly radical way. Personalization and scandalous revelations were used to heighten the appeal of political analysis for relatively unsophisticated readers.' The papers continued to use, well into the late part of the century, 'Old Corruption' as their main political framework.[93]

Biagini and Reid have argued that:

the central demands of progressive popular politics remained largely those of radical liberalism well into the twentieth century: for open government and the rule of law, for freedom from intervention both at home and abroad, and for individual liberty and community-centred democracy. Some of these themes were voiced in popular slogans like 'anti-corruption' and 'fair play', usually directed against familiar 'parasites' like the landed aristocracy, financiers, and the established Church.[94]

There is little doubt that such ideas continued to influence much of working-class politics in London in this period. But in parts of the East End such beliefs could lead to quite diverse political outcomes.

As discussed earlier, general working-class respect for the church was noted by the clergy and others to have increased in the late Victorian period. But Richard Free, based in the Millwall dock area on the Isle of Dogs, still found the church to be linked by some number of his parishioners to a social 'parasitism': 'The parson stands to him for the conservative selfishness of the rich and privileged, for the tyranny of those inexorable powers which have combined to keep him tied hand and foot to that station of life to which a cruel destiny had called him.' He described a scene: ' "Look at it! That's where our money goes!", cried an old man in the railway-train, pointing me out with the finger of scorn—the notion being that this gentleman, and all other gentlemen of the same class, were taxed to keep me in idleness.'[95] The persistence of such ideas may have been influenced by what seems to have been a more powerful Nonconformist presence in Free's Millwall area than in many riverside districts. The School Board visitor for the area told Potter of the 'difference of class of Millwall dock employees. Many country folk. Long hours and hard work . . . Resemble stevedores. Dissenters and

---

[92] Joyce, *Visions*, 68.   [93] Berridge, 'Popular Sunday Papers', 257–9.
[94] Biagini and Reid, *Currents of Radicalism*, 5–6.   [95] Free, *Seven Years*, 248 and 228.

know each other.'[96] Free also pointed out, quite specifically, that '*Lloyd's* and *Reynolds'* form the staple Sabbath diet of the Millwall working man'.[97] Such old radicalism seemed vibrant in this part of the Isle of Dogs at the end of the century, but with surprising political results.

An area with a strong Nonconformist conscience and with relatively prosperous workers could be thought to be the most likely scene for the pure acceptance of 'Old Corruption' ideas and the world-view presented in *Reynolds News* and *Lloyd's*. Some of the most specialized workers in the London docks were those who worked at the grain and timber docks in Millwall. Before the 1889 strike they were said to have regular work and to earn from 30*s.* to 35*s.* a week.[98] But as Free pointed out, the Isle of Dogs was 'more remote' from London than 'the remotest of suburbs. The difficulty of getting to it is almost incredible . . . the swing bridges . . . isolate the Island like the drawbridges of a medieval castle.'[99] Bart Kennedy described it as 'a quiet village surrounded by the river'.[100] This isolation, and village-like atmosphere, was reinforced markedly by the background of many of the inhabitants. The Isle of Dogs, said the rector of Poplar, was generally where 'countrymen preponderate'.[101] This was most particularly the case in Millwall. Into the area in the late 1870s had come a large number of country immigrants to replace striking dockers. Into the 1890s they still formed an overwhelming majority in the grain and timber docks.[102] Even more than twenty years after the strike-breakers had first come into Millwall, the area was still 'very countrified . . . The majority of the people are "not a bit like Londoners".'[103] It is likely that immigration from the country continued for a significant period after the first strike-breakers; it was not unusual for those coming from rural areas to seek out previous immigrants from these areas, or for relatives to be 'sponsored' by those who had gained work in the city.[104] This trait in Millwall would probably have continued through to the Edwardian period.

This factor undoubtedly helped to account for the fact that Millwall also had one of the highest levels of church attendance of the areas examined earlier, with 11 per cent of the adult population attending a Protestant church on the survey day.

---

[96] Webb, MS Diary, vol. 11, p. 15, typescript 804. [97] Free, *Seven Years*, 112.
[98] Webb, MS Diary, vol. 10, p. 146, typescript 785. [99] Free, *Seven Years*, 2.
[100] B. Kennedy, *London in Shadow* (1902), 56.
[101] The Revd A. Chandler, Booth MSS B169, 3.
[102] See Booth MSS B141, 7–8; Potter in Booth, *Life*, 1st series, vol. 4, p. 16; Thompson, *Socialists, Liberals and Labour*, 49; and Stedman Jones, *Outcast London*, 144.
[103] The Revd D. G. Cowan, Booth MSS B169, 69.
[104] See Arthur Baxter in Booth, *Life*, 2nd series, vol. 3, p. 178.

Richard Free noted generally the area's 'affectionate clannishness'.[105] Although heavily dominated by dock employees,[106] Millwall also was home to a 'large number of . . . Scotch-engineers'.[107] Many of these were associated with the Presbyterian churches established to cater for them.[108] In addition, there was a growing number of engineering factories and mills starting to form a 'ring' along the waterside.[109] This isolated area, with few places of entertainment or other facilities, was described by Smith and Nash as having a character 'more like a provincial town than a part of East London'.[110] Workers lived 'chiefly on the island and do not often seek work elsewhere'.[111]

Despite the circumstances in which many of the dockers first came to Millwall, workers there very early entered into the 1889 strike, and their solidarity during the dispute was extremely strong.[112] From 1891, as the dockers' union started to collapse numerically across London, it was notable that Millwall was one of the very few areas where numbers and organization held.[113] In 1889, just as agreements were being reached to end the Great Strike, a number of workers had rebelled and, in a move which epitomized much of what was discussed earlier in this chapter, rejected the authority both of 'corrupt' supervisors and of their union officers. In this they also showed that they perhaps had a much more localized perception than their union leaders of their most pressing industrial needs. Leading this action were the grain workers at Millwall, who, immediately after a general agreement had been reached in the strike and workers were returning, stood their ground and 'disclaimed all obedience to Burns and Tillett and pressed forward a demand for the abolition of the middleman or foreman. As they were not immediately granted this, they consulted with other men, and ceased work.'[114]

---

[105] Free, *Seven Years*, 91.   [106] See Booth MSS B346, 3–7.

[107] M. E. Arber, 'Millwall', *Biblewomen and Nurses*, 15 (1 Mar. 1898), 51.

[108] The Presbyterian church in St Cuthbert's, one of the parishes of Millwall, in 1902 had a adult congregation equal to 10.2% of the adult population of the parish, although of course this was also drawn from surrounding areas. See also the comments of Lizzie Alldridge, 'East India Dock Road (Presbyterian Church)', *Biblewomen and Nurses*, 15 (1 Nov. 1898), 207, and the Revd David McQueen, Booth MSS B171, 22–3.

[109] See the evidence of W. G. Martley, COS. *Unskilled Labour* report, q. 9, and Bedarida, 'Urban Growth', 178.

[110] Smith and Nash, *Dockers' Strike*, 16.

[111] Webb, MS Diary, vol. 11, p. 21, typescript 808.

[112] See *East London Advertiser*, 6 July 1889, p. 5 col.g, for an example of early action by the Millwall dockers.

[113] Thompson, *Socialists, Liberals and Labour*, 52.

[114] *East London Advertiser*, 21 Sept. 1889, p. 6 col.b.

The strength of worker solidarity, and their willingness to take action, is hard to question for the Millwall docks, yet the politics of the area again suggests the importance of specific local circumstances and milieu in the attitudes of East End workers. Despite very high levels of trade-union membership and the suggestions of acceptance of the Radical beliefs touched upon earlier, workers in Millwall also seem to have supported the Conservatives more strongly than almost anywhere else in the East End. The main factor here seems to have been the strength of what Joyce, in reference to the cotton-factory workers of northern England, has called the 'sense of place and belonging'.[115]

The Millwall ward of Poplar, as noted in Chapter 3, was overwhelmingly Conservative in this period, with fourteen out of fifteen of its councillors in 1900–12 elected as Conservatives, and an average Conservative vote of 66 per cent. In the 1892 general election the Poplar Conservative candidate also claimed Millwall as a stronghold.[116] Despite having a relatively high level of progressive vote fluctuation, indicating again the possible importance of abstention, there clearly was also a solid 'core' of working-class Conservative support here. This came from skilled, reasonably regularly employed, unionized dock and other manual workers.

In the isolated and close-knit environment of Millwall, workplace and local identity could coalesce easily into a general 'sense of place'. As we have seen, workers there seem to have acted with greater solidarity than those elsewhere in the area against the authority and role of 'corrupt' supervisors. (In Millwall there was a particular three-tier system of employment on the docks, and the term 'contractors' equated more closely to the large dock companies elsewhere.[117]) Yet in Millwall generally, relations between workers and the peak employers were exceptionally good. Potter's informant thought it worth noting that in the Millwall docks 'Labour contractors take interest in their people'.[118] One of the reasons why the dockers' organization remained strong there after 1891 was because 'the employers preferred to work through the union'.[119] The relationship of employer and union in Millwall was made clear by Colonel Birt, the general manager of the docks, to the Royal Commission on Labour:

I am altogether in favour of labour unions . . . I should like the power of the unions to be stronger. All the little difficulties we have are from men who break the rules of

---

[115] Joyce, *Work, Society*, 93.   [116] *Eastern Post*, 9 July 1892, p. 5 col.c.
[117] See the evidence of Colonel Birt, general manager of the Millwall docks, *SC Sweating*, 1888 XXI.
[118] Webb, MS Diary, vol. 11, p. 15, typescript 804–5.
[119] Thompson, *Socialists, Liberals and Labour*, 52.

the Union, and to get them put right we have to appeal to the executive of the Union ... we have got on very well with the Union, and I do not object to the men belonging to the Union. On the contrary, when sometimes men ask me whether they shall join the Union I say it is a matter entirely for themselves, but I think if I were they I should do the same as my mates did.[120]

Workplace relations on the docks seem to be typical of the approach of major employers in this isolated milieu. The major force in Conservative politics in Millwall, and candidate for Poplar in 1895 and 1900, was F. A. Bullivant, the owner of a large wire-making factory in the area. Bullivant's local activities—in an area where 'They have no amusements. No music hall'[121]—included running popular concerts to compensate for this lack of entertainment, and encouraging temperance beliefs amongst his workers. He was also, apart from the Church, the most 'benevolent' force in Millwall.[122] Clearly his activities reinforced the strongly paternalist employer tone in this 'provincial' district.

The Millwall area combined a significant level of factory employment with a skilled and heavily unionized dock workforce. Yet, as Joyce has noted in the case of the textile town of Blackburn, the particular nature of pervasive 'localism' and paternalist workplace relationships in Millwall meant that it too could combine the 'most evidently appreciative response to a far-reaching paternalism, with the highest degree of ... trade unionism'.[123]

At least some Conservative support in Millwall was based upon what Potter found to be an unusually 'Strong feeling in favour of protection'.[124] This could well have been related to the experience of economic depression, from the late 1870s, in the agricultural districts unprotected against foreign grain imports, which undoubtedly was a factor persuading many of the migrant strike-breakers to migrate to London. But reinforcing this were the relationships in the area, such as Joyce describes, where there could also be a 'displacement of blame' away from a paternalistic employer to an 'external enemy', through a recognition of the common interests in the 'trade'.[125]

In contrast to the image of Conservatism flowing from a 'fragmented, impoverished' workforce in the East End, the example of Millwall shows

[120] *RC Labour*, Group B, vol. 1, P.P. 1892 XXXV, qq. 6961–2 and 7161.
[121] The Revd Father Egglemeers, Booth MSS B180, 51.
[122] See Booth MSS B173, 1–13.
[123] Joyce, *Work, Society*, 68. See also Savage, *The Dynamics of Working-Class Politics*, 47–8, on the effectiveness of paternalism in some factory and similar employment.
[124] Webb, MS Diary, vol. 11, p. 21, typescript 808. Cf. Tanner, *Political Change*, 171.
[125] See Joyce, *Visions*, 119.

active working-class Conservatism in an area with one of the highest levels of social cohesion in the district. Factors similar to those at work here can be shown to have influenced the politics of, in particular, more prosperous workers in other parts of the East End.

Spread around the Old East London Cemetery, the Stepney Gas Works, and the Chemical Works in Ocean Street, was the East Centre ward of the Stepney constituency (Mile End Old Town vestry). It was described by Duckworth as generally 'purple' to 'light blue' (standard poverty), and occupied by gas stokers, carmen, costermongers, and women workers in confectionary and other factories.[126] Until 1900 this ward was said to be where 'the strength of the Labour party lies' in Stepney. From the time of the reorganization of the vestry in 1894, the weakness of the Liberal organization meant that the members of the Stepney Labour League, formed around a number of prominent trade unionists who happened to live in the area, 'have practically had this ward left in their charge'. In the 1898 guardians election it was considered that the ward would 'remain true to its Labour tradition'. Labour League candidates were dominant in most annual vestry and guardian elections in the ward from 1894 to 1899. The ward was also said to have provided Bill Steadman, the Labour League Liberal candidate in the 1898 parliamentary by-election, with his majority.[127]

With the creation of the boroughs in 1900 the East Centre ward was joined with part of the West Centre ward to form (not surprisingly) the Centre ward. But following this, through all the borough elections between 1900 and 1912 in the Centre ward, Labour, Progressive, or Socialist candidates did not win even one seat. It is clear that this dramatic turnaround was related to the addition of the section of the old West Centre ward. Comparing the last vestry elections of 1899 in East Centre ward to the first borough election in 1900 on the new boundaries, the progressive vote increased by only 173 votes, while the Conservatives nearly quadrupled their previous total, increasing by 522 votes. More significantly, the average number of voters supporting progressive candidates in 1900–12 was only around 50 per cent above that in the smaller East Centre ward (in the less popular vestry elections). The number of Conservative voters, on the other hand, was almost 200 per cent higher than in the previous period. Clearly the portion of West Centre ward which was added brought with it very few active progressive voters.

[126] See Booth MSS B350, 55–63.
[127] *East London Advertiser*, 20 Oct. 1900, p. 8 col.d; 15 Dec. 1894, p. 8 col.a; 2 Apr. 1898, p. 8 col.b; and 12 Mar. 1898, p. 8 col.b.

The added area was centred around Stepney Green, was described as generally 'pink' (comfortable working class) or 'pink-barred' (middle and working class mixed) by Booth's investigators,[128] and was dominated in part by blocks of model dwellings, such as the 'Cressy Buildings. 4 storied, red brick, belonging to the East End Dwellings Society, here taken [*sic*] up the whole of the triangle made by Daniels Row, Hannibal Rd and Cressy Place—A very mixed class in the buildings—a curate—lady worker—County Council architect . . . as well as artisans . . . 111 lettings in the buildings . . . 6/- for 2 rooms . . . the demand is for 2 roomed holdings.' On the other side of Stepney Green additional model dwellings—the Dunstan Houses—were added in 1899, and others were built later.[129]

Centrally placed in this relatively compact, comfortable working-class area, in Stepney Green itself, was the Stepney Tabernacle, part of the Primitive Methodist Church, usually regarded as one of the most working-class and radical of the Nonconformist sects.[130] The Tabernacle was dominated by the Kemp family, its founders, owners of a large oven-building factory in the area. The family was extremely prominent, and well regarded as doing 'good works' in the area.[131] The Tabernacle drew a reasonably good, essentially working-class congregation from the immediate area and, very unusually for an East End Nonconformist church, house-to-house visiting and church clubs and activities were undertaken by a 'Sister of the People', twenty-eight Sunday School teachers, and nineteen other workers. Significantly, a great deal of this activity directly involved the Kemps and also the Cade family, coal merchants. Clubs and other activities, and the mothers' meetings held by the church, for example, seem to have been strongly associated with the 'Misses Kemp' and the Cades.[132]

Linked to the importance of church activities was the role of the Kemps as employers. The *East London Advertiser* reported that: 'The hold which the Kemp family has over the Stepney people was never more clearly shown than on the return of the employees of their firm from the annual excursion on Monday. Seldom has Stepney seen such a spectacle. The Green was lined by thousands of persons, nearly every one of whom seemed to be

---

[128] Booth MSS B350, 53–5.

[129] Ibid. 71–3. See also Gardiner, *John Benn*, 36, and the evidence of William Johnson, *RC Alien*, P.P. 1903 IX, q. 8651.

[130] See McLeod, *Class and Religion*, 108 and 178.

[131] See *East London Advertiser*, 7 July 1900, p. 5 col.h, and 24 Nov. 1900, p. 8 col.f.

[132] For all this see the *East London Advertiser*, in 1898: 9 Apr., p. 8 col.b, and 16 July, p. 5 col.h; and 1899: 7 Jan., p. 7 col.f; 4 Mar., p. 8 col.e; 20 May, p. 8 col.b; 2 Dec., p. 7 col.f; and 16 Dec., p. 8 col.e; Booth MSS B183, 133–5 and B385, 23.

letting off fireworks in honour of this occasion.'[133] The patriarch of the family, John Dewson Kemp, was said to have been a 'most liberal subscriber, not only to his own denomination, but to various local charitable organizations . . . That gentleman had been a figure head for many years in the Hamlet of Mile End Old Town.'[134] The 'sense of place and belonging' which Joyce suggested could be appropriated by an employer is precisely what the *East London Advertiser* seemed to point to when it said that 'the Kemp family is one of the oldest families in Stepney, and is a name that is almost synonymous with Stepney'.[135]

Certainly synonymous with politics in the area, it seems. Holding progressive inclinations into the 1880s, Kemps were elected to local positions as Liberals in that period, often topping the poll even in these limited and far less party-political elections. But by the early 1890s they were, like a number of other elite Nonconformists, solidly Conservative. From 1894 a Kemp—often two—won in each vestry contest for West Centre ward, most often topping the poll, and often elected to the Board of Guardians as well. A Kemp then managed to be elected as part of the Conservative borough election victories in Centre ward in both 1900 and 1903.

The 'tone' of paternalism and support for the Kemps must have existed more broadly than merely amongst Kemp employees to produce these political results. But it can be said that such support existed generally amongst regularly employed factory employees[136] in an area with relatively prosperous workers and a 'mixed' social environment. Here the closeness of the link between work and neighbourhood, and the general sense of identification with 'place', could overcome the social isolation and political ambivalence that were seen in Chapter 3 to be common amongst such workers. Again, as in many cases, the total milieu was the key.

The model of abject poverty leading to the Conservatism of the East End again seems weakened by this example. The following chapter will examine some further influential, historical 'models' of politics in the East End, and we will again see the importance of the exact 'mix' of beliefs and local-community dynamics in creating the varying responses across groups and areas in the—certainly less than uniform—politics of East London.

---

[133] 23 July 1898, 8 col.a.

[134] Editorial comment, and condolence speech of Dr Reilly on the Mile End Board of Guardians, on the death of J. D. Kemp, *East London Advertiser*, 7 July 1900, p. 5 col.h.

[135] Ibid., 8 Sept. 1900, p. 8 col.c.

[136] See Ch. 1 regarding the regularity of employment of most East End factory workers.

5

Myths and Models

The historiography of the street sellers—costermongers—of London's East End in the nineteenth and early twentieth centuries touches upon many of the general issues concerning how studies of London's working class and their politics have been approached. There are a number of 'myths' that exist regarding the attitudes of the costers, and it is also clear that they had an organizational and political complexity, and a significance in the political battles of the time, that has largely gone unnoticed.

The costermongers have, most typically, been portrayed as personifying, in the extreme, aspects of the nature of the Victorian and Edwardian London working class. Mayhew's representation of the 'tribes' of the poor in mid-century London reached its zenith with the costers: 'They appear to be a distinct race . . . seldom associating with any other of the street folks, and being all known to each other.'[1] As Stedman Jones has shown, during the latter part of the nineteenth century the images of the coster and that of the generalized 'cockney' became entwined, and in this representation the coster also came to be the embodiment of the cockney 'virtues' of good-naturedness, determination, and individualism.[2] This composite image of the coster as representing much that was London working class, but being also separate from it, is one that has persisted, and has figured in the few historical treatments of this group. McKibbin has explicitly used these concepts in his discussion of the politics of the costers and associated workers:

In many ways they had what we take to be the essential characteristics of the Edwardian working class, yet in them a collective sense of class was aetiolated almost to non-existence: on the contrary, a jaunty and attractive individualism was essential to their lives. While they were fairly well aware of where they stood on the social ladder, they were almost entirely outside a conventional political culture. Indeed,

---

[1] H. Mayhew, *London Labour and the London Poor*, 4 vols. (1861; repr. New York, 1968), i. 6.
[2] G. Stedman Jones, 'The "Cockney" and the Nation, 1780–1988', in Feldman and Stedman Jones, *Metropolis*, esp. 294–300.

their occupational world of chance and quick-wittedness was in many ways ab-
solutely opposed to collectivist politics.[3]

These same concepts are inherent in Thompson's briefer point that, although industrially organized in a manner similar to other members of the
working class: 'Certain trade unions, such as the Watermen and Costermongers, catering for privileged workers and small tradesmen, were regarded as traditionally Conservative, at least until 1906.'[4] Henry Pelling
makes the image of 'within but different' even more explicit: 'Costermongers, who pursued a middle-class occupation at a working-class level of
life, were also Conservative in London.'[5]

   Such images constitute the historical view of costers and politics. But a
closer examination of the evidence upon which this perspective is based begins to show the unrecognized complexity of the political positions adopted
by the costers. It demonstrates again the importance of the local and the
personal, rather than simply the economic, in East End politics.

   The evidence Thompson refers to for his assertion of the 'traditional'
Conservatism of the costermongers is a bitter attack made upon the polit-
ical stance of the costers by Frank Brien in 1901. Brien was acting as an elec-
tion agent in Bill Steadman's campaign to hold his Stepney seat on the
London County Council for the Progressives. Brien wrote to the *East
London Observer*:

The action taken against the Progressive party, and especially against Mr W. C.
Steadman, in Stepney, by the Whitechapel Costermongers Union, in circularizing
the ratepayers asking them to vote for the Moderates, is not only mean, but it is, in
my opinion, contemptible, and unbecoming any Trade Union . . . Whatever, or
whoever, was behind the scene of that letter, I think any Trade Union would be ill-
advised in placing obstacles in the path of progress. We have certainly enough en-
emies without looking for them in the ranks of organised workmen. What I fear
most, Mr Editor, is that if a strict enquiry is not gone into by the London Trades
Council as to the cause of this, the action taken by them will rebound on their own
shoulders, and that ere long.[6]

The very aggrieved tone of Brien's letter indicates at least two things. First,
as will be discussed further below, that the position taken by the local

---

   [3] McKibbin, 'Marxism', 4. While McKibbin refers in this passage also to other workers in
the 'service sector', it is clear from the references he provides that this argument comes essentially from images of the costers.
   [4] Thompson, *Socialists, Liberals and Labour*, 87.
   [5] Pelling, *Social Geography*, 425.
   [6] *East London Observer*, 9 Mar. 1901, p. 3 col.c, and see Thompson, *Socialists, Liberals and
Labour*, 87, n. 1.

costers was seen as being of some significance in East End elections (the Whitechapel union certainly would have had coverage into the western Mile End area which formed the Stepney seat). But also, the 'shock' inherent in the letter, and the call for an enquiry by the Trades Council, do not suggest that this attack was directed merely at a further anti-Progressive stance by a 'traditionally Conservative' union. It suggests instead that it was an attack upon a departure by the union from the conduct expected of it. There is little doubt that, contrary to Thompson's interpretation, Brien's main complaint was that a normally progressive union had turned on Steadman.

The evidence for this appeared in the following edition of the paper, in a reply to Brien from the secretary of the Whitechapel costermongers' union, Benjamin Davis:

The action taken by the Whitechapel Costers Union complained of so much by Mr Frank Brien concerned Mr Steadman only and not the Progressive party as a whole, because if our friend had made enquiries, which he should have done, he would have found that they were strongly supporting and working for the following candidates:—Prof J. Stuart, Lord Monkswell [Haggerston], Bertram Straus, R. Seager [Mile End], H. L. Lawson, W. C. Johnson [Whitechapel], and several others of the Progressive party . . . We, as an organised body, had worked extremely hard for Mr Steadman, not only on his last County Council election, but also on his Parliamentary election, which was partly the means of his being returned by a small majority.

Davis declared that Steadman had been singled out by the union because of what they regarded as his dishonesty towards them regarding the proposed Shop Hours Bill. At a meeting of the costers' union, Steadman, said Davis, 'openly declared that he would not support the Shop Hours Bill, seeing that it meant utter ruin to all the small tradespeople and costers'. But the costers had discovered that Steadman had also gone to the East London secretary of the shop assistants' union and pledged his support for the bill and to 'fight it through on their behalf'. Steadman, said Davis, had 'tried to catch a weasel asleep and failed in his attempt'.[7]

It was their perception of this dishonesty by Steadman which had alienated the costers. They continued to support others of his party, and perhaps it was an assumption by Steadman that this union was solid in its support for the Progressives that had led him to ignore their sensitivities, because it is clear that Thompson's evidence for his assertion of coster union Conservatism concerned a organization that was, if anything, quite the opposite

---

[7] *East London Observer*, 16 Mar. 1901, p. 3 col.d.

and was (to use his phrasing) 'traditionally' progressive. When first established in 1894, the Whitechapel costers deliberately chose to call themselves a 'Labour Union', seemingly to indicate open solidarity with the wider labour movement.[8] As Davis noted, they supported Steadman as a Liberal in the Stepney by-election of 1898, and a range of LCC Progressives in 1901. In the 1900 general election they campaigned in neighbouring Hoxton, and 'addressed an appeal to their "brothers and sisters" behind the barrow . . . to guard their interests by voting Liberal', while circulating similar material in support of S. M. Samuel in Whitechapel.[9] At a rank-and-file meeting of the union in 1905, Samuel was 'loudly cheered upon entering the hall'.[10] In 1910 a notice advertising a mass meeting for Samuel stated that his supporters there would include the president and secretary of the union.[11] Finally, around the period of the First World War, the Whitechapel union affiliated at a local level with the Labour party.[12] Its personal dispute with Steadman, and Brien's letter, seem to be the only evidence available of any 'Conservatism' on the part of this union.

Yet it is as nonsensical to claim that the evidence of the Whitechapel union's political activities means that 'the costers' union' was generally progressive, as it was for Thompson to use this evidence to assert its Conservatism, because Whitechapel was only one of very many coster organizations. It is useful to look at this fact in association with another historiographical theme, this time originating with Henry Pelling.

In also asserting the Conservatism of the London costers, Pelling makes specific claims about the political motivations of costers in one area of the East End. He argues that in the Hoxton constituency in Shoreditch, in the 1900 general election, the Conservative candidate, Claude Hay, had the support of 'almost all the costermongers, who were no doubt hostile to the rules and regulations of the LCC which was virtually under Liberal control'. From this East End example, he later broadens his argument to say that costers generally were Conservative in London, because of their 'resentment' of 'restrictions imposed upon them by the progressive majority on the LCC'.[13] He provides no evidence for this claim; neither does Stedman Jones, who repeats Pelling's general claim almost exactly,[14] nor

---

[8] See letter from Benjamin Davis, *Jewish Chronicle*, 20 Mar. 1895, p. 8.
[9] *Daily News*, 28 Sept. 1900, p. 3 col.e, and 1 Oct. 1900, p. 3 col.d.
[10] *Jewish Chronicle*, 14 Apr. 1905, p. 28.
[11] *East London Observer*, 15 Jan. 1910, p. 7 col.g.
[12] *Street and Market Trader*, 2: 14 (Feb. 1923), 20.
[13] Pelling, *Social Geography*, 48 and 425.
[14] Stedman Jones, 'Working-Class Culture', 213.

Kenneth and Jane Morgan, who similarly repeat his specific Hoxton claim.[15] Pelling's work in this area has clearly been influential in perpetuating a belief in the conservatism of the costers, but it is also as clearly wrong in its ascribing of political motivation to them.

London's costermongers began to form themselves into distinct organizations to a significant extent in the early 1890s. Coster 'defence societies' or associations existed in St Luke's and Hammersmith and a few other areas in the mid-1880s.[16] But the major growth in unionization amongst the street sellers began around 1892, particularly associated with a bitter dispute involving the Farringdon Road costers and attempts to remove them from their informal market in that road. The 'consternation', as one source put it, that this and similar moves caused generally amongst the costers led to a rapid flowering of unionism.[17]

The Clerkenwell (Farringdon Road) union was formed, followed quickly by the Hoxton, St George's, and Whitechapel organizations and other smaller groups. Harold Hardy, writing for Booth in 1896, said that the costers' union had five branches in London, with 800 to 1,000 members.[18] But it is important to recognize that these were not 'branches' of the one union, but autonomous groups formed around specific market locations. They had no central organization or officers, they did not share a common name, and, for example, the St George's group refused, at its first meeting, an approach regarding federation by the Farringdon Road union.[19]

The dispersion of their organization was in many ways appropriate, for their motivation for unionization was very localized. Unlike Pelling's (and others') claims, the main focus of the disputes between the costers and local government was not with the London County Council, but, before 1900, with the vestries and local boards of works, and later with the borough councils. As a brief chronicle of significant disputes between costers and local authorities, through the period of the establishment of the LCC and up to 1900 (including areas outside the East End), the following can be

[15] K. and J. Morgan, *Portrait of a Progressive: The Political Career of Christopher, Viscount Addison* (Oxford, 1980), 10.

[16] See *The Times*, 19 Nov. 1884, p. 13 col.c, on Hammersmith, and *Weekly News and Chronicle*, 17 Sept. 1892, p. 5 col.e, on St Luke's.

[17] See, for background, *Judgements on Election Petitions—St. George's Division of Tower Hamlets*, P.P. 1896 LXVII, 464, and see *Weekly News and Chronicle*, 3 Sept. 1892, p. 6 col.e; 10 Sept., p. 2 col.e; 17 Sept., p. 5 col.e; 24 Sept., p. 6 col.d; and 1 Oct., p. 5 col.e, on the resistance of the Farringdon Road costers; and *Hackney and Kingsland Gazette*, 10 June 1892, p. 3 col.f, and 13 June, p. 3 col.f, on similar, but more successful, moves in that district.

[18] Booth, *Life*, 2nd series, vol. 3, p. 270.

[19] *East London Advertiser*, 29 Oct. 1892, p. 8 col.d.

listed: 1884, with the Fulham Board of Works; mid-1880s, with St Luke's Vestry; 1888, with Bethnal Green Vestry; 1889, with Holborn Board of Works; June 1892, with Hackney Board of Works; September 1892—the major Farringdon Road dispute, again with the Holborn Board of Works; 1895, with the City of London; 1898, with Wandsworth Board of Works.[20] Most of these disputes were the major catalyst for the formation of coster unions in the affected areas. There appears to be no evidence of any major coster dispute with the London County Council in the period up to and including 1900, the year in which Pelling claims the Hoxton costers fell in behind the Conservatives because of their resentment of the LCC.

Pennybacker has supported much of Pelling's general claim, in her work on public reactions to the social 'interference' of the Progressive LCC. She says that the council's actions meant that many people 'who had not confronted the state in this form before, became objects of LCC policy'. As part of this she refers to the action of the LCC to 'clear the streets of barrows blocking the business of more respectable grocers'.[21] Yet the Hoxton costers, Pelling's case in point, had a very different view of which level of local government they were forced to deal with. In 1902, less than two years after their supposed anti-LCC Conservatism was noticed, the chairman of the Hoxton costermongers' union, William Ball, was examined by the Royal Commission on Alien Immigration and asked why his union was formed, and what happened when shopkeepers complained about the costers:

We found the local authorities were interfering with us, and we thought it was better to amalgamate and see if we could do more in a body than we could do single handed . . .

7906. What is the procedure of the local authorities?—First, they give you a notice to clear out by a certain date, and if you do not clear out by a certain date, then they take out a summons against you . . .

7909. Who gives you this notice?—The borough council . . .

7911. Your great difficulty arises from the fact that the local authorities throw obstacles in your way?—Yes . . .

7914. Have you, as the representative of your union, come into direct contact with the local authorities?—Yes, we have been to see them, and interviewed a lot of members of the borough council.[22]

---

[20] See, as examples, *The Times*, 22 Nov. 1884, p. 12 col.a; 23 Oct. 1888, p. 3 col.e; 3 Dec. 1889, p. 6 col.f; 18 Sept. 1895, p. 5 col.c; and 12 Dec. 1898, p. 4 col.e; *Hackney and Kingsland Gazette*, 10 June 1892, p. 3 col.f; *Weekly News and Chronicle*, 17 Sept. 1892, p. 5 col.e.

[21] Pennybacker, 'The Millennium by Return of Post', 143–4.

[22] *RC Alien*, P.P. 1903 IX, qq. 7903–14.

The LCC is not mentioned by Ball in his evidence. Similarly, in Hardy's description of the costers' situation in the mid-1890s, he refers only to the 'frequent attacks' on the costers' 'customary privileges made by the Vestries and District Local Boards'.[23] The LCC itself, even when pushed, refused to acknowledge any interference with the costers. George Gomme, clerk to the LCC, when questioned in 1903 by the Royal Commission on London Traffic regarding LCC regulations, was at great pains not to assume responsibility for clearing costers from the streets. When asked, concerning the legal right to clear coster 'obstructions' from thoroughfares, 'would the County Council claim the right to do that?', he replied: 'No, certainly not.'[24] At the hearings of this Royal Commission there was, again, no mention of coster disputes with the LCC, only of those with borough councils.[25] The London County Council was not the focus of coster discontent over restrictive regulations.

It is important to note here the extent of unionization amongst the costers. For the whole of London the 1901 census counted 12,000 'costers and hawkers', with 4,000 in the East End.[26] But the assistant commissioner of Police for the metropolis, from a street count of 'pitches', believed there were only around 7,500. This broadly concurs with other studies undertaken by the LCC, and is likely to be the more accurate figure.[27] The census-enumeration techniques for this occupational area were less than satisfactory. Street sellers with a stall or barrow in a particular market were usually quite different from those 'hawkers' or 'travellers' who moved from town to town selling goods. The costers themselves drew this distinction.[28]

<hr/>

[23] Booth, *Life*, 2nd series, vol. 3, p. 263.

[24] *Royal Commission on London Traffic*, P.P. 1906 XL, q. 3809. (Evidence given 12 June 1903.) The LCC formalized the arrangement of borough councils having responsibility for such action in its General Powers Bill that year. See the letter from Gomme to Town Clerk, Hackney Borough Council, dated 24 June 1902, Hackney Archives Department, Rose Lipman Library, Borough Engineer and Surveyor's Department file H/E/68/2, 'Street Markets'.

[25] In the most dramatic example, the Southwark borough engineer told the Commission that action there to move the costers had meant that 'Indignation meetings were held at street corners, and candidates from among the costermongers were nominated at the election of Borough Councillors . . . The officials were insulted in the Police Courts, the streets, and at the polling booths.' Memorandum of evidence handed in by Arthur Harrison, Borough Engineer and Surveyor of the Borough of Southwark [Dec. 1903], *RC Traffic*, P.P. 1906 XLI, App. No. 20, p. 382.

[26] Including the boroughs of Stepney, Bethnal Green, Shoreditch, Poplar, and Hackney.

[27] Memorandum of evidence handed in by Sir Alexander Carmichael Bruce [Nov. 1903], *RC Traffic*, P.P. 1906 XLI, App. No. 13, p. 330; and see S. Ruck, 'The Street Trading Community', in H. Llewellyn Smith, *The New Survey of London Life and Labour: Vol. III, Survey of Social Conditions (1) The Eastern Area* (1932), 320–8.

[28] See evidence of Henry Blake, *RC Alien*, P.P. 1903 IX, qq. 7792–3.

Yet it is clear from the manuscript census material that occupations such as traveller were included with the numbers for costers—with the registrar often specifically noting on the schedule that this classification was to be used—and that there was a great deal of inconsistency regarding classification.

The figure for the East End alone is not easily calculated from this, as one set of figures relates to those living in the area, and the other to those working within it. But given the generally lower figure suggested above, an estimate of 3,000 male and female costers living in the East End seems reasonably accurate. The discrepancy in numbers would also have been to a minor extent explained by husband-and-wife or family groups working the one 'pitch' in a market. This point is important for the issue of union coverage, as it is likely (given that there was a subscription payable) that the unions would only have been able to enrol one member for each family 'pitch'. So the 7,500 figure for London costers overall should be seen as a maximum possible coverage for the unions. Many other 'occasional' street sellers took to the streets in summer and around Christmas, but these may be more usefully considered as underemployed members of other trades— they would have still described themselves as, to take one example, 'labourers' rather than 'costers'. They did not generally share the concerns or social relationships of the 'regular costers', and tended to be shunned by the unions.[29]

Hardy said in 1896 that the union had five branches in London, with nearly 1,000 members. In the first decade of the new century there were nearly three times this number of unions,[30] and two of them alone, those covering the City and Whitechapel, had probably 1,200 members between them. The City union was said to have as members 'the great majority' of 'year to year' regular costers who worked in the area.[31] While these were

---

[29] On this, see letter from Christopher Addison to Winston Churchill, 15 Mar. 1910, pp. 2–3, Addison Papers, Bodleian Library, Oxford, Box 80, File 'Costermongers 1910'; R. Samuel, 'Comers and Goers', in H. J. Dyos and M. Wolff (eds.), *The Victorian City: Images and Realities*, Vol. 1 (1973), 133–5; Stedman Jones, *Outcast London*, 62 and 81.

[30] See *RC Alien*, P.P. 1903 IX, evidence of Benjamin Davis, q. 19934, and Henry Blake, q. 7696. Some of the London unions in 1903 included Whitechapel, Battersea, Holborn, North London (Hackney), South London, Hoxton, Limehouse, Fulham, Clerkenwell, and Southwark, followed soon after by, at least, unions in the City, Dalston, Woolwich, and Walthamstow.

[31] See evidence of John Lyons, Chairman of the Whitechapel union, *RC Alien*, P.P. 1903 IX, q. 19883; *The Times*, 24 Apr. 1913, in Stuart Montagu Samuel Cuttings Book, House of Lords Record Office, 42; and *The Times*, 26 Nov. 1918, p. 8 col.d, which indicates that that the Whitechapel union had doubled in size by the First World War; see also draft open letter (election leaflet) on Addison's work, written by William Shepperley, Union of City Hawkers, dated

undoubtedly the largest unions, others, such as Clerkenwell, were strong, and with the continual emergence of unions in this period, it is very likely that the majority of the costers across London were associated with a union. In the East End this is even more likely to have been the case, particularly given the strength of the Whitechapel union, and the fact that many East End costers worked in other areas where there had been significant disputes and therefore the development of strong organizations—Hackney, Farringdon Road, and the City. With some exceptions,[32] the regular costers in the East of London were very heavily organized by around the turn of the century.

The focus of the costers organizationally was towards their quite separate unions and the local authorities with whom they were in dispute. They did not move en masse to the Conservative side as a result of LCC actions, as Pelling suggests. There is a possibility that, in areas where one side was in power at a local level for a long period, that interference may have become associated with one particular party,[33] but this seems an inadequate explanation for the diversity of coster politics, and the fact that simple 'anti-statist' reactions against interference seem not to have been the major determinant in their political choices. For the costers were, or appeared to be, very divided in their politics. Whitechapel aside, it is nearly always possible to find evidence from within a particular area of costers supporting both (or all) sides of politics. Harding remembered of Bethnal Green in the years before the First World War that: 'In those days all the costermongers were Conservatives. They used to have all their stalls decorated with the colours on election day.'[34] But the Liberal *Daily News* reported in 1906 that in Bethnal Green North East the 'orange and yellow [colours of the Liberal candidate] flamed in every street . . . Barrows and costers' carts were decorated with the same brilliant favours'.[35] Also in Bethnal Green, *The Times* noted in 1911 that the Socialist candidate for the South West seat by-election 'has already obtained a good deal of support among the costermongers and

24 November 1910, Addison 80/'Costermongers', and undated cutting from *News of the World*, attached to a letter from Shepperley to Addison dated 21 July 1910, same file.

[32] The *Street and Market Trader*, 1: 7 (July 1922), 9, noted futile attempts since 1892 to unionize the costers at the Chapel Street market, Finsbury. The paper said this was 'due in great measure to the influence of interested politicians'. Poplar also seemed slow to obtain union coverage.

[33] There is some suggestion of this in Walworth in South London, where perhaps consistent Progressive local dominance in Southwark authorities encouraged a strong Conservative coster reaction. But there are also suggestions that memories of Conservative actions on the Battersea vestry helped John Burns amongst the costers in that constituency. *Daily News*, 29 Sept. 1900, p. 2 col.e.

[34] Samuel, *East End Underworld*, 262.   [35] *Daily News*, 17 Jan. 1906, p. 7 col.f.

street dealers'.[36] The *Eastern Argus* acknowledged that, in this by-election, 'the coster vote is divided'.[37]

Such division on politics does not seem consistent with any central or localized 'trade defensive' position against interference. It is more easily explainable when seen in terms of the organizational diversity of the coster unions. As noted above, the unions were formed around the focus of particular market locations. So union membership was not based upon where a costermonger lived, but upon which market he or she normally worked. Costers who lived in Shoreditch, for example, could be members of one of a range of unions—covering the City, Hackney, Whitechapel, or other areas. Costers did not always work in streets close to home, and often went significant distances.[38] This meant that, although union membership was extensive, a local coster union (apart from the generally problematic nature of representation) did not necessarily speak on behalf of the costers of that area. This point was made explicitly by William Shepperley, general secretary of the Union of City Hawkers, in a letter to Christopher Addison, Liberal MP for Hoxton, at the time of the Bethnal Green South West by-election discussed above. Despite the fact, said Shepperley, that Bethnal Green costers' union members 'were tied, it appears, by order of their "Executive" to the coat-tails of the Tory candidate', the members of his union who lived and had the vote in the constituency 'did their duty' and supported the Liberals.[39] As a further example, although it appears that the Hoxton[40] costers' union remained generally more conservative in the pre-war period—its secretary, George Cook, was elected as a Municipal Reform borough councillor in 1912—again, those members of the City Hawkers' Union who lived in Shoreditch seem to have rallied to the progressive cause. The *Bromley Chronicle* reported during the December 1910 general election that: 'The members of the London Street Hawkers' Union have worked out a plan of campaign, and fully a score of the men who are engaged in street trading have been told off to speak and to canvass on

---

[36]   *The Times*, 25 July 1911, p. 13.

[37]   *Eastern Argus and Borough of Hackney Times*, 29 July 1911, p. 4 col.e.

[38]   See 'Petition on behalf of the Costermongers of Hoxton who are going to be ejected from the City of London', Addison 80/'Costermongers'. The Union of City Hawkers also held 'crowded' meetings in Spitalfields, which indicates that it had a number of members from that area: see undated *News of the World* cutting, attached to 21 July 1910 letter, same file. See also list of costers summoned for obstruction while working in Farringdon Road in 1892. They included traders from Bethnal Green, Shoreditch, and from as far away as Walworth: *Weekly News and Chronicle*, 1 Oct. 1892, pp. 5–6.

[39]   Letter dated 31 July 1911, Addison 80/'Costermongers'.

[40]   Around 1910 this union seems to have renamed itself the Borough of Shoreditch Costers' Union.

behalf of Dr. Addison, M.P. for Hoxton.'[41] Other costers campaigned for the progressives in Shoreditch, even though their trade may have taken them elsewhere and into a different union. W. J. Paterson, who was a member (and later became secretary) of the Hackney union, was also, like Cook, elected to the Shoreditch borough council in 1912, but this time on the Progressive side.[42]

The political character of the Hackney union, like the Whitechapel and City unions, seems to have been generally to the left. Also active in this union for a long period had been Morris Lewis. He became a coster at Kingsland Plain in the mid-1890s, after leaving tailoring because his 'outspoken ways were reducing his chances of employment'. Around the same time he joined the Social Democratic Federation, and was used extensively by this organization as a speaker and was involved in many other political activities. He became chairman of the Hackney and Kingsland costers' union, and ultimately vice-chairman of the post-war Federation of Costers' Unions.[43]

Costers generally, or a 'costers' union' as a whole, or even costers who lived in a particular locality, did not hold common party-political attitudes. It seems more likely that it was the individual coster unions that had, and retained, distinctive political characters themselves, at least in the latter part of the period under study. Some of the reasons for this, and the effects flowing from it, can be seen by examining a number of themes in the development of coster union politics.

The major push of coster unionism, in the late 1880s and early 1890s, coincided with the growth of 'new unionism' and significant political and industrial activity within many occupations. The costers were, at least initially, associated with this general movement. This can be seen in the reports of the early protest meetings on behalf of the Farringdon Road costers. The *Weekly News and Chronicle* reported on such a 'splendid demonstration' which took place on Sunday, 25 September 1892. Taking part, the paper said, were the: 'St. Luke's, Hoxton, Walworth, Kingsland, Islington Costers Societies, and the Patriotic, East Finsbury, Gladstone and United Cocoa [Radical] clubs, and the General Railway Workers, Spitalfield Porters, Green Fruit Porters, Dock Labourers and several other

---

[41] *Bromley Chronicle*, 1 Dec. 1910 (cutting in Addison Papers, Box 103).

[42] See *Daily Herald*, 2 Nov. 1912, p. 3 col.b, and *Street and Market Trader*, 1: 11 (Nov. 1922), 21. This journal noted that, during a dispute in 1922 over endorsement by the costers of Labour candidates in local elections, Paterson was said to have 'proceeded to give a speech on the policy and programme of the Labour Party in general'.

[43] See *Street and Market Trader*, 1: 8 (Aug. 1922), 8–9.

similar bodies.'[44] This was typical of a series of meetings which took place over a number of weeks, aimed at the Holborn Board of Works, at which resolutions were often moved by costers and seconded by Radical club members. (This also suggests a point to be looked at below, that is, the desire by politicians to associate with coster organizations.) Banners held by costers in processions to the meetings included slogans such as 'The Costermonger—the Poor Man's Friend' and 'United we stand, divided we fall'.[45] The coster bodies continued to identify themselves as trade unions and as part of the broader labour movement. It was noted earlier that the Whitechapel union called itself a 'Labour Union' in this period. In 1895 the Clerkenwell union—that of the Farringdon Road costers—formally registered itself as an industrial organization, as, in subsequent years, did other coster unions.[46] It was said at a meeting of the St George's-in-the-East and Wapping Street Traders' Protection Association in 1893 that 'the interests of the working classes—the costers were most typical of the labour interests—could best be served when its association was managed by themselves. (Hear, hear.)'[47] Such connection to the overall solidarity of the union movement, and association with broader 'labour' ideals, seems to have continued into the late 1890s. Costermonger groups were prominent in an 'East London Trades Union Sunday' organized in 1897.[48] The solidarity they exhibited with general working-class movements and causes, as well as within their own market groupings, belies the claim of the overriding importance of 'individualism' in their lives and attitudes.

In 1898–9, despite the unions being very separate organizations, a Federation of coster unions was starting to be established, with Benjamin Davis of the Whitechapel union as its first secretary. It was registered as an industrial organization in 1899.[49] But at around this time it also began to collapse, as did any solidarity amongst the coster organizations. Davis told the Royal Commission on Alien Immigration that this was because

it was found that there was so much anti-Semitic feeling on the part of Mr. Blake [chairman of the Federation] and some of the Farringdon Road people that my union threw the whole thing up. Other unions did the same, e.g. North London and Limehouse, and the so-called federation was simply a federation of anti-Semitic costermonger societies. The so-called federation did not represent one-twentieth of the costermongers in London.[50]

---

[44] *Weekly News and Chronicle*, 3 Sept. 1892, p. 6 col.a.
[45] See ibid., 3 Sept.–1 Oct. 1892.   [46] *Labour Gazette*, 3: 11 (Nov. 1895), 352.
[47] *East London Advertiser*, 11 Feb. 1893, p. 8.   [48] Ibid., 31 July 1897, p. 8.
[49] *Labour Gazette*, 7: 12 (Dec. 1899), 384.   [50] *RC Alien*, P.P. 1903 IX, q. 19934.

The Whitechapel union was predominantly a Jewish organization, though not exclusively so—its chairman said that 'a very large number' of its members were gentiles. Additionally, it had an associated branch in Southwark, of around 150 members, the majority of whom were not Jewish. A number of other unions which were not predominantly Jewish, such as the Hackney union, seem not to have associated with the 'anti-alien' movement on the part of some coster organizations. Davis claimed that the unions in the remaining federation covered no more than 5 per cent of London costers, and it is likely that his union alone covered more costers than did the Federation at that time.[51] But this issue did mark a split within coster ranks industrially. Politically, the period 1900 to 1906 is also that from which most reports of coster Conservatism have come. But, although this was certainly associated with the issue of anti-alienism, it is clear that the latter issue was also greatly intensified by localized, personal, factors.

By far the most extreme opponents of the increasing number of new 'foreign' costers on the streets seem to have been the Hoxton union, and probably also the Bethnal Green organization. In Haggerston, when costers (almost certainly from the Hoxton union) campaigned for the Conservatives in 1906, their 'particular grievance' was 'the competition they are meeting with from a host of alien costermongers'.[52] Certainly this was the main grievance expressed by the Hoxton union secretary to the Alien Immigration Royal Commission in 1903, and contrary to Pelling's argument about the LCC, is much more likely to have been the reason why the Hoxton costers were said to have supported Hay in 1900. It is significant, however, that the Dalston costers, who were previously covered by the Hoxton union, broke away and formed their own union at the height of this issue, taking perhaps 100 members with them.[53]

After 1906 the anti-alien issue began to fade. But what was significant both before and after this date was the extent to which individual coster unions retained their own very solid, opposing, political standpoints. Although there were some minor splits,[54] those unions which had apparently

---

[51] The federation claimed 409 members in 1901 (and 74 in 1904). See *Reports of the Chief Registrar of Friendly Societies*, 1901 and 1904, Part C, P.P. 1902 XCVI and P.P. 1905 LXXV.

[52] *Daily Mail*, 11 Jan. 1906.

[53] See *Reports of the Chief Registrar of Friendly Societies for the Year 1913*, Part C, P.P. 1914 LXXVI, p. 720.

[54] Christopher Addison could claim as one of his supporters in 1910 the secretary of the Hoxton union (who had been in office since at least 1902), although it does appear that this man was removed from office soon after. Leaflet for Addison, Dec. 1910 election, Political Cuttings File, Hackney Archives S/LD1/23. It is significant that Addison claimed the support of the 'Executive Committee' of the City union on this leaflet, but only the secretary alone of the

moved to Conservatism on the anti-alien issue seem to have generally retained this character, even as this issue declined in importance. At the same
time, other coster unions retained their more progressive stance. One of the
major reasons for this continuing split seems to have been a 'political socialization' process within the unions, similar in many ways to that noted by
John Davis as occurring in the working-men's clubs. No doubt a significant
factor in such a process was the great deal of attention given to coster unions
in this period by politicians of both sides and their agents. The coster
unions had clearly become recognized as useful bodies to have 'on-side',
and this had important consequences for their political development. In
many ways, as we have seen throughout this study, the political importance
of an 'issue' was often greatly intensified by specific local, personal factors.

It is clear that contemporary political observers saw significance in the
costers' political role. Press reports of East End elections frequently noted
how the 'coster vote' was looking, while often making little specific mention
of other local groups or trades. Typical of the prominence given was a report in *The Times* from before the 1906 election: 'At a meeting of the South-
West Bethnal Green Conservative and Unionist Association, held last
night, Mr S. Forde Ridley, MP for the division, was unanimously adopted
as the candidate. The committee of the association has 400 working members, and the president of the Costermongers' Union, a locally strong body,
was among those supporting Mr Ridley.'[55] From the nature of the meeting
and the report it is clear that this point was felt important enough by the Association itself for it to wish to emphasize it to the newspaper. This prompts
an interesting speculation, that the apparent strength of political splits in
coster ranks may have been highlighted by the desire of all sides of politics
to 'claim' the coster vote, thereby multiplying the amount of contradictory
evidence from the period.[56] The coster support given to the Socialist nom-
inee in Bethnal Green South West in 1911 was again almost the only item

Hoxton union. William Shepperley indicated also that a number of Bethnal Green members
broke from their executive to vote Liberal around this time. Letters to Addison dated 31 July
1911, Addison 80/'Costermongers'.

[55] *The Times*, 2 Jan. 1906, p. 4.

[56] This process was perhaps more clearly illustrated in some examples from South London.
The Liberal *Daily News* was keen to exhibit coster support and published a special article on
the 'Coster Vote in Battersea'—29 Sept. 1900, p. 2 col.e. In 1895 it appeared concerned to
counter claims of coster support for Conservatives in Walworth. It published an account of a
meeting for the Liberal candidate which included: 'At this juncture the banner of the "Pro-
tective Costermongers No. 1 Union" was carried into the crowd, amid cries of "Bravo
costers".' This sounds so unlike most coster union names that suspicion is raised that the
whole event may at least have been "exaggerated" to emphasize coster support. *Daily News*,
12 July 1895, p. 7 col.a.

that *The Times* felt newsworthy enough to print about this candidate in its whole coverage of the by-election.

Of course, it was not only in Bethnal Green that costers were noticed. The *Daily Mail* suggested that in Haggerston, in the 1906 election, 'Some of the most effective speeches' on behalf of the Conservative candidate were made by 'a small party of costermongers, who address little knots of people in the side streets from their own carts or barrows'.[57] In the *Standard*'s list of factors influencing the 1900 Hoxton election, it said: 'Last, but not least, there are the costermongers.'[58]

Voters apparently often shared this view of the importance of the stance taken by the costers. Harding remembered that in the Bethnal Green South West seat, immediately pre-war, 'the Conservative candidate was head of the costermongers union, that's how he got in, because the costermongers were the chief people with influence'.[59] Political operatives also showed their desire for coster support. Frank Brien's bitterness at the Whitechapel costers' support going to the Moderates was noted earlier. One of the chief accusations brought in corrupt-practice proceedings against Harry Marks, Conservative candidate for St George's-in-the-East in 1895, was that three years earlier he had sought to gain favour with the local costers by 'financially assisting' the formation of their union.[60] The charge was dismissed, but it was clear that Marks and other candidates often exerted themselves strongly to support issues raised by their coster constituents. Christopher Addison, in Hoxton after 1910, lobbied constantly for the rights of costers who had 'pitches' within the boundaries of the City. Even though most of these traders came from outside his constituency, he devoted a great deal of time to their cause, with numerous meetings and parliamentary deputations.

It was noted above that Radical clubs were quick to support the cause of the costers in their bitter disputes of 1892. So too did the Conservatives. John Lowles, Central Hackney LCC member, and later MP for Haggerston between 1895 and 1900, supported the Hackney costers at a crowded public meeting in June 1892, and moved the 'emphatic' protests of the meeting regarding the 'harsh treatment' the costers had received. He was

[57] *Daily Mail*, 11 Jan. 1906. [58] *Standard*, 27 Sept. 1900, p. 4 col.b.

[59] Samuel, *East End*, 262. Harding remembers the candidate as Major White, and this is interpreted in the book as Major Sir Matthew Wilson, Conservative candidate for Bethnal Green South West in the by-election of 1914. It seems Harding may have confused the candidate with Captain White, a radical who 'organised the Citizen Army in Dublin', and who spoke at meetings on behalf of the Socialist candidate in the same election. See *Daily Herald*, 17 Feb. 1914, p. 5 col.b. Presumably Wilson was honorary president of the union.

[60] *Judgements on Election Petitions*, P.P. 1896 LXVII, pp. 464–5.

careful, however, not to go too far in criticizing members of his own party in the majority on the local authority, and added that the actions had been taken 'contrary, it is believed, to the wishes of the majority of the members of the District Board of Works'.[61]

The politicians 'worked' the costers' unions strongly, and associated closely with them. It was claimed that the Conservatives in Bethnal Green 'used to take them out on holiday runs'.[62] The honorary presidents of these unions were usually political figures, as in the Bethnal Green case above (the chairman was the true administrative head). The president of the Whitechapel union in 1910 was a Stepney borough councillor, and the vice-president a Finsbury borough councillor, as was the president of the Far-ringdon Road union in the same year.

As noted above, *The Times* reported that the unnamed president of the Bethnal Green costers' union attended a selection meeting in 1906 for a Conservative candidate. Yet it is equally certain that the president of the White Cross costers' union, covering a market area of perhaps 200 pitches near the Shoreditch boundary, was attending Progressive selection meetings at around the same time. This was Edward Garrity, trade unionist and editor of the working-men's clubs' *Club Life* magazine, and variously also president of the Finsbury Radical Club and Labour Party. He had been in-volved with the costers since the earliest days, initially in the Farringdon Road dispute.[63]

Why was coster support given such significance by politicians and ob-servers? The costers were not numerous enough as a trade to threaten sig-nificant 'block' voting against any party. There were likely to have been only just over 2,000 male regular costers in East End areas in 1901, from a total male working-age population of close to 400,000. Even in their areas of greatest concentration the costers could not have exceeded 1 or 2 per cent of the adult male population. There is no suggestion that they differed greatly from other working-class groups in the extent of their registration to vote.[64] They consequently formed a relatively minor proportion of voters in East End seats.

The costers possessed political influence for other reasons. It seems likely that they were able to 'deliver' support for a candidate in a much more

[61] *Hackney and Kingsland Gazette*, 22 June 1892, p. 3 col.c, and for Lowles, see *Daily Graphic*, 29 Sept. 1900.

[62] Samuel, *East End*, 262.

[63] See *Street and Market Trader*, 1: 7, (July 1922), 8–9, and B. T. Hall, *Our Fifty Years: The Story of the Working Men's Club and Institute Union* (1912), 307–8.

[64] See Ch. 2, Tables 1–3.

organized and effective, and publicly visible, way than many other groups; they seemed to possess significant personal respect amongst other members of their local communities; and they were also, perhaps, symbolically important to the cause of the politicians.

The coster unions were able to deliver support effectively 'on the street' partly because they were very small, localized organizations. In 1902 the Whitechapel union was undoubtedly the largest. But apart from Middlesex Street (Petticoat Lane) in that area, 200 stalls per market was the maximum. The Hoxton and Dalston union in 1902 covered perhaps two markets this size, as did the Bethnal Green group later.[65] Generally, coster organization involved lobbying and social contact with no more than a few hundred traders, an easily covered, and probably more cohesive group. The leaderships of these organizations were likely to be influential in gathering and delivering support amongst their small number of members. Davis's arguments regarding the artisan working-men's clubs (which had similar sized memberships in this period) again seem relevant: 'associational politics still required opinion formers, and it is likely that their expertise and articulacy gave them a greater influence than they often acknowledged.'[66] Interestingly, this has similarities with Mayhew's statement about costers in the mid-century: 'in every district where the costermongers are congregated, one or two of the body, more intelligent than the others, have great influence over them . . . their pecuniary and intellectual superiority cause them to be regarded as oracles. One of these men said to me: "The costers think that working-men know best, and so they have confidence in us."'[67] Thomas Wright, in 1892, gave a description of 'Bookey' Bishop, who espoused popular radical ideas at meetings and on street corners. He 'was a fish-hawker of the humbler kind . . . He was something of an orator, and among his own class was regarded as something of an oracle also.'[68]

There certainly were costers in the ranks and leadership of the unions with the 'expertise and articulacy' to give them influence amongst their peers. We have noted Morris Lewis in Hackney. The Union of City Hawkers, which put so much pressure on Addison in Hoxton, had been founded by its then secretary, William Shepperley. He was described as 'quite an orator' and was in demand as a public speaker.[69] He was a poet too, and also a strong supporter of the Progressive cause, as can be seen in his extremely

[65] See lists of markets in Ruck, 'Street Trading', 320–4.
[66] Davis, 'Radical Clubs', 116–17.   [67] Mayhew, *London Labour*, i. 20.
[68] T. Wright, *The Pinch of Poverty* (1892), 79.
[69] *Daily Chronicle*, 25 Nov. 1910, cutting in Addison Papers, Box 103 [file 56.1]; Newspaper Cuttings, 30.

articulate correspondence with Addison. He attacked the newspaper *City Press* as being of the 'fossil-tory' type. He referred to Winston Churchill as 'our beloved Home Secretary' and to Charles Masterman as 'one of the best' and the 'noblest member' Bethnal Green had ever had. He referred to his members voting Liberal as doing 'their duty'.[70] Examples of articulate and active coster leaders on the Conservative side included George Cook in Shoreditch, a former actor who had taken to street trading, and earlier, Henry Weston Blake, who contributed to *Pall Mall Gazette*.[71]

When, around 1900, some coster leaders headed towards an anti-alien stance, the translation of this into backing for Conservative politics would have been strengthened and given greater depth by support offered by interested politicians. As Moss Phillips, past-president of the Whitechapel union, noted in 1903 about the new 'federation', there were 'plenty of political people and agitators' willing to help them in their anti-alien cause.[72] Such attention would have helped to bring the union leaders more permanently into the Conservative fold, and to establish a continuing link between these unions and local Conservative politicians.

The influence of the political articulacy and commitment of the coster 'opinion formers' would have been reinforced as professional politicians moved into positions associated with the unions. Officials became closely associated with political figures and were supported by parties in their activities. In the period around 1910–14 the Whitechapel, Shoreditch, Clerkenwell, Whitecross, Bethnal Green, and Hackney unions, at least, had local borough councillors or political candidates from the respective sides as honorary members, or had had members from within their ranks elected to such bodies as party representatives.

Apart from political 'socialization' by existing members, union leaderships could also try other methods to influence costers who did not support the union 'line'. Shepperley claimed that the Bethnal Green executive threatened to 'kick out of the union' any member not supporting the Conservative candidate in 1911.[73] But it is much more likely that less aggressive methods were generally used to gather support. Given the secret ballot, union executives could not on their own ensure that members voted the

---

[70] See letters from Shepperley to Addison dated 13 July 1910 and 21 March and 31 July 1911, and a printed work by Shepperley, *Fishes of the Dead*, in Addison 80/'Costermongers'. Shepperley had works of poetry published.

[71] See *Street and Market Trader*, 1: 4 (Apr. 1922), 9, and 'The Alien Coster' by 'HWB', *Pall Mall Gazette*, 24 Mar. 1902, 2.

[72] *RC Alien*, P.P. 1903 IX, q. 19996.

[73] Letter to Addison dated 31 July 1911, Addison 80/'Costermongers'.

'right' way, and, as noted above, the coster vote in itself was not of great significance in parliamentary constituencies. But a display of support by the costers (even those without the vote) could be extremely useful for a campaign, was easily verifiable by union and political leaders, and would be subject to either overt or subtle social pressures. The display of a candidate's colours on a large number of costers' stalls lining a street market was undoubtedly a very effective form of political advertising. Its impact in Bethnal Green was noted above, and such displays were seen as important in other areas.[74] But coster support purely as a 'vehicle' for advertising would not have been important. It is likely that the parties in the East End also saw importance in the fact that costermongers seemed to enjoy a good deal of public working-class support. When the first Farringdon Road dispute occurred in 1889, according to the *Weekly News and Chronicle*, 'public opinion strongly protested against the high-handed proceeding'. During this dispute costers gathered 10,000 signatures on petitions in their support. In the Hackney dispute of 1892 there were 'large attendances' at public meetings to back the costers, and the *East London Advertiser* noted that the Hackney Board of Works had sought to reach a compromise 'with a view to removing the stigma cast upon them of being harsh with the costermongers'.[75]

Such public support was likely to have been partly due to the association of the role of the costermongers with the need of the poor for cheap food. Certainly, this was often used as an argument by those supporting coster markets.[76] When John Raphael, honorary secretary of the Whitechapel union, stood as a union-endorsed 'independent and people's' parliamentary candidate, he specifically made this connection, and in terms with clear echoes of radical politics, suggesting that costers were interested in 'fair play for the small trader, good and cheap food for the people'.[77] S. M. Samuel

---

[74] Walworth was a good example. See *South London Press*, 20 July 1895, p. 5 col.f; *Standard*, 5 Oct. 1900, p. 5 col.c; *Daily News*, 15 Jan. 1906, p. 7 col.f.

[75] *Weekly News and Chronicle*, 3 Sept. 1892, p. 6 col.a; *The Times*, 3 Dec. 1889, p. 6 col.f; *Hackney and Kingsland Gazette*, 22 June 1892, p. 3 col.c; *East London Advertiser*, 10 Sept. 1892, p. 8 col.c.

[76] See e.g. article by James Greenwood, *Hackney and Kingsland Gazette*, 27 June 1892, p. 3 col.d.

[77] This was in 1918. Raphael stood as an independent costers' union candidate, against three other candidates, including one from the Labour party, in the Whitechapel and St George's constituency. As the union seems to have been affiliated with the Labour party at this time, and Raphael himself was elected as a Labour party representative on the borough council less than a year later, his candidacy seems likely to have been either some attempt to draw votes from other non-Labour candidates, or perhaps the result of a temporary factional dispute over candidate selection. *The Times*, 26 Nov. 1918, p. 8 col.d.

had made a similar connection in his campaign in 1910, targeting the tariff-reform policies of his opponents. He claimed that 'any restriction of the freedom of trade' would mean that 'the costermongers would disappear, for there would be no cheap food to handle'.[78] When the Camberwell Vestry in 1885 discussed action against the costers, part of the debate was said to turn on 'the claims of the "people"' and 'the summonses against the "people's caterers"'. Vestrymen described the street traders as 'the donors of a boon to hundreds of poor people', and few failed to publicly declare their admiration for them.[79] It was said in Newington that some vestrymen 'feared to lose their seats' by a vote restricting the costers.[80]

Association with the costermongers, then, seems to have been a useful symbolic way of indicating one's empathy with the economic needs of poorer working-class constituents. It would also have been an effective method of communicating this message to those to whom other propaganda was difficult to deliver. Unlike other examples, such as those given by Lawrence regarding Wolverhampton, where politicians sought to associate themselves with football and similar clubs to demonstrate their 'localism',[81] association by East End politicians with costermonger bodies may have made a 'policy' statement as well. This would have been very useful to politicians, particularly in the period of the tariff-reform versus free-trade debates of the latter part of this period. It is interesting that Christopher Addison in Hoxton, for example, was very keen to include on his leaflets in 1910 that he had the support of the City costers' union, when only a small number of their members were his constituents, and even fewer could actually vote for him. It seems that he had a much broader audience in mind.

The East End costermongers were not 'traditionally Conservative', and for the most part, were not Conservative at all. The anti-alien agitation of 1900 to 1906 seems certainly to have caught up groups of costers, particularly in Hoxton, Bethnal Green, and Clerkenwell, but in purely numeric terms they would still have been outnumbered in the East of London by the demonstrably more progressive and stronger Whitechapel, Hackney, and City coster organizations. After 1906 it appears that even the more conservative unions began to have some members moving towards Liberal or Socialist support, and in many ways the latter seems to have been the more 'natural' position of the costers politically. 'Trade defensiveness' seems not to have been a significant factor in the costers' political decisions; their trade

---

[78] *Daily News*, 8 Jan. 1910, p. 7 col.c.
[79] *Camberwell and Peckham Times*, 17 Oct. 1885, cutting in Southwark LSL file 658.842.
[80] *The Times*, 12 Jan. 1886, cutting in Southwark LSL file 658.842.
[81] Lawrence, 'Class and Gender', 640–1.

'disputes' were with local authorities too diverse to result in a consistent political trend towards one party. The division of the coster support for parties, even within the same area, suggests the influence of more complex factors.

Although the union leaderships have received a good deal of attention above, it is clear that large numbers of ordinary costers too participated in political activities, from canvassing and voting to displaying colours on their stands. The union leaderships, and their political 'patrons', were likely to have been very important in forming members' political stances, through a number of influences, social and intellectual. The small size of most coster unions was important in their 'socializing' effect. Politicians were keen to gain coster support, partly because of their usefulness in the public display of the candidate's material, but also because the coster gave politicians something desirable in the eyes of poorer constituents—a 'legitimacy' in the claims of concern for their needs.

Stepney and the Temperance Vote

The evidence used to support the accepted 'model' of costermonger Conservatism clearly has a number of weaknesses, and the politics of this group was much more complex than has previously been portrayed. This is also the case with a number of other 'models' applied to East End politics, and examination of these can provide a clearer understanding of where the 'core' support of the parties in East London was most likely generated, as well as again putting to the test the type of evidence upon which previous characterizations of East End politics have been based.

The examples of Millwall, Stepney Centre ward, and the costers have shown the key importance of 'localized' loyalty in assisting candidates. The Millwall example showed most clearly how a Nonconformist-influenced popular radicalism could coexist easily with a paternalist social and political setting in the East End. Thompson suggests that in London, at least in 1886 and 1900, 'both Nonconformity and Liberalism benefited from a backbone of artisan and lower middle class support'.[82] Undoubtedly this can be said of Nonconformity, but whether any specific correlation of this with Liberal strength can be made is certainly less clear. There is little reason to suggest that either the lower middle class or Nonconformism delivered a great deal of support to progressive politics in East London. This can be seen by looking in more detail at the Stepney seat.

[82] Thompson, *Socialists*, 20.

We saw earlier the great range of large Nonconformist and evangelical centres bordering the Stepney constituency. In contemporary assessments of politics, it was commonly noted that the 'Nonconformist character of Stepney is a most important consideration'.[83] To some extent Stepney was the one area where 'marginal' religious attachment was also strong in relation to the Dissenting churches (as in the case of the Kemps).

A reporter asked a Liberal election agent: 'Stepney has always been regarded as a Nonconformist stronghold. How was it the Liberal party lost in 1886?'[84] Stepney had been won by the Liberals in 1885, but then was held by the Conservatives in all seven general elections from 1886 to January 1910, falling to the Liberals only in a by-election in 1898, and then again in the second general election of 1910.

Undoubtedly the seat was a 'stronghold', at least of Nonconformist religious effort. The Revd Sissons of the Wycliffe Chapel, situated at the Western end of the constituency, painted the picture for George Arkell in 1898 of Nonconformist ministers almost tripping over each other in their endeavours. He told Arkell that the 'place is crowded with chapels. District is better provided with places of worship than any other in London. There is not enough population to work on.'[85] A London City Missionary and Congregationalist thought that his part of Stepney was 'well worked and . . . [that] he is not needed in the district which is well looked after compared to others'. He visited other areas 'where the people are neglected', and wondered why 'he is not sent to such a place as that'.[86]

The Stepney constituency, which was relatively wealthy in East End terms, had at least a dozen Nonconformist chapels and missions operating within it or on its boundary streets. Not only Nonconformity, but also the Established Church, was strong in parts of Stepney and surrounding areas.[87] Despite only average attendance figures for churches within the constituency, the evidence suggests strongly that a large number of those attending the nearby vast evangelical and Nonconformist centres came from within Stepney.

But politically, in many ways Stepney seems to have exemplified a model of London Nonconformist drift away from the Liberals from the mid-1880s onwards, as has been described by Bebbington and Stephen Koss. Many Nonconformists, already unhappy with Liberal actions such as the 1870 Education Act, moved to the Liberal Unionists in response to Gladstone's

[83] *East London Advertiser*, 2 July 1892, p. 8 col.c. See also *East London Observer*, 6 July 1895, p. 6 col.b.

[84] *East London Advertiser*, 6 Aug. 1892, p. 8 col.b.   [85] Booth MSS B223, 15.

[86] Mr H. Carnall, Booth MSS B223, 129.   [87] See Booth MSS B182, 45.

Home Rule proposals in 1886. While some later moved back towards Liberalism, others drifted closer to the Conservatives. Intra-party dissension over the South African War again pushed a number of voters, particularly Wesleyans, away from the Liberals, and despite a coming together against the Conservative's 1902 Education Act, the tie of religion and politics was dissipated.[88] This pattern can be seen amongst the Nonconformists of Stepney, with the exception that there the drift seems not to have been even temporarily reversed by the Education Act alliance after 1902. Stepney—the Nonconformist 'stronghold'—elected a Liberal member in 1885, the only one of the four 'classic' Conservative-voting East End seats of Stepney, Mile End, Limehouse, and St George's to do so; but after that the Conservatives became increasingly dominant.

In 1897 a Nonconformist minister could be welcomed back into the Liberal fold, having 'left the Unionist ranks'.[89] But more usual were cases such as that of O. W. Peacock, a prominent member of the Stepney Wesleyan Temple Church and superintendent of the Sunday School, who after having a 'coat of many colours' politically for some time, threw in his lot wholeheartedly with the Conservatives in the midst of the South African War in 1900, and was elected as a Moderate to the borough council, in the Stepney South Ward.[90] That in doing so he became more closely aligned politically with most members of his congregation is suggested strongly by an examination of his church and his ward.

The Wesleyan Temple Church in Commercial Road is one of the very few for which an employment breakdown of membership is available. In 1898 its minister, the Revd John Howard, gave Booth's inquirer a list of the occupations of nearly all of the church's full members,[91] the main employment categories being as follows:

    26 artisans
    20 warehousemen, dray-, and carmen
    18 clerks
    18 teachers, postmen, policemen, nurses, and other professionals
    15 regularly employed dock workers
    14 casual labourers
    10 shopkeepers and assistants
     6 servants.

[88] Bebbington, 'Nonconformity and Electoral Sociology', 644–6, and S. Koss, *Nonconformity in Modern British Politics* (1975), *passim*.
[89] See *East London Advertiser*, 27 Feb. 1897, p. 3 col.b.
[90] See ibid., 8 Sept. 1900, p. 8 col.b, and *East London Observer*, 27 Oct. 1900, p.8 col.d, and 3 Nov. 1900, p. 5 col.e.   [91] Booth MSS B184, 25–9.

Those female members who were employed generally worked at the type of jobs taken up by the wives of even the lower middle class and regularly employed artisans—such as jam- and sweet-making, dressmaking, laundry work, and charring.[92] The vicar said that although this list covered only the church membership of 250, those 'who come to services and meetings [at least 500 of a Sunday evening] are of exactly the same class as the members . . . living for the most part in half a small house, or with two rooms'.[93]

The church was within the small area Booth described as 'A respectable block. Houses generally small but neatly kept. Great majority of the people are in regular steady work; artisans, postmen, policemen, clerks, shop assistants, and many others engaged in one branch or another of the shipping trade.'[94] Clearly the church was representative of the population of its surrounding streets. This block also formed the core of Stepney South ward, and in Stepney it was the South ward where the 'Temperance Party'—based heavily upon Nonconformist support—was 'particularly strong'. This ward was indeed a Nonconformist stronghold, with very little Church of England attendance registered in 1902–3, but with a strong temperance movement and many in the ward undoubtedly attending the Nonconformist churches just outside the ward boundaries. In the South ward in 1898 the temperance 'party' was able to deliver nearly one-third of the total vote (on a 50 per cent turnout) to its independent candidates, against the combined strength of both major parties, when it objected to a political compromise which would have seen a publican elected to the vestry.[95]

But the South ward also was one where the Conservatives normally 'romped in'. From 1900 to 1912 it elected only Conservative councillors to the Stepney borough council, with an average Conservative vote of over 64 per cent, peaking at 78 per cent in 1906. Before that, the ward had also 'been known for its moderate propensities'.[96] It is also relatively easy to determine that it was the block containing the Temple Church that provided the bulk of Conservative support in the ward. This is because of boundary changes associated with the formation of the boroughs in 1900: newspaper commentators identified a new area added to the ward as significantly weakening the Conservative hold, yet the strength of the Conservative vote in

---

[92] See evidence of Alexander Horn of Clarke, Nickolls & Coombs, confectioners, COS, *Unskilled Labour*, qq. 1839–40.

[93] Booth MSS B184, 33.   [94] Booth, *Life*, 1st series, vol. II, App., area 77B.

[95] See *East London Advertiser*, 14 May 1898, p. 7 col.e; 28 May, p. 7 col.d; and 11 June, p. 7 col.d; and also P. Clarke, 'Electoral Sociology of Modern Britain', *History*, 57: 189 (Feb. 1972), 41.

[96] *East London Advertiser*, 27 Oct. 1900, p. 8 col.g, and 8 July 1902, p. 8 col.a.

the old part of the ward managed to retain it for the Conservatives for the next twelve years—in borough elections, in any case. There is very little to suggest that the strength of Nonconformism, or the social make-up of this ward, was assisting the progressive vote to any significant extent.

Samuel Montagu implied that temperance adherents played a large part in the poor performance of the Liberals in Mile End in the Home Rule election of 1886. Noting that the turnout of electors dropped considerably in that election, he complained that he 'could understand abstainers refusing to vote for a brewer [Charrington, Cons.], but they might have voted for a brewer's opponent'.[97] The direct effect of Home Rule on the voting intentions of many Nonconformists, particularly Wesleyans, in London is clearly shown by Bebbington. But he qualifies the impact of this issue by noting that a continuing trend through the late nineteenth century was the weakening community influence of the chapel upon party allegiance, particularly amongst the more prosperous of the members of the congregation, and especially in London. He quotes Ostrogorski's comment from 1902, that 'Dissent . . . formed, according to Mr Gladstone's expression, the backbone of the Liberal Party. The joints of the backbone are beginning to get dislocated . . . [this] is not a little helped by the social ambitions which are infecting the richer members of the Nonconformist sects and making them keep to themselves amid their coreligionists, even in the places of worship.'[98] 'No longer', says Bebbington, 'would the deacons of a chapel automatically assemble after morning service and allow the conversation to turn to their common political concerns.'[99]

None of this denies, of course, that very many of the most prominent members of the Nonconformist churches continued to support the Liberals. The association of Nonconformity with Liberalism, and most of Anglicanism with Conservatism, is usually assumed on the basis of the professed stands of activist clergy and prominent laypeople. Many examples of Nonconformist ministers in Stepney showing their support for the Liberals can be found. An extreme example can be seen in the complaint by a correspondent to the *East London Advertiser* in 1900, that the Revd Atkinson at the Latimer Congregational Church in Stepney had concluded a sermon with: 'In the name of humanity, in the name of justice and . . . as a Christian minister, in the name of God, I ask you to vote for Steadman [the Liberal

[97] Ibid., 25 Dec. 1886, p. 5 col.d.

[98] M. Ostrogorski, *Democracy and the Organization of Political Parties* (1902), quoted in Bebbington, 'Nonconformity and Electoral Sociology', 647.

[99] Ibid. 647.

candidate].'[100] But as Cox has said, it may be that 'even outright Tories were crowding into Edwardian chapel pews, [but] they were forced to listen cheerfully or at least passively to a great deal of Progressive rhetoric'. He has found similar evidence in his study of Lambeth to suggest a political split between ministry and membership in the London Nonconformist churches by the end of the nineteenth century. The minister of the Surrey Strict Baptist Tabernacle believed that 'the majority of his congregation was Conservative, although he himself was a strong Liberal', and other divisions are apparent between pastors and activists.[101] Bebbington too argues that 'a significant proportion of nonconformists was abandoning liberalism for unionism before the First World War . . . Particularly among the upper echelons of the middle class and particularly around London, a process of transfer was well under way by 1894. The political solidarity of the chapels was decaying.'[102] Again, it was the weakening community influences of the chapel which perhaps most clearly enabled this decay and allowed the political move of Nonconformists to the Conservatives in response to Home Rule and other issues.

In the Centre ward of Stepney, where the Primitive Methodist Tabernacle and at least five other Nonconformist churches were located, the only non-Conservative candidate to be elected at the five borough-council elections 1900–12 was again a temperance candidate, the Revd W. G. Boyd of St Faith's mission church, whose nomination was thought to be 'calculated to injure the Moderate cause' and 'was bitterly resented by the Moderates, for it was felt that this splitting of the votes would cause the loss of a seat', which it did.[103] The temperance movement in this ward was again based mainly on Nonconformist organizations, largely the Congregational Stepney Meeting House.[104] Yet this election showed again what was certainly believed by the local Conservatives—that Nonconformist temperance and Conservatism were not incompatible. It seems apparent that in these areas of the East End the most prosperous working-class and middle-class temperance advocates could come together specifically on that issue to support a temperance candidate. But in purely party-based electoral contests, the more generalized association of the Liberals with the temperance cause was insufficient to attract many of their votes.

---

[100] 13 Oct. 1900, p. 3 col.d. See also 21 Nov. 1891, p. 8 col.b, and 16 July 1898, p. 8 col.e; and *Eastern Post*, 23 Feb. 1895, p. 2 col.e.

[101] Cox, *Churches*, 172.

[102] Bebbington, 'Nonconformity and Electoral Sociology', 654.

[103] *East London Advertiser*, 31 Oct. 1903, p. 8 col.a.

[104] See article from *Chart and Compass* in Booth MSS B172, between 19 and 20.

THE RACE ISSUE

Somewhat surprisingly, after the Revd Boyd's 'temperance' victory in Stepney Centre ward, the *Jewish Chronicle* also made the claim that Boyd won largely 'through the votes of Jews and the instrumentality of Jewish canvassers'.[105] That a temperance campaigner who clearly won by splitting the Conservative vote should have relied significantly on Jewish support seems a bizarre possibility, but it is one that ties in closely with other similar evidence.

Stepney was the constituency after 1900 of Major William Evans-Gordon. Evans-Gordon was a principal force behind the anti-immigration Aliens Act of 1905, and it has been often claimed that he held Stepney for the Conservatives against the general Liberal swing of 1906 largely on the basis of popular support for his restrictionist activities.[106] The generally assumed central place of race in the political divide of the East End was described in the Introduction. But a fact of great interest is that, within the Stepney constituency over much of this period, the one voting ward with an overwhelmingly large Jewish population—the West ward—was also considered to be 'a hotbed of Toryism'. Indeed, the West ward was said to have helped overturn a looming Progressive victory in the Stepney LCC contest in 1904.[107]

In fact, it is clear that until well into the Edwardian period, as Garrard and Geoffrey Alderman have shown, those Jews who possessed the vote in the East End and elsewhere often used it in support of Conservative candidates, despite the exhortations of many Liberals who believed that they were the 'natural' party for the Jewish community.[108] The Jewish vote was often significant in deciding results in some of the East End seats.

On the general question of whether a Jewish 'block' vote existed, the *Jewish Chronicle* asserted that: 'Surprise or no surprise, Jews actually do support Radicals; wonder or no wonder, Jews are often Tory. The fact is that Jews have become so thoroughly English that they regard their responsibility as voters entirely as Englishmen.'[109] Across the East End

---

[105] *Jewish Chronicle*, 6 Nov. 1903, p. 26.

[106] See Pelling, *Social Geography*, 46; Husbands, 'East End Racism', 9; Feldman, 'The Importance of Being English', 70; and Garrard, *The English and Immigration*, 74.

[107] *Jewish Chronicle*, 12 Oct. 1900, p. 7, quoted in Garrard, *The English and Immigration*, 118, and G. Alderman, *The Jewish Community in British Politics* (Oxford, 1983), 46; *East London Advertiser*, 12 Mar. 1904, p. 8 col.d. On the population of the area see *East London Advertiser*, 19 Aug. 1905, p. 8 col.a, and *London City Mission Magazine*, 67 (May 1902), 90–1.

[108] See Garrard, *The English and Immigration*, 113–19.

[109] *Jewish Chronicle*, 26 Nov. 1885, p. 9, quoted ibid. 116.

constituencies, and for most of the period, observers, including Jews and Liberals, noted the often strong support of Jewish voters for the Tories. In St George's in 1886, 'the English Jews . . . were almost unanimous in favour of Mr Ritchie [Conservative]'.[110] In Mile End in 1895 the Jewish vote 'went solid', it was said, for the Conservatives, with the *Jewish Chronicle* noting in 1905 that the 'majority of Jewish electors' had been Conservative in that seat.[111] In Stepney in 1889, 'a large percentage of the aliens voted for the Conservative candidate', and in 1898 the Jewish vote 'formed a great bulk of the Unionist poll'.[112] David Dainow found generally 'a large amount of Tory opinion amongst Jews in East London'.[113]

It is apparent also that the mere fact of a candidate being Jewish did not guarantee support from Jewish voters. Bertram Straus was the Jewish Liberal candidate for St George's in 1900. His Conservative opponent was T. R. Dewar, who made his 'speciality' for the election his promise to 'do everything in his power to restrict the immigration of foreign aliens . . . the canker that is eating out the life blood of St George's'.[114] A witness at a meeting of Jewish voters in that election recalled later that:

> it was the Jewish vote and Jewish influence that secured the seats of St. George's and Stepney for their present occupants [Conservatives]. I still remember with shame and disgust the proceedings of a meeting of Jewish voters called together in support of Mr. Dewar's candidature. The principal speaker of the evening . . . [who] was stated to be the private secretary and right hand of Lord Rothschild, enlarged upon the friendship and goodwill of the Conservative Party for the Jewish people . . . it was the cherished wish of 'our Lord' that the Jews should return the Conservative candidate. This had the desired effect and the Jewish vote, with few single exceptions, went solid for Mr. Dewar. Similar things happened in Stepney.[115]

This writer implies an importance for 'influence' in the actions of Jewish voters. In other elections it was stated that letters from Rothschild supporting East End Conservatives would influence 'to a large extent' Jewish voters,[116] even against Jewish candidates. But perhaps much more important in this case, as in so many others, were specifically local, personalized effects. The president of the St George's Conservative Association in 1900

[110] *East London Advertiser*, 14 Aug. 1886, p. 5 col.b.

[111] *Eastern Post*, 20 July 1895, p. 5 col.b, and *Jewish Chronicle*, 13 Jan. 1905, 10.

[112] Letter to the editor, *East London Advertiser*, 27 July 1889, p. 6 col.g, and ibid., 12 Mar. 1898, p. 8 col.b. See Alderman, *Jewish Community*, 45, for further similar examples from these and other East End constituencies.

[113] D. Dainow, 'The Jewish Vote', *East London Advertiser*, 1 Jan. 1910, p. 8 col.d.

[114] *Eastern Post*, 6 Oct. 1900, p. 4 col.f.

[115] Letter to the editor, *Jewish Chronicle*, 7 Mar. 1902, p. 6.

[116] See e.g. *East London Observer*, 13 July 1895, p. 6 col.d, and 20 July 1895, p. 6 col.e.

was Joe Abrahams, who was supremely confident of delivering the Jewish vote. Abrahams was said to be 'one of the oldest inhabitants in St. George's ... and his influence is undoubtedly great'.[117] He was also undoubtedly successful, for after the election Straus bitterly complained that 'the great Jewish race had, in St. George's East, sold their birthright for mess of pottage, or something else'.[118] Apparently also able to swing enough Jewish support away from the Conservatives in Stepney Centre ward to the Revd Boyd, to deliver to him the seat, was the Revd Stern of the Stepney Synagogue. Stern backed the Independent Boyd against Jewish candidates endorsed by the parties, against some protest but, it seems, very effectively.[119]

It is very clear, as noted above, that Jewish voters, voting as 'Englishmen', did not just support candidates because they were of the same religion. But it seems likely that they were subject to the same localized or community-based influences that we have noted characterizing much of the voting patterns of other voters in the East End. In the creation of the 'sense of place' which we have seen as significant, the role of race or religion was of course important. But other aspects were perhaps more consequential, and the extent to which influential members of a community could 'work' on voters was perhaps the key. It is noticeable that reports of meetings of the 'Tory hotbed' Stepney West ward Conservative Club were dominated by members with Jewish names.[120] The chairman of this club for a significant period was the Jewish MP Wooton Isaacson. The teachers of the Stepney Jewish schools were said to have 'put in an immense amount of hard work' for Isaacson in 1895.

In Whitechapel, also with a very high Jewish population, but by contrast always won by the Liberals, the local Jewish community was swayed politically to a large extent, as David Feldman suggests, by the 'network of influence which circulated around Samuel Montagu and the Federation of Synagogues' (of which Montagu was president).[121] Alderman suggests that the 'Jewish vote which Montagu created was, in the deepest sense, a personal vote built upon a very personal relationship between MP and constituents'.[122] Tied to this was the fact that the Federation of Synagogues was more closely linked to more recent Jewish immigrants, in contrast to

[117] *East London Observer*, 25 Sept. 1900, p. 3 col.a, and see Garrard, *The English and Immigration*, 118, n. 1.

[118] *Eastern Post*, 6 Oct. 1900, p. 5 col.b.

[119] See debates in *Jewish Chronicle*, Nov. and Dec. 1903.

[120] See *East London Advertiser*, 17 Dec. 1887, p. 6 col.b, and 1 June 1889, p. 7 col.a.

[121] D. Feldman, *Englishmen and Jews: Social Relations and Political Culture 1840–1914* (1994), 386.

[122] Alderman, *Jewish Community*, 45.

other, more established, sections of the London Anglo-Jewish community. This was politically more advantageous in Whitechapel, with a much higher number of immigrants, meaning that even the relatively low percentage of these who became naturalized and possessed the vote were able to have a significant impact.[123] In other parts of the East End, for most of this period, the majority of Jewish voters were those who had been in the country longer, often in business or of wealth, and their descendants. In St George's in 1886 it was said that the 'English Jews, who may be called the party of order, were almost unanimous in favour of Mr Ritchie [Con.]; whilst the German and Russian Jews, men of revolution, most of whom are non-voters, were wild in favour of the Separatist candidate [Mr Eve, Lib.], for whom they shouted and cheered in a most frantic manner'.[124]

The politics, occasionally socialist and revolutionary, of relatively newly arrived European immigrants lies outside the scope of this study. But the politics of the established Jewish community in the East End may in fact have been significant in the strong Conservative vote that has, in many cases, been used as evidence of anti-alien sentiment amongst the working class. Wealthy and well-placed, often Conservative, local Jewish leaders could be extremely influential in swaying the votes of the relatively close-knit, long-established Jewish communities. This could, in some instances, have had a decisive effect on election results, particularly in closely fought seats such as St George's. A detailed case could be made, from the evidence noted above, that without the Jewish vote St George's would have been won by the Liberals in every election from 1892 to 1910, a result which would turn much of the assumed political impact of anti-alienism in the East End completely on its head.

But Feldman suggests that the extent of anti-alienism in the East End cannot be seen through election results, given the restricted level of enfranchisement. Instead, he argues, one needs to look at the support given to organizations such as the purportedly working-class anti-alien British Brothers' League, and also at the very localized attacks made upon Jews moving into parts of the East End.[125]

---

[123] Of 140,000 foreign-born residents in London in 1901, only 5,500 were naturalized British subjects, *Census*, P.P. 1902 CXX, p. 173. In the St George's North ward area analysed in Ch. 2, of 499 identifiable voters, only 12 had not been born in Britain or Ireland. It was said that in Whitechapel between one-quarter and one-half of voters were immigrants. See newspaper clippings in D. H. Kyd Papers, British Library of Political and Economic Science, Vol. 1, pp. 54 and 59; Vol. 2, pp. 5 and 14.

[124] *East London Advertiser*, 14 Aug. 1886, p. 5 col.b.

[125] Feldman, 'The Importance of Being English', 70–2.

The evidence we have of who participated in the BBL mass demonstrations is very general, by far the most specific being a description of stewards at a 1902 meeting in Mile End, who were 'big brawny stalwarts, dock labourers, chemical workers from Bromley, and operatives from Bow, Bethnal Green and Mile End'.[126] But certainly the most infamous incidents of direct action by East End residents to exclude immigrant Jews occurred in the streets of St George's.[127] Cornwall Street, in the North ward of St George's, was, as Bernard Gainer describes, 'inhabited by dock labourers and carmen, with a smaller proportion of coal porters, building trade labourers, and the like, [and] was the scene of frequent disturbances'.[128] These reached their peak in October 1901, in an incident which was widely reported at the time, and has been widely used since by historians as a key example of the anti-alienism of the East End. Jewish tenants were attempting to move into the street, when 'the natives, some three or four hundred strong, made a rush for the van. The occupants beat a hasty retreat, while the crowd pulled the furniture out of the van, smashing it to pieces, and afterwards wrecked the van itself.'[129] But the direct political importance of such incidents is difficult to gauge. In Duckworth's tours for Booth in 1898 he visited the streets adjoining Cornwall Street, and found them similarly inhabited by coal- and other dock and general labourers, carmen, and costers. He described the block as 'rough and poor, probably dark blue', noting a decline in the character of the area since the earlier maps had been prepared. Duckworth also found in one of these streets, Tarling Street, 'In the windows of most of the houses portraits of the two progressive candidates [for the LCC] C. Balian and C. Barratt, both shopkeepers in Watney Street. Balian is known locally as the "Toffee Cooler", he is a confectioner. Motto "For progress and the people".'[130] These candidates were successful in the election. At a presentation to Mr Barratt the previous year, the 'Wapping Gas-stokers Brass Band assembled at Gladstone House before the concert, and marched to the Town Hall, where they gave selections during the evening'.[131] Even more representative of localized support,

[126] *East London Observer*, 18 Jan. 1902, 2. See Feldman, 'The Importance of Being English', 71.
[127] See *East London Advertiser*, 26 Oct. 1901, p. 7 col.c; *RC Alien*, P.P. 1903 IX, qq. 2612–17; T. Kushner, 'Jew and Non-Jew in the East End of London: Towards an Anthropology of "Everyday" Relations', in G. Alderman and C. Holmes (eds.), *Outsiders and Outcasts: Essays in Honour of William J. Fishman* (1993), 39.
[128] B. Gainer, *The Alien Invasion: The Origins of the Aliens Act of 1905* (1972), 58.
[129] *East London Advertiser*, 26 Oct. 1901, p. 7 col.c.
[130] Booth MSS B350, 187–9.
[131] *East London Advertiser*, 27 Aug. 1897, p. 8 col.d.

Barratt also ran for election in the ward vote in the first borough-council elections in 1900, and easily topped the poll.

But most significantly, these 1900 borough elections were held only four weeks after the general parliamentary election, which in St George's had been made by Dewar, the Conservative candidate, into a poll on the issue of Jewish immigration. Barratt still clearly drew a great deal of support from this 'anti-alien' area. It was claimed that in Sheridan Street, near Tarling Street the display of election posters in the 1900 general election was 'chiefly . . . for Mr Straus [the Liberal candidate]'.[132]

The evidence that issues such as anti-alienism were translated into attitudes towards politics or parties has been thought to lie in the electoral results. But I would argue that the electoral results in the East End are far too confused and conflicting to allow any direct conclusion about the influence of anti-alienism to be reached. The arguments which purport to see anti-alienism in the electoral results of the East End are usually structured similarly to those of Gainer, who suggests that in all elections from 1886 and 1906, 'the Conservative party, which advocated immigration control, polled a consistently larger proportion of the total vote in East End boroughs than the median Conservative proportion in the nation as a whole. All else being equal, the swing reflected anti-alienism.'[133] The problem with this is that all else was not equal. Such a view completely ignores social and political variations within the East End and reasons for strong Conservative performances in some areas, including the franchise provisions and, indeed, the apparent strength of Conservative support amongst Jewish communities. Feldman shows, in contrast, that immigration restriction was pursued more strongly as an issue by London Conservatives in 1892 than in 1895, 'yet in the former year the Conservative candidates were routed and in the latter they made good their lost ground'.[134]

But there were other apparent political manifestations of anti-alienism. The *Eastern Post* reported in 1900 that:

The people of St. George's have a great hatred of other than their own nationality. 'I ain't agoing to vote for anybody,' said a well-known but somewhat illiterate Conservative voter when he had been begged for the twentieth time to come up and give his vote. 'That bloke "De Ware" [Dewar, Con.] is a Frenchman. I can tell by his name, and you can't kid me. The other one Straus [Lib.] is a Jew, and I ain't going to vote for either a Frenchman or a Jew.'[135]

---

[132] *East London Observer*, 2 Oct. 1900, p. 2 col.c.   [133] Gainer, *Alien Invasion*, 59.
[134] Feldman, 'The Importance of Being English', 70.
[135] *Eastern Post*, 13 Oct. 1900, p. 5 col.c.

In 1903 the secretary of the St George's Liberal Association said that he had been 'assured by some score of Liberals in St. George's who have informed me that they will neither work nor vote for our candidates if we attempt to run a person of the Jewish populace'.[136] The Liberals refused to accept a Jewish candidate proposed by the Labour party for a joint ticket. But, strikingly, the Liberal ticket in St George's North, with the Jewish candidate excluded, was completely defeated in the election, with the Conservative candidates dominating, *with* one Jew amongst their number. The *Jewish Chronicle* suggested that its 'enquiries' had shown that the Liberal defeat was 'mainly because of the intolerant and unreasonable attitude adopted towards the Jews'.[137] As Garrard suggests, this incident showed 'how great could be the gap between assumptions about racial hostility . . . and the reality'.[138]

An overestimation of the political importance of anti-alienism seems particularly to have been a failing of the Liberals, who were exceedingly frightened of the immigration issue in the East End in this period.[139] It is possible, on the other hand, that the Conservatives were confident enough of holding much of the 'English' Jewish vote to attempt to 'have it both ways'.[140] All four central East End seats in which anti-immigration sensitivity has usually been argued to have been strongest[141]—Mile End, Stepney, Limehouse, and St George's—were represented for some part of this period by Jewish members. In Mile End, Harry Lawson [Con.] held the seat from a by-election in 1905 to 1906 and from 1910 to 1914. In the intervening period it was held by Bertram Straus. These men were the only candidates for the seat from 1905 to 1914. In Stepney, Wooton Isaacson [Con.] held the seat from 1886 to 1898. In Limehouse, Harry Samuel [Con.] was the member from 1895 to 1906. Harry Marks [Con.] held St George's between 1895 and 1900.

The Conservatives in particular were happy to continue to run Jewish candidates, even in seats such as St George's, and they were usually successful. Clearly, in these seats the Conservative vote was at least partly based on winning a sizeable percentage of Jewish support, which held for much of this period. It is likely that, until 1906, the Conservative vote itself included a higher percentage of Jewish voters than of voters who had switched from being Liberal to Conservative on the basis of anti-alienism.

[136] *Jewish Chronicle*, 9 Oct. 1903, p. 20.
[137] Ibid., 6 Nov. 1903, p. 26, and see Garrard, *The English and Immigration*, 135–6.
[138] Garrard, *The English and Immigration*, 136.   [139] See ibid. 137–40.
[140] See Alderman, *Jewish Community*, 68.
[141] See Pelling, *Social Geography*, 44–6.

We also saw earlier that strong opposition to 'alien' traders was exhibited by some groups of costers between 1900 and 1906. But it was apparent that the translation of this feeling into politics was greatly assisted by the actions of local politicians, who saw the community importance of the costers and flocked to associate with and to influence them.

As mentioned above, the most commonly quoted evidence for the importance of anti-alienism in the East End is the performance of Evans-Gordon, who claimed much of the credit for the 1905 Aliens Act, in easily holding the Stepney seat in the face of the Liberal landslide in 1906. The possibly significant role seen earlier of wealthier Nonconformist and Jewish voters in the continuing strong Conservatism of Stepney somewhat undermines the argument that voting patterns in that constituency were affected to any great extent by anti-alienism. But it has been thought that the passage of the Aliens Act by the Conservative government made many Jewish Conservatives switch, at least temporarily, to the Liberals. Given this, Garrard suggests, Evans-Gordon's victory was 'a doubly eloquent tribute to the popularity of the Aliens Act amongst the Gentile voters in his constituency'.[142] The *East London Advertiser* made the same assumption, and admitted that it thought the Stepney West ward would, 'by reason of its large Jewish population, show a large majority for Mr Stokes [Lib.]. As it happened, however, when the votes were counted it was seen that the candidates had almost equally divided the votes.'[143]

Indeed, one factor which has been ignored in the results in this constituency is the basic stability of the Stepney vote. In 1906 the fall in the Conservative share of the vote in Stepney was 4 per cent, which, although smaller than in most other East End seats, was the same as the fall in Whitechapel, which had a great many Jewish voters. Garrard says the smallness of the swing in Whitechapel was 'scarcely significant' in assessing the effect of the anti-alien issue, because this 'invariably Liberal constituency never recorded more than a 5.7 per cent swing either way in all the elections from 1885'.[144] Yet this was almost exactly the same maximum variation as occurred in Stepney across the period.[145]

Between 1900 and 1906, with a quickly increasing percentage of immigrant residents in the constituency, the number of voters on the register in

---

[142] Garrard, *The English and Immigration*, 121, n. 3, and see 112–13.
[143] *East London Advertiser*, 20 Jan. 1906, p. 8 cols.d–e.
[144] Garrard, *The English and Immigration*, 74.
[145] The maximum vote-shift in Whitechapel was in fact 6.0% from 1892 to 1895. This is confirmed in Pelling, *Social Geography*, 43. The maximum shift between general elections in Stepney was 6.4% between 1885 and 1886.

Stepney dropped by 12 per cent. Yet in 1906 the actual number of voters voting Liberal was 8 per cent higher than in 1900, while the actual number of Conservative voters fell by 11 per cent. In real terms, this meant that the Liberals increased the number of their voters turning out from the available electorate by around 20 per cent, comparable to the result in a seat such as Poplar, which was also a relatively stable voting area. That the Liberals did not achieve an even higher percentage increase in their vote, and victory, in Stepney was probably due largely to organizational issues.[146]

But of all East End residents, the most anti-alien were often claimed to be the Irish in parts of the south of St George's and surrounding areas, who have been represented as the classic xenophobic labouring poor. In that district, it was said, there was 'a bold and hardy race with a fierce prejudice against foreigners. They are nearly all Irish.'[147] As Feldman says, 'it was well known that there were few Jews in the south ward of St. George's because the largely Irish inhabitants of the neighbourhood would not let them settle'. But 'Irish' politics were largely concerned with other issues of identity. Feldman goes on to state that Irish anti-alienism may not have turned in a political direction, 'because the language of nation and empire employed by the leaders of organized anti-alienism found little resonance among a population retaining strong links to Ireland and Catholicism'.[148]

Lynn Lees's conclusion on Irish politics in London at the end of the century emphasizes the multivariate influences on these voters:

the impact of the Irish vote was limited because of the tripartite political ties of the Irish community. Priests' commitments and the issue of education drew Catholics to the Conservatives; desire for home rule produced loyalty to the Liberals; and the growth of unions among the unskilled fostered ties to the Socialist clubs. The Irish vote therefore was split and usually as a bloc politically ineffective.[149]

Contradictory claims were made as to the key influences upon the East End Irish voter. In 1906 the *Eastern Post* argued that the education issue would

---

[146] Between 1900 and 1906 the Liberal party structure, already weak, completely collapsed in Stepney. The Liberal Association was said to have 'died' by 1902, with the 'only Progressive body in existence' in the constituency being the Stepney Labour League discussed earlier: London Municipal Society collection, Guildhall Library, cuttings book, 192, 54, said to be *Daily Chronicle*, 24 Oct. 1902 (but see Thompson, *Socialists, Liberals and Labour*, 172, for a discussion of its source). The League essentially only had organizational ability in the Centre ward. It was also weakened immeasurably in 1906 by the ill-health of Frank Brien. See *East London Advertiser*, 25 Aug. 1906, p. 8 col.b, 6 Oct., p. 5 col.f, and 6 and 17 Nov.

[147] *East London Advertiser*, 9 Sept. 1905, p. 3 col.d.

[148] Feldman, 'The Importance of Being English', 72.

[149] L. H. Lees, *Exiles of Erin: Irish Migrants in Victorian London* (Manchester, 1979), 237. See Thompson, *Socialists, Liberals and Labour*, 167–8, for a similar argument.

swing most Catholic votes in St George's because, 'After all, most Irish Catholics put religion before politics'. At the next general election the *Daily Telegraph* noted of the same constituency that, despite the Catholic clergy working hard for the Conservative candidate, 'there was little doubt that the whole of the Catholic Irish voted against him. That means they followed the Nationalist leaders and not the priests'.[150] The *Observer* similarly thought that 'Wapping, where the Irish dockers live' (generally separate from the small Wapping polling district, discussed in Chapter 3 in relation to the model dwellings) 'prides itself on freedom from priestly influence and is fond of declaring that Wapping is not in Ireland'.[151] The Catholic priest for the Isle of Dogs agreed that the political views of the church hierarchy had little effect on parishioners. He said of the 1,000 or so Roman Catholics in his area that: 'Everyone of his people are radical. They don't much approve of the Cardinal because they think he is Conservative.'[152]

Both parts of Wapping, and the Isle of Dogs, as we saw earlier, were 'cut off' from the rest of the East End in many ways, and self-contained. Sections of this area of south St George's were described as: 'almost like a village shut in as they are by the dock waters and the bridge and the river, the people are much less migratory than in some parts of East London and many of those who leave come back again partly because of the church partly because of the general associations and friendliness.'[153] Lovell says that the Irish lived in 'a compact neighbourhood', which they dominated. 'Unionism took root quickly among this coherent group, and the district soon became the most active in the union'. But their approach included 'the greatest opposition to central direction', and in disputes they generally 'conducted the strike and negotiations with scant reference to the wishes of Mann or other union leaders'.[154] The dock unionists, both here and in Millwall, as discussed earlier, showed a great deal of independence in regard to the union's central body, and it seems that a very similar independent attitude towards at least the upper reaches of the Catholic Church was shown by the Irish who lived there.

But it appears likely that a paternalist relationship, which we saw could develop and have significant political effects in such 'isolated' areas as Millwall, did not become of importance for the Irish residents in Millwall or St George's. A number of factors, including religion, were needed to

---

[150] *Eastern Post*, Supplement to 6 Jan. 1906 edn., p. 10 col.c; *Daily Telegraph* quoted ibid., 22 Jan. 1910, p. 5 col.d.
[151] 27 Feb. 1910, in Stansgate Papers, ST/11 Cuttings, 37.
[152] The Revd Father Egglemeers, St Edmunds, Booth MSS B180, 45.
[153] Booth MSS B222, 45.   [154] Lovell, *Stevedores*, 116–17.

sustain this relationship, and in this sense the Irish were 'outside' the terms of the bond and the 'common life' with employers.

Attempts to assess the direction and importance of the Irish vote in London have been very limited, and relatively superficial. Lees notes that many of the Irish worked in the docks, and she assumes that they were the least likely to gain the vote in a restricted franchise: 'franchise requirements and polling hours kept many Irish out of English elections . . . low-paid workers who moved frequently were unlikely to be on the electoral register.'[155] Thompson also utilizes a number of the stereotypes of the poor East End working class in discussing the influence of the Irish. He argues that the conflicting influences to which the Irish were subject meant that they 'were the most unstable element in London politics'. They had low levels of registration because of their extreme defensiveness against the outsider 'English Liberal agent', and their 'main effect was simply to add to the apathy and unreliability of the poorest riverside constituencies'.[156]

The Irish did not form a majority of voters in any East End area, with the 'effective' Irish community comprising, at most, 20 per cent of the electorate in an area of highest concentration, such as St George's.[157] But certainly in terms of enfranchisement they were not as dissimilar to the rest of the working class as Lees and Thompson suggest. Many of the best-paid and most regularly employed of the dock and wharf workers were Irish. It was said in 1901 that the Irish 'form the most permanent element in that class of labour . . . many Irish families have gained their livelihood on the riverside for generations'. Of the best-paid trades, the 'stevedores are a compact body of men, largely Irish, who form a river-side aristocracy . . . The coal-whippers also contain a strong Irish element, and their wages work out at some 25s. a week.'[158] The Irish in south St George's were said to include a number of watermen and lightermen, and a number of the unionized Irish wharf workers in that district were working regularly in 1892 at rates of from 30s. to 36s. a week.[159] Lovell says of the Irish dockers in London after the middle of the nineteenth century that, 'in the better paid work their dominance was permanent . . . the second generation of Irish inherited the pick of the work along the waterfront'.[160]

[155] Lees, *Exiles*, 237. [156] Thompson, *Socialists, Liberals and Labour*, 27.

[157] See *Morning Leader*, 27 Feb. 1910, cutting in Stansgate Papers ST/11, 15; A. O'Day, 'Irish Influence on Parliamentary Elections in London, 1885–1914: A Simple Test', in R. Swift and S. Gilley (eds.), *The Irish in the Victorian City* (1985), 99; and Joyce, 'Work', 142–3.

[158] Anon., 'The London Irish', *Blackwood's Magazine*, 170 (July 1901), 129 and 130.

[159] *East London Advertiser*, 9 Sept. 1905, p. 3 col.d, and 30 Apr. 1892, p. 8 col.e.

[160] Lovell, *Stevedores*, 57.

In the St George's North ward area analysed in Chapter 2, the Irish-born in fact had a somewhat higher level of enfranchisement than British-born adult males.[161] This suggests, as Alan O'Day argues, that the 'bias against the Irish in London of the registration system must have been comparatively slight'.[162] It may even have been a positive bias in some areas. But significantly, those regularly employed and more prosperous Irish who would have been on the voters' registers in the East End were not subject to the same type of influences experienced by many of the working-class voters discussed in previous sections. They were much less likely to act in an 'isolated' manner within their communities. The largely Irish coal-whippers, for example, were an 'extremely close-knit group', and generally the Irish 'lived and worked in self-contained communities, quite apart from other workers in neighbouring districts and trades'.[163] In Limehouse, Potter was told, if the Irish 'like the circle of their friends they go round and round within a certain area they work for each other'.[164] Lovell argues, in fact, that the 'clannish' Irish were part of the cause of the fragmentation of the London waterside workers into 'little isolated groups',[165] with the often-assumed implications of this for working-class solidarity and politics in the East End. Yet it seems apparent that the Irish were one of the strongest support groups for progressive politics in the East End in this period. This was, of course, for a number of very specific political reasons, but was also made more pronounced, by comparison with other working-class voters, by their relative isolation from other 'outside' influences. By being part of more 'self-contained' communities, those who became voters in these areas were subject more strongly to the enforcement of neighbourhood 'norms'.

This can be seen in a series of examples of political 'enforcement' that occurred in poorer, largely Irish areas of St George's. Mary Shaw, charged with causing a disturbance, told the local police court in 1895 that, since her husband had voted for the Conservative candidate in the election, 'the neighbours had not let her have any peace'. Presumably the neighbours found out her husband's politics through some display of support. In two further incidents, Hannah May and Elizabeth Wells also sought redress in the police courts after they, respectively, were assaulted and had windows smashed for displaying posters supporting Conservative candidates.[166] In

---

[161] On a relatively small sample of Irish born. Of 108 Irish-born adult males, 43 were on the voters' register, compared to 444 British-born voters from 1,355 adult males.

[162] O'Day, 'Irish Influence', 102.   [163] Lovell, *Stevedores*, 55 and 58.

[164] Webb, MS Diary, vol. 11, pp. 37–8, typescript 818–19.   [165] Lovell, *Stevedores*, 58.

[166] *East London Advertiser*, 27 July 1895, p. 6 col.f; 13 July 1895, p. 7 col.d; and 23 July 1892, p. 7 col.b.

all these cases it is clear that the message from within the local area was that it was not socially acceptable to display one's Conservative leanings. Noticeably, these seem to have been disputes involving women, who in other poorer, more 'neighbourly' areas usually assumed the important role of maintaining the community's mores or 'public opinion'. Significantly, also in the St George's area, as noted earlier, there occurred incidents of community boycotting of shopkeepers who supported the Conservatives. Peter Clarke has said, of earlier in the century, that the 'power of the radical mob, based on physical intimidation, was perhaps most effective in the 1830s. It was in the practice of exclusive dealing (i.e. with sympathetic retailers) that the mass of non-electors turned the economic modes of 'influence' against their betters.'[167]

In the only significant attempt to analyse the political effects of the Irish in London, O'Day has concluded that the Irish were 'overwhelmingly Liberal' after 1885 and 'were generally part of the anti-Conservative electorate'.[168] Certainly this was the case in seats such as St George's, where the sizeable Irish vote seems to have held strongly to the Liberals throughout the period. The community nature of this support is also seen in the description of the 1910 election, when the Liberal candidate 'toured the constituency in an illuminated motor-car . . . The St. Patrick's band, a well known local band which has many members of the United Irish League in its ranks . . . put off an engagement in order to be able to head the procession.'[169] In 1886 the *East London Advertiser* said that in St George's, 'the question has arisen who supplied green paper bonnets and flags, bearing the name of Mr Eve [Lib.], to some 40 or 50 well-known immoral women . . . and who hired and paid for the band, which, headed by Mr Eve's flags, paraded the streets and played Irish tunes!' Similar scenes occurred in parts of Poplar, most likely in the Isle of Dogs.[170] Most importantly, this closeness of the community and its link to politics meant that it was less likely that the more prosperous workers who became voters would be influenced by factors which tended to inhibit progressive support amongst other working-class voters in parts of the East End. Significantly, in Mile End, where the Irish were less 'self-contained', where such an overlap of identities for Catholics was less strong, and where the community was more 'integrated',

[167] Clarke, 'Electoral Sociology', 39–40.
[168] O'Day, 'Irish Influence', 103.
[169] *Morning Leader*, [n.d.] Feb. 1910, in Stansgate Papers ST/11, Newspaper Cuttings, 16.
[170] *East London Advertiser*, 10 July 1886, p. 6. See also *Eastern Post*, 20 July 1895, p. 5 col.b, on Whitechapel.

it was said in both the 1904 LCC elections and the 1905 parliamentary by-election that the Catholic vote would be cast in favour of the Conservative.[171]

Although there is some suggestion that religious feeling against the Irish and Catholicism played some part in making the non-Irish vote more Conservative in St George's in particular, there is very little to suggest that this factor was significant. It certainly never developed into the political importance of the extreme popular Protestantism of parts of Lancashire and elsewhere.[172] The more generalized influence of Irish Home Rule as an issue, of course, cannot be denied.

Amongst the Irish voters in the East End, although the evidence is very limited, the cohesiveness and self-containment of their communities seems to have helped to reinforce political support for causes of importance for these communities, even amongst the more prosperous who had gained the vote. This contrasted with the influences acting against a clear political allegiance amongst many other such working-class voters, as we have seen throughout this study. The important point, to be emphasized again, is that the significance of the milieu and personal contacts of the voter in translating underlying political beliefs into action has to be recognized, as well as those beliefs themselves or the rhetoric of politicians.

[171] *East London Advertiser*, 5 Mar. 1904, p. 8 col.d, and *Eastern Post*, 7 Jan. 1905, p. 5 col.e.
[172] See O'Day, 'Irish Influence', 101, and Vernon, *Politics and the People*, 179–80.

Conclusion

The image of a populist Conservatism and a political apathy growing in the late Victorian and Edwardian period out of an abjectly poor East End is wrong. The examination, in the previous chapter and throughout this book, of 'models' put forward by historians to support this idea has suggested that few were built upon a solid base of evidence, and that they often relied heavily upon superficial and unjustified assumptions regarding poverty, race, and religion. The politics of the East End working class were far more complex than these models allow.

It has been the argument of this study that 'East End Conservatism' was the result of a range of interconnected factors and impressions, some of which related specifically to East London, while others applied more broadly to working-class life in London and elsewhere.

Only four of the eleven constituencies within the East End—St George's, Stepney, Mile End, and Limehouse—voted Conservative in any consistent way in this period. But it is upon the evidence of the electoral results in these seats that much of the impression of the politics of the area has been based. In the other seven constituencies, the Conservative vote was in fact well below the average in other London working-class seats.[1]

Of the four 'Conservative' seats in the East End, two—Mile End and Stepney—were overwhelmingly the wealthiest in the area, and amongst the wealthiest 'working-class' seats in London. Nearly 75 per cent of residents in Mile End Old Town, the district which covered both constituencies, were living 'in comfort', according to Booth's survey. Extreme East End poverty seems to have been the least likely reason for Conservatism in these seats.

The statistical material in Chapter 3 also suggested similar, tentative links between relative wealth and apparent Conservatism in areas of Poplar and Bow and Bromley. An examination of the effects of the franchise provisions in East London made the point even more strongly that electoral Conservatism did not occur as a response to poverty.

In Chapter 2 it was shown that the predominance of sub-letting of accommodation across most of the East End meant that most voters in the

---

[1] See Pelling, *Social Geography*, Table 3, 43. The average Conservative vote 1885–1910 in these seven constituencies was 44.7%. In the other 13 non-East End constituencies defined as working class by Pelling, the average Conservative vote was 48.4%.

area were those who were wealthy enough to be principal tenants—either able to take a house by themselves, or to accept the risk of sub-letting parts to raise the whole rent. This meant that, in all areas of the East End, instead of the electoral results representing the populist reactions of a degraded poor electorate, as is often implied, voting patterns demonstrated the views, mostly, of a more prosperous working-class and middle-class section of the population.

It was in the poorest, but very high-rent, riverside areas closest to the inner city that this division between the status of the voter and the non-voter was at its most extreme—that is, specifically in the other two 'Conservative' constituencies, St George's and Limehouse. We saw in Chapter 3 that, in these constituencies, the most Conservative sections were not those dominated by poor voters, but instead by those lucky and financially secure enough to live in the model block dwellings which extended across large parts of Shadwell and Wapping, where their residents dominated the electoral registers. Again, this suggested that it was the more prosperous areas which delivered apparently greater support to the Conservatives in these 'classic' East End 'Conservative' seats.

It was also noted that in other areas, such as Poplar and Bethnal Green, the effects of sub-letting were minimized by the number of small houses in the areas. This meant that in these seats a larger number of poorer residents were likely to have the vote, and indeed, these were areas where the progressives tended to do best.

But locally specific demographic and franchise factors only worked to create the impression of dominant Conservatism in some parts of the East End because of more general social influences acting upon the politics of the prosperous working class most likely to be on the electoral register in these areas.

Conservative parliamentary victories in the pre-war East End were due in large measure to significant numbers of the working class not bothering to turn out to vote at elections. This could be thought to imply the political apathy considered characteristic of a poorer working class, particularly in the East End. Instead, it was suggested in Chapter 3 that at least part of this response was the result of a political neutrality fostered amongst the more prosperous working class by a combination of the effects of a growing social isolation of more 'respectable' workers, and a continuing marginal attachment to the Church of England in working-class London. These factors acted together to greatly increase the potential personal influence of largely middle-class and similar activists, such as Anglican church visitors and those who ran religiously based clubs and other activities, with whom many of these working-class families were likely to come into contact. The direct 'political' influence exerted by such activists was largely limited to the passing on of judgements or information as to the moral or religious traits of various candidates, usually to the detriment of the Conservatives' opponents. This did not lead to direct Conservatism amongst the working class, but the effect on individual voters appears to have been simply, as Thorold Rogers put it, that they were 'rendered indifferent' to the progressive candidate.[2] When the issues of the day and transitory party difficulties were added to this, it meant that the progressive cause could be more easily abandoned by these voters, at least temporarily.

The further material in Chapter 3 suggested that areas with higher levels of working-class church attendance, and also of marginal attachment to the Church of England, experienced some of the highest levels of such voter abstention. But in areas where Church of England contacts were more likely to be with progressive rather than Conservative elements, such as in Bromley South East, these vote fluctuations virtually disappeared. A conflict between political and 'moral' influences was not leading voters here to neutrality and abstention.

This Conservative church influence, and its effects on politics, was to some extent only possible because of a continuing general belief amongst many sections of the working class in the importance of the 'moral' in society. We saw many aspects of this in Chapters 3 and 4. Amongst both the 'respectable' and poorer working class, any scandalous stories about public figures could be politically important. For the more prosperous working-class voters, as described above, such scandal could involve accusations of atheism or other moral failings brought by church and similar canvassers against progressive candidates. As discussed in Chapter 3, these could be transmitted through contacts largely made by women, into 'gossip' networks that existed amongst their husbands.

But generally, the degree of importance given by the East End working class to the issue of 'character' amongst political and other leaders was greatly increased by a number of factors. First, because of the way in which the franchise favoured principal tenants, who tended to be older and with a number of children, voters in the East End were, on average, on the register for relatively short periods. This was particularly the case with that minority of voters from less-skilled and poorer occupations, who tended to gain the franchise only when they had adult children living at home. This is likely to have meant that there was a lower level of party-political allegiance

[2] Rogers, 'Confessions', 691.

amongst such voters, because they had only rarely performed the loyalty-generating act of actually voting. Political scientists have emphasized the central role that the non-party, personal attributes of candidates play in discussions between voters around election times. This can only have been increased in importance in this period by such factors.

But a general belief in the central social importance of individual personality was also boosted enormously by the specific economic conditions and structures faced by workers in the East End. The dominant working experience in East London was of being subject to the oppression, fraud, and demands for bribery of the local, low-level, contracting middleman or workgroup foreman. It was the corruption of these supervisors, rather than any systemic injustice, that many workers identified as being the direct cause of their troubles, and this came to personify their view of evil in society. In this context, the use, particularly by many of the new trade-union leaders amongst the unskilled from the late 1880s, of ideological concepts with a base still within a continuing Radical stream of politics, was significant. They emphasized, even within an apparent socialist framework, continuing political ideas of Old Corruption, 'Good' and 'Evil' as basic dividers of society, and also the need for the moralizing of the workplace. These arguments connected well with East End workers' own knowledge of corruption, and their day-to-day perception of being 'robbed' of their fair wages. But their personal experiences meant they saw these ideas in very much localized, personalized terms, and these Radical ideas merely acted to emphasize the central importance of individual character, rather than structural change, in seeking reform. Their anger would be directed at a corrupt foreman rather than the employer's system of wages, or indeed the capitalist economic structure itself, and in politics the 'good man' may have been more likely to benefit from their support. This latter reaction, of course, has been demonstrated elsewhere to have been a widespread and common response in politics through the nineteenth century and later, but it was also a response that was strongly fostered by the specific conditions of the East End. Particularly in areas which were culturally isolated from other parts of East London, and had their own developed sense of 'place', such as Millwall, we saw that such working-class experiences and views meant that local paternalist employers and politicians were more likely to gather support.

But some aspects of an emerging class identification were apparent in another side to the working-class interest in political morals. This was through the interest shown by a number of—particularly the poorer—working class in any moral scandal amongst politicians. This interest appears likely to have been at least partly a response to the inferiority the working class were made to be feel by the derogatory language used by the middle and upper classes regarding the assumed moral and spiritual condition of the poor. As one part of a continuing struggle to establish some degree of respect and personal self-esteem, it appears that some number of working-class voters could eagerly seize upon discrepancies in the personal behaviour of middle- and upper-class politicians. With the casting of their vote, they could seek to at least symbolically retaliate against their treatment, by imposing some form of moral equality in punishing and bringing any of the hypocritical 'high and mighty' back down to earth. The interest in scandal amongst working-class voters, used by Stedman Jones and others to suggest a political immaturity and lack of understanding, was instead possibly a very clear form of symbolic social 'rebellion' by some voters.

But again, it is likely that even such 'retaliation' against their treatment by the middle and upper classes was directed by the fundamental beliefs of the poorer working class more strongly towards criticism of morals and character than towards other aspects of social conflict or reform. Their class identification was diminished by their general distrust of human nature, and a belief in the dominance of corruption in society, as felt through their own experiences. As Free put it, workers in his area often exhibited a 'strange distrust' of all others.[3] Trust, or willing acceptance of the knowledge or views of others, might on occasion extend only to those in a very small surrounding circle. This attitude can be seen reflected in the overwhelming political and social influence enjoyed by an articulate select few, regarded as 'oracles' within small, localized, social or work groups. Because of this influence, locally specific economic conditions and structures in the East End could be very important in how political beliefs or messages were 'filtered' or received by the parts of the working class.

This can be seen most obviously within some of the most desperate of all conditions in the East End, in the common lodging houses, as discussed in Chapter 1. Here economic and social ills threw together in common circumstances the poorest manual worker and the underemployed declined artisan or professional. The articulacy of those who had been in 'better' positions was extremely important in presenting their world-views to the many unskilled workers who lived and developed common bonds with them. With many of these 'declined' skilled workers blaming foreign imports for the loss of work in their trade, this localized and very personal alliance between artisans and the most casually employed of manual

---

[3] Free, *Seven Years*, 81.

workers became a significant conduit of protectionist politics to parts of the poorer working class, while such policies seem to have been less readily adopted by other workers. Economic structures (in this case small street-market sizes) meant as well that the politics of the costermongers, for example, was also influenced strongly by the views of a range of articulate individuals, and this was reflected in the variety of political approaches of their union branches, as we saw in Chapter 5.

But if local and personal influences and issues were the most important for much of the East End working class, it seems that a sense of class political identification was growing amongst some other, wealthier segments of the East End population, at the expense of older forms of group loyalty. The Conservative influence, mentioned above, of Church of England activists upon the politics of the more prosperous working class was strengthened by the weakness of working-class Nonconformity in London. Any marginal working-class religious attachment and influence was much more likely to come through the Established Church. But we saw in Chapter 5 that even in areas of relative Nonconformist strength in parts of the East End, particularly in the Stepney constituency, there appears to be little evidence that this provided any significant electoral support to Liberalism. The areas identified as including the largest Nonconformist groups, in the South and West Centre wards of Stepney, were solidly Conservative. These areas had large numbers of Nonconformist chapels, and were largely dominated by upper working-class or 'mixed' lower middle-class and artisan populations, the most promising groups for Nonconformist membership (and also those most likely to be on the electoral register). Yet the politics of these areas do not seem to have been significantly influenced by those issues believed to connect Liberalism to the Nonconformist cause. It appears, for example, that many voters who would strongly support the single-issue temperance candidates who stood in some elections in these areas would still, in a straight contest, swing their support behind the Conservatives even against the restrictionist Liberals.

We saw also that amongst the Jewish community in East London religion was not dominant in their politics, even in the face of the bitter political fight over the immigration of their co-religionists into London. It appears likely that large numbers of the established members of the Jewish community strongly backed the Conservatives in most elections in the East End in this period, even on occasion against Jewish progressive candidates. Leaders of the community used their personal influence to gather this support. The 'Anglo-Jewish vote' seems to have been very important in the victories of the Conservatives in St George's, Stepney, and other constituencies on a number of occasions before the First World War. It is likely that this vote itself contributed significantly to the perception of 'East End Conservatism'. This is many senses reverses the widely accepted argument that Conservative support in the East End in this period was built largely upon the anti-alienism of the poorer working class. Established Jewish Conservatism seems to have been a stronger force than racist anti-immigration Conservatism in East London.

Many 'myths' about East End working-class politics have been tackled in this study. It appears that very few of them have much substance. East End Conservatism and apparent working-class political apathy were not caused by extreme poverty. To emphasize the point, even the extent of poverty itself in the district was shown in Chapter 1 to be far less widespread, and economic conditions far more diverse, than is normally assumed.

In place of many of these generalized myths, this study has provided a model that does not seek to explain the politics of the East End in full, but suggests instead that we can understand politics, and the formation of political attitudes, in the East End or any other area only through a very detailed examination of specific localized community and workplace structures.

There was a vast array of factors which combined to create the impression of Conservative dominance in the area. The interrelationship of the particular East End demographic and economic conditions with more general factors acting upon working-class politics in London created a web of important influences, often very personalized, which can only be explained and understood within this very specific and detailed context.

A homogeneous 'poor' politics in the East End has often been assumed, with even such indicators as clear variations between the election results in different East End seats often being ignored. The complexity of social, economic, and personal factors in the development of politics in the area had little chance of recognition. Politics in the East End did not involve simplistic and one-dimensional reactions to either economic conditions or the rhetoric of politicians. As was said at the start of this study, historians of other parts of Britain have well described the rational and multifaceted basis to working-class politics in those areas. An outcome of this study, it is hoped, might be to show the East End, similarly, the respect of treating its politics seriously.

APPENDIX 1

Charles Booth's Social Classifications

In his studies of London, Booth used a variety of systems to classify social and economic conditions, with social classes and areas being described by a series of colours, numbers, or letters. These are called upon at various points in this study as historically well-accepted 'shorthand' descriptions, but for clarity, Booth's exact definitions of each category are listed in full below. (For details see Charles Booth, *Life and Labour of the People in London*, 1st series (1902), i. 33–62 and ii. 40–1.)

Classes of People

A. The lowest class of occasional labourers, loafers, and semi-criminals.
B. Casual earnings—'very poor'.
C. Intermittent earnings.
D. Small regular earnings [C and D together—'the poor'].
E. Regular standard earnings—above the line of poverty [approx. 22s. to 30s. a week].
F. Higher class labour [generally 30s. to 50s. a week].
G. Lower middle class.
H. Upper middle class.

Booth defined the 'poor' as those 'who have a sufficiently regular though bare income, such as 18s. to 21s. per week for a moderate family'. The 'very poor' were those 'who from any cause fall much below this standard'.

Booth translated these categories into colours for the maps he produced to socially define each street in London. These colours meant:

Black—'The lowest grade (corresponding to Class A), inhabited principally by occasional labourers, loafers, and semi-criminals—the elements of disorder.'

Dark Blue—'Very poor (corresponding to Class B), inhabited principally by casual labourers and others living from hand to mouth.'

Light Blue—'Standard poverty (corresponding to Classes C and D) inhabited principally by those whose earnings are small (say 18s. to 21s. a week for a moderate family), whether they are so because of irregularity of work (C) or because of a low rate of pay (D).'

Purple—'Mixed with poverty (usually C and D with E and F, but including Class B in many cases).'

Pink—'Working class comfort. (Corresponding to Classes E and F, but containing also a large proportion of the lower middle class of small tradesmen and Class G.) These people usually keep no servant.'

Red—'Well-to-do; inhabited by middle-class families who keep one or two servants.'

Yellow—'Wealthy; hardly found in East London and little found in South London; inhabited by families who keep three or more servants, and whose houses are rated at 100 pounds or more.'

The figures calculated by Booth for each area in the East End of those in poverty (Classes A to D) and 'comfort' (E to H) are shown in Table 8.

TABLE 8. *Booth's social categories in areas of the East End (%)*

Census area (and constituencies)	In poverty	In comfort
Shoreditch (Haggerston and Hoxton)	40.2	59.8
Bethnal Green (B.G. North-East and South-West)	44.7	53.3
Whitechapel	39.2	60.8
St George's-in-the-East	48.8	51.2
Stepney (Limehouse)	38.1	61.9
Mile End Old Town (Stepney and Mile End)	26.2	73.8
Poplar (Poplar and Bow and Bromley)	36.5	63.5

Source: C. Booth, *Life and Labour of the People in London*, first series (1902), i. 36.

APPENDIX 2

Parliamentary Electoral Results in the East End, 1885–1914

TABLE 9.1. *Bethnal Green North East*

Year	Winning party	Con.	Lib.	Other
1885	Lib.	1,844	3,095	
1886	Lib.	1,906	2,278	
1892	Lib.	2,321	2,918	Lab. 106; Ind. 23
1895	Con.	2,591	2,431	
1900	Con.	2,988	2,609	
1906	Lib.	2,130	4,127	
1910 (Jan.)	Lib.	2,435	3,842	
1910 (Dec.)	Lib.	2,037	3,188	

TABLE 9.2. *Bethnal Green South West*

Year	Winning party	Con.	Lib.	Other
1885	Lib.	2,200	3,088	
1886	Lib.	2,001	2,550	
1892	Lib.	2,171	3,206	
1895	Lib.	2,324	2,603	
1900	Con.	2,862	2,514	
1906	Lib.	2,064	3,542	
1910 (Jan.)	Lib.	2,350	3,328	
1910 (Dec.)	Lib.	2,086	2,768	
1911 (by-election)	Lib.	2,561	2,745	Soc. 134
1914 (by-election)	Con.	2,824	2,804	Soc. 316

TABLE 9.3. *Bow and Bromley*

Year	Winning party	Con.	Lib.	Other
1885	Lib.	2,738	3,419	
1886	Con.	2,967	2,396	
1892	Lib.	3,649	4,072	
1895	Con.	4,339	3,178	
1899 (by-election)	Con.	4,238	2,123	
1900	Con.	4,403		Soc. 2,558
1906	Lib.	3,974	4,596	
1910 (Jan.)	Con.	3,695	2,167	Lab. 2,955
1910 (Dec.)	Lab.	3,452		Lab. 4,315

TABLE 9.4. *Haggerston*

Year	Winning party	Con.	Lib	Other
1885	Lib.	1,259	2,736	
1886	Lib.	1,677	2,054	
1892	Lib.	1,622	2,543	
1895	Con.	2,269	2,229	
1900	Lib.	2,266	2,290	
1906	Lib.	2,371	2,772	
1908 (by-election)	Con.	2,867	1,724	Soc. 986
1910 (Jan.)	Lib.	2,585	3,041	Soc. 701
1910 (Dec.)	Lib.	2,641	3,046	

TABLE 9.5. *Hoxton*

Year	Winning party	Con.	Lib.	Other
1885	Lib.	2,047	3,084	
1886	Lib.	2,079	2,324	
1892	Lib.	2,114	3,410	Soc. 19
1895	Lib.	2,862	2,990	
1900	Con.	2,868	2,595	
1906	Con.	3,489	2,753	
1910 (Jan.)	Lib.	3,398	3,736	
1910 (Dec.)	Lib.	2,795	3,489	

TABLE 9.6. *Limehouse*

Year	Winning party	Con.	Lib.
1885	Con.	2,566	1,676
1886	Con.	2,230	1,428
1892	Lib.	2,305	2,475
1895	Con.	2,661	2,071
1900	Con.	2,608	2,070
1906	Lib.	2,007	2,981
1910 (Jan.)	Lib.	2,395	2,826
1910 (Dec.)	Lib.	2,126	2,557

TABLE 9.7. *Mile End*

Year	Winning party	Con.	Lib.	Other
1885	Con.	2,091	1,442	'Independent Lib.' 420
1886	Con.	2,110	1,281	
1892	Con.	2,204	1,931	
1895	Con.	2,383	1,516	
1900	Con.	2,440	1,280	
1905 (by-election)	Con.	2,138	2,060	
1906	Lib.	2,169	2,295	
1910 (Jan.)	Con.	2,333	2,276	
1910 (Dec.)	Con.	2,179	2,177	

TABLE 9.8. *Poplar*

Year	Winning party	Con.	Lib.
1885	Lib.	2,113	4,090
1886	Lib.	2,827	2,903
1892	Lib.	2,975	5,007
1895	Lib.	3,110	3,939
1900	Lib.	2,840	3,992
1906	Lib.	2,235	4,546
1910 (Jan.)	Lib.	3,115	4,172
1910 (Dec.)	Lib.	2,148	3,977

TABLE 9.9. *St George's-in-the-East*

Year	Winning party	Con.	Lib.
1885	Con.	1,744	1,180
1886	Con.	1,561	1,076
1886 (by-election)	Con.	1,546	889
1892	Lib.	1,263	1,661
1895	Con.	1,583	1,579
1900	Con.	1,437	1,141
1906	Lib.	1,064	1,685
1910 (Jan.)	Lib.	1,134	1,568
1910 (Dec.)	Lib.	1,022	1,401

TABLE 9.10. *Stepney*

Year	Winning party	Con.	Lib.
1885	Lib.	2,035	2,045
1886	Con.	2,237	1,735
1892	Con.	2,292	2,203
1895	Con.	2,346	1,876
1898 (by-election)	Lib.	2,472	2,492
1900	Con.	2,783	1,718
1906	Con.	2,490	1,853
1907 (by-election)	Con.	2,299	1,350
1910 (Jan.)	Con.	2,102	1,866
1910 (Dec.)	Lib.	1,811	1,926

TABLE 9.11. *Whitechapel*

Year	Winning party	Con.	Lib.
1885	Lib.	1,972	2,353
1886	Lib.	1,592	2,179
1892	Lib.	1,800	2,327
1895	Lib.	1,977	2,009
1900	Lib.	1,608	1,679
1906	Lib.	1,569	1,925
1910 (Jan.)	Lib.	1,402	1,963
1910 (Dec.)	Lib.	1,191	1,731
1913 (by-election)	Lib.	1,556	1,722

APPENDIX 3

Average Length of Time on Electoral Registers in the East End

The estimate provided in Chapter 2 of the *maximum* average length of time that voters remained on the electoral register was based upon the following method of calculation:

For each 10-year cohort of voters, the average period of registration was calculated on the basis of the existing, and assumed to be static, age breakdown of the register. For example, for voters aged 21–30, the maximum time each voter could have been on the register varied from 0 to 10 (the last figure if they were about to turn 31). The average maximum for this group could be roughly assumed to be 5. In the case of older voters, a more complex formula applied. If the age breakdown of the register (again, assumed to be static) was that there were 500 voters aged between 21 and 30, and 1,000 voters aged between 31 and 40 (a ratio fairly close to reality), then for 500 of the older voters their maximum period of enrolment varied from 10 to 20 years, and averaged 15. But for the other 500 voters their maximum varied from 0 to 10, and averaged 5, simply because they (theoretically again) could not have been on the register for the longer period, as only 500 voters first registered in that earlier age cohort, and the second 500 of the older group must have come on later. So in fact the average for this whole older group becomes (500 × 15) + (500 × 5)/1000 = 10. The overall average maximum period of registration can be roughly calculated for the whole register by using this method for each age cohort, and by taking into account the overall age profile to estimate when sub-groups theoretically could have come onto the register.

Undertaking this calculation for the St George's North register analysed in Chapter 2 gave a figure of 20 years for all voters except labourers, and just over 16 years for labourer voters. These figures, by common sense, overstate reality, as it is unlikely, for example, that every one of the very few voters aged 75 came onto the register at 21, yet, because it is faintly possible, these figures include that assumption. The figure of 20 years suggests that the entire register would (theoretically) turn over in the space of four general elections, or that 25 per cent of the electorate would be new voters at each scheduled five-yearly election. As these figures are maximum, it is likely that the true figure was closer to a full turnover every three general elections, or 33 per cent of the electorate being new at each election. In the case of labourers, 16 years implies a full turnover after every three-and-a-bit elections, and in reality, a turnover perhaps every two-and-a-half elections, or 40 per cent of the labourer electorate being new voters at each election.

But these figures are based upon the age breakdown of only the 1891 electoral register, and it is likely that the electorate profile did change to some extent over the period examined in this study, because gaining registration became easier than it had been when those aged in their fifties, sixties, or seventies in 1891 were young. This would have meant more in those age groups on the register at the end of the period, and so slightly longer average periods on the register. But this was probably only of minor significance to these figures, as the total size of the electoral registers, even in stable areas such as Poplar and Bow and Bromley, which were little affected by factors such as immigration, hardly changed across the period. The total electorate in Poplar and Bow and Bromley in 1891 was 21,035. In 1910 it was 20,188.

APPENDIX 4

Correlations of Voting Patterns with Booth's Data and Church-Attendance Evidence

There are a number of points to be made regarding the evidence used for the analysis made in Chapter 3 to determine any possible links between socio-economic conditions, as represented in Booth's data, Protestant church-attendance figures, and 'Conservative' voting patterns. There are also some issues to be specifically addressed in regard to the validity of the use of Poplar and Bow and Bromley figures for this purpose.

First, it does not seem that the connections that were made in the chapter between church attendance and Conservative voting patterns were a function of, for example, a greater number of churches being placed in particular types of areas, and so by default showing greater apparent attendance. This is shown by the separate Church of England figures—counting only church, not 'mission', attendance—with only one church to be counted in nearly all the areas, and with usually a 'contained' catchment area of the parish. These figures, with one or two exceptions, show very much the same trend (see Fig. 5) as the total Protestant attendance correlation, as do those for Nonconformist attendance (Fig. 6). Importantly, as Jeffrey Cox notes, for local studies combined figures are the most accurate measure of attendance,[1] but these graphs, when taken together, do suggest that the will to attend church in either the established or dissenting churches was generally higher in the same areas where Conservativism was also apparently stronger.

The church attendances used for these correlations also did not reflect any popularity of 'generous' churches to which large numbers of the poor may have flocked. Statements by the ministers concerned show that these were not the types of congregations reflected in the highest levels of attendance. The vicar of the extremely well-attended St Matthias's, Poplar, did not 'believe it is the duty of the Church to give help'. At the very popular St John's, Cubitt Town, the vicar similarly said they had a deliberate policy to 'confine their relief as far as possible to the old, widows, and the sick',[2] and certainly not to those who may have just come along on a Sunday in hope of assistance.

A further consideration for these figures was that they may have been significantly distorted by differences in the number of Irish Catholics in the population of wards, so affecting the relative numbers of potential Protestant churchgoers. This factor could also, of course, directly affect the political character of wards. But the number of Irish in the Poplar and Bow and Bromley constituencies was relatively

---

[1] Cox, *English Churches*, 31.   [2] Booth MSS B169, 61 and 83.

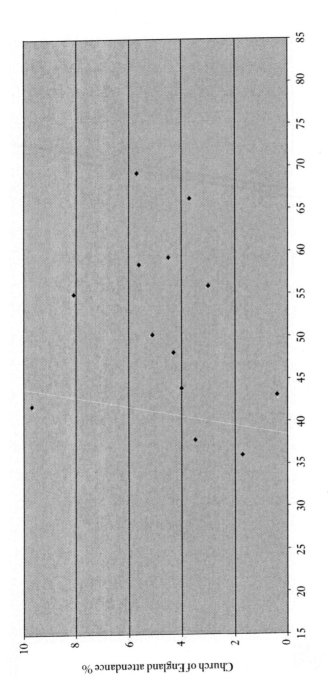

Fig. 5. Church of England attendance/Conservative vote

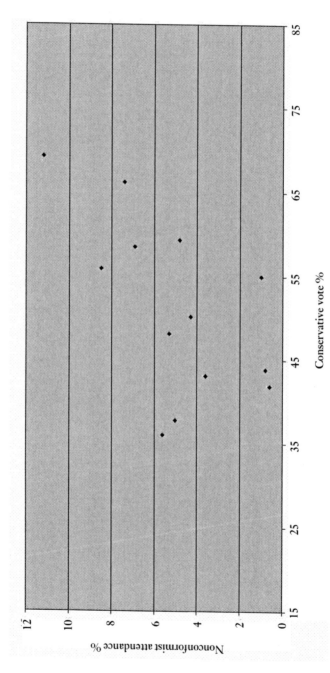

Fig. 6. Nonconformist attendance / Conservative vote

low, in the order of 5–6 per cent of the population,[3] and only in one area—the 'Fenian Barracks' area around Devons Road—was the concentration significantly higher than this. Otherwise, the number of Irish in each ward was insufficient to directly distort the Protestant church-attendance figures. Similarly, unlike other areas of the East End, the percentage of Jewish immigrants in Poplar was too small at this stage to affect these calculations.[4] Finally—and this applies to both social indicators and church attendance correlations—the use of only Poplar and Bow and Bromley in this exercise raises the possibility that circumstances—including a relative social 'stability'—were different in these areas, and any conclusions cannot be applied to other areas of the East End. Reasons why the same type of analysis was less applicable to other areas were discussed in Chapter 3, and evidence from elsewhere was discussed throughout, which does show that similar conclusions can most likely be reached for the East End as a whole. But the issue of the political representativeness for the East End of Poplar and Bow and Bromley's electoral results, particularly given that area's stronger socialist movement, is important, as will be discussed below, and this also touches upon the use of the overall term 'Conservative' in analysing these results.

Electoral Material

In regard to the local electoral material used in the chapter, the ward is clearly the smallest political entity upon which a localized political analysis can be attempted for this period, if the evidence is limited to voting figures. Yet ward-level voting results are only available in the East End for this period for local-government elections. For these to be of assistance in indicating the political 'complexion' of an area, there needs first to have been a genuine party-political contest reflected by the results. As Davis and Thompson both note, until the late 1880s such contests were rare in both vestry and board-of-guardians elections, and it was only in the mid-1890s that party divisions became relatively clear in these elections.[5] But even after this, voter turnout in these elections remained low, and only increased significantly when the vestries were replaced by the borough councils in 1900. As an example, voter turnout in the wards of Bromley increased from 26.4 per cent in the second-last vestry election, in 1898, to 46.2 per cent in the first borough election two

---

[3] In 1881 the percentage of Irish residents in Poplar borough was calculated at 6.87% of the population, compared to 26% in St George's-in-the-East, 22% in Whitechapel, and 13% in Limehouse (Stepney registration district). See Stedman Jones, *Outcast London*, 148. In 1897 the Catholic priests in Poplar estimated the Catholic population at just below 5% of the total. See Booth MSS B180, 19, 45, 55, and 83.

[4] The total 'alien' population of Poplar in 1901 was only around 1%, and had grown by only 526 people in the previous twenty years. See *RC Alien*, P.P. 1903 IX, Tables LIX–LX, 1011–1013.

[5] Davis, *Reforming London*, 25–9, and Thompson, *Socialists, Liberals and Labour*, 79–83.

years later. By 1912 the turnout in the area was 54.8 per cent.[6] While these figures are still below the parliamentary election turnouts of the period, which averaged from 70 to 80 per cent, a turnout of around 50 per cent across the borough elections of 1900–12 seems a relatively good indicator of *voter* inclinations, and certainly is likely to be more accurate than the results for the previous local bodies. This ignores, for the moment, the question of the representativeness of the franchise and those actually voting, as has been touched upon elsewhere. Board-of-Guardian elections, which continued throughout the period and also provided ward results, had voter turnouts significantly lower than the borough contests—although they were relatively high in Poplar—and tended to be less political in nature and more 'confused' in results. Ward boundary changes in 1900 also meant that such results could not be compared between the two periods. All this suggests that the 1900–12 borough-council ward results provide the most useful *localized* electoral evidence for the East End in this period.

However, there is the problem of whether these results can be used in arguments regarding influences upon parliamentary elections in the same area. The major technical difference between the two types of election was that the borough franchise included women. Women constituted around 15–16 per cent of the municipal electorate, but their turnout seems, in London at least, to have been somewhat lower than men's.[7] It has been suggested that some women did vote in a slightly less 'politicized' and more 'moral' way, as discussed in Chapter 3, but it also seems likely that this tendency may have been strong, but unrecognized, amongst men. The borough results were probably not 'distorted' as an indicator of parliamentary preferences because of the different franchise. It was also argued in the Introduction and Chapter 4 that it seems unlikely that voting patterns were significantly altered by the different issues that applied in local and parliamentary elections, but that it is possible that the personalized influences which may have been acting to a greater extent within localized election campaigns may have acted to maintain the Progressive vote at a higher level than that of the Conservatives.

Duncan Tanner has examined some of the advantages and disadvantages of using municipal ward results as indicators, and has concluded that 'the differences between the municipal and parliamentary franchises evidently did not have a considerable political impact before 1914'.[8]

Calculating the level of 'Conservatism' in each ward raised a number of difficulties. First, there was the issue of identification of party alignment amongst the myriad of descriptions used by, particularly Conservative, municipal candidates in this period, and also the many inaccuracies regarding this in press reports of results.[9] While in parliamentary elections, as seen above, very few party labels were

---

[6] See *East London Advertiser*, 28 May 1898, 7 col.d and 10 Nov. 1900, 8 col.a, and *London Statistics*, vol. 23 (1912–13), 32.

[7] See Hollis, *Ladies Elect*, 38, and *North Eastern Leader*, 2 June 1894, 2 col.d.

[8] Tanner, 'Elections, Statistics', 905 and *passim*.

[9] See ibid. 894 and Husbands, 'East End Racism', 8, for discussions of this issue.

necessary (although the 'Conservative' candidate could be Conservative, Liberal Unionist, or Conservative and Unionist), in municipal elections the party nomenclature used was much more varied and confusing, particularly amongst the Conservatives. Very broadly, it could be said that the Conservatives adopted the label 'Moderates' in local elections, while the Liberals came under a 'Progressive' umbrella,[10] but all this could vary considerably. The Conservatives, in fact, often ran under the guise of local ratepayers' or other such organizations, and as 'Municipal Reform' or similar groupings (as will be discussed specifically regarding Poplar below).

The major groupings counted as 'Conservatives' in borough-council elections for the purposes of analysis in this study included the Union of Stepney Ratepayers, the Municipal Alliance, the Municipal Reform party, the Ratepayers' Union, and the Moderates, as well as a range of clearly Conservative 'Independents' in each round of elections. Interestingly, the Liberal/Progessive side also ran under such groupings as the Stepney Council of Public Welfare.

The problem of identification was most pronounced in areas such as Stepney, but could be overcome by using evidence such as newspaper discussions of alignments, checking past party identifications of 'Independents', and cross-checking a wide range of local reports. In Poplar and Bow and Bromley, a more fundamental problem concerned the role of the anti-Socialist Municipal Alliance group, which started to play a major role from the 1906 municipal elections onwards. The votes for this group were counted as forming the majority of 'Conservative' support in the area for the correlations in the later part of the period examined. The difficult issue is the extent to which this group was actually gaining votes from both Liberal and Conservative supporters as a united reaction against the strength of socialism in the Poplar borough, as Thompson and others have suggested.[11] If this was significant, the local 'Conservative' results in this borough cannot be seen as sufficiently representative of alignments in other areas of the East End, and the connections made in Chapter 3 cannot be seen to be more widely applicable. However, an analysis of the Conservative vote in the elections of 1900, before the Alliance was active, and the average Alliance vote across the three elections 1906–12, show that there was very little difference either in the ranking of wards according to the relative Conservative or Alliance vote, or in the actual percentage of votes they gained in wards in each of the periods. This is illustrated in Table 10. This suggests a very close alignment indeed between 'traditional' Conservative support and that later gained by the Municipal Alliance. But it could be argued that the Alliance in Poplar and Bow and Bromley maintained the non-Socialist/Progressive vote at a high level in the area at a time when it should have been in decline after peaking in 1900. But the years from 1906, when the Alliance became active, were also very good ones for the Conservatives generally across London in local elections. This can be seen by comparing the voting patterns in borough elections in Poplar with other areas of the East End

[10] See Thompson, *Socialists, Liberals and Labour*, 80–1.
[11] See ibid. 83 and 187.

TABLE 10. *Comparison of Conservative vote and ranking across wards, 1900 and 1906–1912*

Ward	1900 vote (%)	1900 rank	1906–12 rank	Average 1906–12 vote (%)
Bromley				
North-West	74.4	1	3	69.9
Bow South	71.6	2	1	78.9
Poplar East	68.0	3	4	64.1
Millwall	62.0	4	2	70.8
Poplar West	59.1	5	5	60.2
Bow Central	59.1	6	6	59.8
Poplar				
North-West	53.0	7	8	49.0
Cubitt Town	50.0	8	7	50.1
Bromley				
South-West	49.7	9	14	38.1
Bow North	47.7	10	9	45.6
Bromley				
South-East	45.1	11	10	45.0
Bow West	45.0	12	12	43.0
Bromley				
North-East	44.7	13	11	44.6
Bromley Central	27.0	14	13	38.8

which were not influenced by a strong Socialist party. The average Conservative/Alliance vote in Poplar and Bow and Bromley increased by 2.1 per cent from 1900 to 1906 (the election in which the Alliance became genuinely active). In the wards of the three surrounding seats of Stepney, Mile End, and Limehouse, the average Conservative municipal vote also increased, by a very similar 1.1 per cent, between the same two elections, suggesting that the Alliance itself had only minimal effect on voter alignments.

From this it seems likely that the Alliance vote and its social and geographic basis did not differ greatly from a base Conservative vote, so it can be broadly used for the correlations undertaken in Chapter 3 and as indicative of 'Conservative' factors elsewhere in the East End. Throughout the study it is further discussed why the influences on politics in Poplar and Bow and Bromley can be seen as not dissimilar to those in other areas of the East End, despite the stronger and earlier growth of socialism there.

Calculating the actual strength of the Conservative vote in each ward also posed difficulties, given that the multi-member system meant that each voter usually had three votes to distribute across a range of candidates. I calculated party strength in two ways. First, by the percentage of 'Conservative' councillors elected in each ward respectively across the five borough elections. This could, of course, distort the comparison of wards, as it is possible that 100 per cent of councillors could be elected from one party although the party gained only slightly more than a majority of votes.[12] This is less likely because of what was a normal spread of votes with the multi-member system, and ticket-splitting, but I also calculated the actual 'Conservative' vote in each ward using the following method:

I assumed that with each party 'ticket' in a ward, the solid 'core' party vote was represented by the vote gained by the party candidate with the least number of votes, this being the candidate who was least likely to have received any votes on the basis of local popularity or profile. The 'base' votes of all parties running tickets were calculated, with 'Independents' allocated to parties if it was obvious that they were part of a ticket (either from consistency in voting figures or other evidence). The Conservative percentage of these base votes was then calculated. The suitability of this method was indicated by the fact that it had an over 90 per cent correlation with the percentage of Conservative councillors elected in each ward. It seems sound to combine both these methods as indicators of a ranking of Conservative support across the wards in the five elections, as it is the ranking, rather than the exact level, of Conservative support that is important here.

The method used to calculate vote percentages here had the advantage of minimizing the effect on the results of possible distortion of party support by the local popularity or profile of candidates. This is clearly a more significant issue in local than parliamentary elections, and its partial exclusion from the results used in this chapter means that the factors suggested as influencing the results can be more readily applied also to the parliamentary election results.

Religious Survey

To apply the results of the *Daily News* church-attendance survey to each electoral ward in Poplar and Bow and Bromley, I first adjusted the figures for each parish to provide the total adult parish population and the actual adult congregation for each church. The method was adopted, in a simplified form, from McLeod's analysis.[13] I multiplied the percentage of persons aged 15 and over (the definition of adult by the *Daily News*) in the census district (in Poplar's case, 65 per cent) by each parish population to obtain the adult population. I then took the adult church attendance for each church or parish and multiplied this by 19/22 to eliminate those attending twice in the day.[14] These two figures were then used to calculate the percentage of

---

[12] See Tanner's discussion of this, 'Elections, Statistics', 895.

[13] McLeod, *Class and Religion*, 305. I do not believe that the differences between 1903 and the census date of 1901 justify the statistical complexity of McLeod's method.

[14] See ibid. 25.

adult attendance in the parish, or in only the Anglican or Nonconformist churches in the parish. In the few cases where a ward did not include whole parishes, I calculated as closely as possible the percentage of a parish which was inside the ward and adjusted the figures on this basis. In three-quarters of the cases this was not necessary.

The method of calculating the percentage of working-class people who attended church in the example wards of Bromley North-East and North-West, and Bow North was as follows:

The overall percentage of middle-class and white-collar residents calculated from Booth's tables for the Poplar borough was just over 21 per cent (5 per cent middle class, 16 per cent other non-working class). For individual areas, only the middle-class figure was available.

In Bow North the middle-class figure was 3.6 per cent, so a middle-class and white-collar figure of around 18 per cent could be assumed, and so an 82 per cent working-class population. On the survey day, 376 adults attended a Protestant church in St Mark's, the relevant parish. Assuming, as discussed in the chapter, that 25 per cent of this attendance was working class, then the calculation is 25 per cent of 376 = 94. The working-class adult population was then 82 per cent of the adult parish population of 7,753 = 6,357. So the percentage of adult working class who attended church was 94/6,357 = 1.5 per cent , or 1 in every 66. The non-working-class attendance figure comes out as 20 per cent.

The same calculation method for the two Bromley North wards (middle class 4.5 per cent, assumed middle class and white collar 21 per cent), with a notional 50 per cent working-class congregation as also discussed, gives a figure of 7.5 per cent working-class attendance, or 1 in 13. The non-working-class figure comes out as 28.3 per cent.

Charles Booth Material

The following is a list of the relevant Booth 'blocks' used to calculate poverty and middle-class figures for each ward:

    Cubitt Town—Block 80d
    Millwall—80b and 80c
    Poplar East—81c and 81d
    Poplar West—80a
    Bromley South-East—81b
    Bromley Central—81a and 1/3 81b
    Poplar North West—79c and 1/2 82a and 1/2 79b
    Bromley South West—1/2 82a and 1/2 82b
    Bromley North East and North West—83 a, b, c, and 1/2 82b
    Bow South—84c and 84d
    Bow North—85b

Bow West—1/2 85a
Bow Central—1/2 85a

List of Wards in Descending Conservative Vote Order, as shown in Figures

Bow South—69.2
Millwall—66.2
Poplar East—59.3
Poplar West—58.5
Bromley North East and North West (combined)—55.9
Bow Central—55.0
Cubitt Town—50.2
Poplar North West—48.1
Bow North—43.9
Bow West—43.1
Bromley South East—41.9
Bromley South West—37.8
Bromley Central—36.0

APPENDIX 5

Progressive Vote Fluctuations

The fluctuations in the Progressive vote described in Figure 4 and elsewhere were calculated by averaging the percentage by which the raw Progressive voting numbers changed in a ward from election to election. For example, in Bromley South East the raw Progressive voting figures in the borough elections from 1900 to 1912 were 524, 502, 485, 438, and 421. While this suggests a slow decline in either the total number of voters or overall Progressive support, it does not suggest 'fickle' Progressive supporters who sometimes abstained, and the short-term stability of the Progressive vote in this ward was commented upon. The method of averaging the change in Progessive vote *from election to election* illustrates this most clearly, and in this case the respective changes in percentage terms were 4, 3, 10, and 4, averaging 5 per cent. On the other hand, in Poplar East, which was directly compared to Bromley South East in Chapter 3, the raw Progressive votes were 231, 401, 301, 306, and 240, indicating much more dramatically fluctuating support, even though the actual voting numbers in 1900 and 1912 were very similar. The percentage changes were 74, 25, 2, and 22, averaging 31 per cent, and again this seems to illustrate the voting patterns in this ward in the most effective manner.

BIBLIOGRAPHY

MANUSCRIPT SOURCES

Bishopgate Institute
George Howell Papers
Bodleian Library, Oxford
Christopher Addison Papers
British Library of Political and Economic Science
Charles Booth Collection
D. H. Kyd Papers
Manuscript Diary of Beatrice Webb, Passfield Collection
Guildhall Library
London Municipal Society Collection
Hackney Archives Department, Rose Lipman Library
Shoreditch newspaper cuttings collection
Hackney Borough Engineer and Surveyor's Department Files
Political cuttings file
Hartley Library, University of Southampton
Lord Swaythling [Samuel Montagu] Papers
House of Lords Record Office
Lord Stansgate [Williams Wedgwood Benn] Papers
Stuart Montagu Samuel cuttings book
London Metropolitan Archives (GLRO)
London County Council departmental records
Public Record Office
1891 Census manuscript returns RG12/285, 306, 313
Metropolitan Police files
Southwark Local History Library
Press cuttings files
Tower Hamlets Local History Collection, Bancroft Library
Newspaper cuttings files 320.2, 320.7, 321.5

PRINTED SOURCES

(1) *Primary Sources*

(a) Newspapers and Journals

Biblewomen and Nurses (previously *Missing Link Magazine* and *Bible Work at Home and Abroad*)

Critic
Daily Graphic
Daily Herald
Daily Mail
Daily News
Daily Telegraph
East End News
Eastern Argus and Borough of Hackney Times
Eastern Post
East London Advertiser
East London Observer
Hackney and Kingsland Gazette
Illustrated London News
Jewish Chronicle
Justice
Labour Elector
Labour Gazette
London City Mission Magazine
Morning Leader
Morning Post
North Eastern Leader
Oxford House Magazine
Pall Mall Gazette
Public Health
South London Press
Standard
Street and Market Trader (previously *Costers' World*)
The Times
Weekly News and Chronicle

(b) Parliamentary Papers (volumes to which reference is made)

P.P. 1881 VII — *Select Committee on Artizans' and Labourers' Dwellings' Improvement*

P.P. 1884–5 XXX — *Royal Commission on the Housing of the Working Classes*

P.P. 1886 XXXIV — *Report of the Committee on the Origin and Character of the Disturbances in the Metropolis on 8th February 1886*

P.P. 1887 LXXI — *Statements of Men Living in Certain Selected Districts of London*

P.P. 1888 XX, XXI — *Select Committee on the Sweating System*

P.P. 1888 LXXXI — *Report of an Inquiry as to the Immediate Sanitary Requirements of the Parish of St. Matthew, Bethnal Green*

P.P. 1892 XXXV — *Royal Commission on Labour*

P.P. 1892 LXIII, 1901 LIX, *Returns Relating to Parliamentary Constituencies*
 1911 LXII
P.P. 1893–4 LXXXII *Board of Trade report on Agencies and Methods for Dealing with the Unemployed*
P.P. 1893–4 CIV, 1902 CXX *Census of England and Wales*
P.P. 1896 LXVII *Judgements on Election Petitions—St. George's Division of Tower Hamlets*
P.P. 1902 XCVI, 1905 LXXV, *Reports of the Chief Registrar of Friendly Societies*
 1914 LXXVI
P.P. 1903 IX *Royal Commission on Alien Immigration*
P.P. 1906 XL, XLI *Royal Commission on London Traffic*
P.P. 1906 CIII *Report of the Departmental Committee on Vagrancy*
P.P. 1906 CIV *Report to the President of the Local Government Board on the Poplar Union by J. S. Davy*
P.P. 1908 XCII *Report to the Local Government Board on Dock Labour in Relation to Poor Law Relief*
P.P. 1908 CVII *Report of the Board of Trade Enquiry into Working Class Rents, Housing and Retail Prices*
P.P. 1909 XLIII, XLIV, *Royal Commission on the Poor Laws and the Relief of Distress*
 1910 XLVIII, XLIX
P.P. 1913 LXVI *Report of the Board of Trade Enquiry into Working Class Rents and Retail Prices*

(c) Books and Articles
(Place of publication London, unless otherwise shown.)

ACORN, G., *One of the Multitude* (1911).
Anonymous, 'Leaves from the Life of a "Poor Londoner"', *Good Words* (Aug. 1885).
Anonymous, 'The London Irish', *Blackwood's Magazine*, 170 (July 1901).
'A.P.' [Alexander Paterson], 'The Common Lodging House', I–V, *Toynbee Record*, 31: 4–6, 8, 10 (Jan.–Sept. 1909).
BEVERIDGE, W., *Unemployment: A Problem of Industry* (1909).
BLAKE, J., *Memories of Old Poplar* (1977).
BOOTH, C., *Life and Labour of the People in London*, 17 vols. (1902).
BURKE, T., *The Wind and the Rain* (1924).
Charity Organisation Society, *Special Committee on Unskilled Labour*, report and minutes of evidence (1908).
CORNFORD, L. C., *The Canker at the Heart: Being Studies from the Life of the Poor in the Year of Grace 1905* (1905).
DEARLE, N., *Problems of Unemployment in the London Building Trades* (1908).
Dock, Riverside, and General Labourers' Union, *The Sweating System: The Draft Report prepared by the Earl of Dunraven, K.P.* (n.d. [*c*.1890]).

ENGELS, F. and LAFARGUE, L., *Correspondence*, vol. 1 (Moscow, 1959).

FOAKES, G., *My Part of the River*, combined edn. (1976).

FOX, R., *Smoky Crusade* (1937).

FREE, R., *Seven Years Hard* (1904).

GOLDSMID, H., *Dottings of a Dosser: Being Revelations of the Inner Life of Low London Lodging Houses* (1886).

GOSLING, H., *Up and Down Stream* (1927).

GREENWOOD, J., *The Seven Curses of London* (1869; Oxford, 1981).

HALL, B. T., *Our Fifty Years: The Story of the Working Men's Club and Institute Union* (1912).

HOLMES, T., *London's Underworld* (1912).

HUNT, J., *Pioneer Work in the Great City: The Autobiography of a London City Missionary* (1895).

HYNDMAN, H. M., *The Record of an Adventurous Life* (1911).

JAY, A. O., *A Story of Shoreditch* (1896).

KENNEDY, B., *London in Shadow* (1902).

KRAUSSE, A. S., *Starving London: The Story of a Three Weeks' Sojourn Among the Destitute* (1886).

LINTON, A., *Not Expecting Miracles* (1982).

LOANE, M., *Neighbours and Friends* (1910).

London County Council, *Housing of the Working Classes in London, 1855–1912* (1913).

—— *London Statistics*, relevant volumes.

MCKENZIE, F. A., *Famishing London: A Study of the Unemployed and Unemployable* (1903).

MARSHALL, C. B., 'The Homeless Poor of London', *Economic Review*, 2: 2 (Apr. 1892).

MASTERMAN, C. F. G., *The Condition of England* (1909; edited and with an Introduction by J. T. Boulton, 1960).

MAYHEW, H., *London Labour and the London Poor*, 4 vols. (1861; repr. New York, 1968).

—— *The Morning Chronicle Survey of Labour and the Poor: The Metropolitan Districts*, 6 vols. (Firle, 1981).

MUDIE-SMITH, R., *The Religious Life of London* (1904).

NEWSHOLME, A., 'The Vital Statistics of Peabody Buildings and Other Artizans' and Labourers' Block Dwellings', *Journal of the Royal Statistical Society*, 54 (Mar. 1891).

NORTH, L., *Human Documents: Lives Re-Written by the Holy Spirit* ([1909]).

PAGE, E. M., 'No Green Pastures', *East London Papers*, 9: 1 and 2 (Summer and Winter 1966).

PATERSON, A., *Across the Bridges* (1911).

PEMBER REEVES, M., *Round About a Pound a Week* (1913; 1979).

PIKE, G. H., *Pity for the Perishing* (1884).

POPPLEWELL, F., 'The Gas Industry' in S. Webb and A. Freeman (eds.), *Sweated Trades* (1912).

REYNOLDS, S. and WOOLEY, B. and T., *Seems So! A Working Class View of Politics* (1911).

ROBERTS, R., *The Classic Slum: Salford Life in the First Quarter of the Century* (Manchester, 1971).

ROCKER, R., *The London Years* (1956).

ROGERS, J. E. T., 'Confessions of a Metropolitan Member', *Contemporary Review*, 51 (May 1887).

RUCK, S., 'The Street Trading Community', in H. Llewellyn Smith, *The New Survey of London Life and Labour: Vol. III Survey of Social Conditions (1) The Eastern Area* (1932).

SEXTON, J., *Sir James Sexton, Agitator* (1936).

SMILEY, F., *The Evangelization of a Great City: Or the Churches' Answer to the Bitter Cry of Outcast London* (Philadelphia, 1890).

SMITH, H. L. and NASH, V., *The Story of the Dockers' Strike* ([1890]).

SOUTHGATE, W., *That's the Way it Was* (Oxted, 1982).

THORNE, W., *My Life's Battles* (1925).

THORP, H., 'The Casual Ward System', I–III, *Toynbee Record*, 21: 5, 6, 10 (Feb.–July 1909).

TOYNBEE, H. V., 'A Winter's Experiment', *Macmillan's Magazine*, 69 (Nov. 1893).

WHITE, A., 'The Nomad Poor of London', *Contemporary Review*, 47 (May 1885).

WILLIAMS, M., *Later Leaves* (Macmillan, 1891).

WRIGHT, T., *The Pinch of Poverty* (1892).

(2) *Secondary Sources*

(a) *Books and Articles*

ALDERMAN, G., *The Jewish Community in British Politics* (Oxford, 1983).

ARMSTRONG, W. A., 'The Census Enumerators' Books: A Commentary', in R. Lawton (ed.), *The Census and Social Structure: An Interpretative Guide to Nineteenth Century Censuses for England and Wales* (1978).

AUGUST, A., 'A Culture of Consolation? Rethinking Politics in Working-Class London, 1870–1914', *Historical Research*, 74: 183 (Feb. 2001).

BAILEY, P., '"Will the Real Bill Banks Please Stand up?": Towards a Role Analysis of Mid-Victorian Working-Class Respectability', *Social History*, 12: 3 (Spring 1979).

—— 'Conspiracies of Meaning: Music-Hall and the Knowingness of Popular Culture', *Past and Present*, 144 (Aug. 1994).

BEDARIDA, F., 'Urban Growth and Social Structure in Nineteenth Century Poplar', *London Journal*, 1: 2 (Nov. 1975).

BEBBINGTON, D. W., 'Nonconformity and Electoral Sociology, 1867–1918', *Historical Journal*, 27: 3 (1984).

BERRIDGE, V., 'Popular Sunday Papers and Mid-Victorian Society', in G. Boyce, J. Curran, and P. Wingates (eds.), *Newspaper History from the Seventeenth Century to the Present Day* (1978).

BIAGINI, E. and REID, A. (eds.), *Currents Of Radicalism: Popular Radicalism, Organised Labour and Party Politics in Britain, 1850–1914* (Cambridge, 1991).

BLEWETT, N., 'The Franchise in the United Kingdom 1885–1918', *Past and Present*, 32 (Dec. 1965).

—— *The Peers, the Parties and the People: The General Elections of 1910* (1972).

BOOTH, M. R., 'The Metropolis on Stage', in Dyos and Wolff (eds.), *The Victorian City*.

BREWER, J., 'Theater and Counter-Theater in Georgian Politics: The Mock Elections at Garrat', *Radical History Review*, 22 (Winter 1979–80).

BRYMAN, A. and CRAMER, D., *Quantitative Data Analysis for Social Scientists* (rev. edn., 1994).

BUCK, N. H., 'The Analysis of State Intervention in Nineteenth-Century Cities: The Case of Municipal Labour Policy in East London, 1886–1914', in M. Dear and A. J. Scott (eds.), *Urbanisation and Urban Planning in Capitalist Society* (1981).

BUSH, J., *Behind the Lines: East London Labour 1914–1919* (1984).

BUTLER, D. and STOKES, D., *Political Change in Britain: Forces Shaping Electoral Choice* (Harmondsworth, 1971).

CHESNEY, K., *Victorian Underworld* (Harmondsworth, 1989).

CHILDS, M., *Labour's Apprentices: Working-Class Lads in Late Victorian and Edwardian England* (1992).

CHINN, C., *They Worked All Their Lives: Women of the Urban Poor in England, 1880–1939* (Manchester, 1988).

CLARK, A., 'The Rhetoric of Chartist Domesticity: Gender, Language and Class in the 1830s and 1840s', *Journal of British Studies*, 31: 1 (Jan. 1992).

CLARKE, P., 'Electoral Sociology of Modern Britain', *History*, 57: 189 (Feb. 1972).

COX, J., *The English Churches in a Secular Society: Lambeth, 1870–1930* (Oxford, 1982).

CREWE, I., 'The Politics of "Affluent" and "Traditional" Workers in Britain: An Aggregate Data Analysis', *British Journal of Political Science*, 3 (Jan. 1973).

CROSSICK, G., 'The Labour Aristocracy and its Values: A Study of Mid-Victorian Kentish London', *Victorian Studies*, 19: 3 (Mar. 1976).

DAVIS, JENNIFER, 'Jennings' Buildings and the Royal Borough: The Construction of the Underclass in Mid-Victorian England', in Feldman and Stedman Jones (eds.), *Metropolis London*.

—— 'A Poor Man's System of Justice: The London Police Courts in the Second Half of the Nineteenth Century', *Historical Journal*, 27: 2 (1984).

DAVIS, JOHN, 'Radical Clubs and London Politics, 1870–1900', in Feldman and Stedman Jones (eds.), *Metropolis London*.

—— *Reforming London: The London Government Problem 1855–1900* (Oxford, 1988).

—— 'Slums and the Vote, 1867–90', *Historical Research*, 64: 155 (1991).

—— and TANNER, D., 'The Borough Franchise After 1867', *Historical Research*, 69: 170 (1996).

DIX, B. and WILLIAMS, S., *Serving the Public, Building the Union: The History of the National Union of Public Employees. Volume 1: The Forerunners 1889–1928* (1987).

DUTTON, D., '*His Majesty's Loyal Opposition': The Unionist Party in Opposition, 1905–1915* (Liverpool, 1992).

DYOS, H. J. and WOLFF, M. (eds.), *The Victorian City: Images and Realities*, vol. 1 (1973).

ENGLANDER, D., *Landlord and Tenant in Urban Britain 1838–1918* (Oxford, 1983).

—— and O'DAY, R., *Mr Charles Booth's Inquiry: Life and Labour of the People in London Reconsidered* (1993).

—— —— (eds.), *Retrieved Riches: Social Investigation in Britain 1840–1914* (Aldershot, 1995).

FELDMAN, D., 'The Importance of Being English: Jewish Immigration and the Decay Of Liberal England', in Feldman and Stedman Jones (eds.), *Metropolis London*.

—— *Englishmen and Jews: Social Relations and Political Culture 1840–1914* (New Haven and London, 1994).

—— and STEDMAN JONES, G. (eds.), *Metropolis London: Histories and Representations Since 1800* (1989).

GAINER, B., *The Alien Invasion: The Origins of the Aliens Act of 1905* (1972).

GARDINER, A., *John Benn and the Progressive Movement* (1925).

GARRARD, J., *The English and Immigration 1880–1910* (Oxford, 1971).

GILLESPIE, J., 'Poplarism and Proletarianism: Unemployment and Labour Politics in London, 1918–1934', in Feldman and Stedman Jones (eds.), *Metropolis London*.

GOODWAY, D., *London Chartism 1838–1848* (Cambridge, 1982).

GREEN, E. H. H., 'Radical Conservatism: The Electoral Genesis of Tariff Reform', *Historical Journal*, 28: 3 (1985).

—— *The Crisis of Conservatism: The Politics, Economics, and Ideology of the British Conservative Party, 1880–1914* (1995).

HAMMERTON, J., 'The Targets of "Rough Music": Respectability and Domestic Violence in Victorian England', *Gender and History*, 3: 1 (Spring 1991).

HARRIS, J., *Private Lives, Public Spirit: A Social History of Britain* (Oxford, 1993).

HARRISON, B., 'The Sunday Trading Riots of 1855', *Historical Journal*, 8: 2 (1965).

HIMMELFARB, G., *The Idea of Poverty: England in the Early Industrial Age* (New York, 1984).

HIGGS, E., *Making Sense of the Census: The Manuscript Returns for England and Wales, 1801–1901* (1989).

HOBSBAWM, E., *Worlds of Labour: Further Studies in the History of Labour* (1984).

HOLLIS, P., *Ladies Elect: Women in English Local Government, 1865–1914* (Oxford, 1987).

HOWELL, D., *British Workers and the Independent Labour Party* (Manchester, 1983).

HUCKFELDT, R., *Politics in Context: Assimilation and Conflict in Urban Neighbourhoods* (New York, 1986).

HUSBANDS, C. T., 'East End Racism 1900–1980: Geographical Continuities in Vigilantist and Extreme Right-Wing Political Behaviour, *London Journal*, 8: 1 (Summer 1982).

INGLIS, K. S., *Churches and the Working Classes in Victorian England* (1963).

JOHNSON, P., *Saving and Spending: The Working-Class Economy in Britain 1870–1939* (Oxford, 1985).

JOYCE, P., 'Work', in F. M. L. Thompson (ed.), *The Cambridge Social History of Britain*, Vol. 2: *People and their Environment* (Cambridge, 1990).

—— *Work, Society and Politics: The Culture of the Factory in Later Victorian England* (1980; repr. Aldershot, 1991).

—— *Visions of the People: Industrial England and the Question of Class, 1848–1914* (Cambridge, 1994).

—— (ed.), *The Historical Meanings of Work* (Cambridge, 1987).

KIRK, N., '"Traditional" Working-Class Culture and "the Rise of Labour": Some Preliminary Questions and Observations', *Social History*, 16: 2 (May 1991).

KOSS, S., *Nonconformity in Modern British Politics* (1975).

KUSHNER, T., 'Jew and Non-Jew in the East End of London: Towards an Anthropology of "Everyday" Relations', in G. Alderman and C. Holmes (eds.), *Outsiders and Outcasts: Essays in Honour of William J. Fishman* (1993).

LAWRENCE, J., 'Popular Politics and the Limitations of Party: Wolverhampton, 1867–1900', in Biagini and Reid (eds.), *Currents of Radicalism*.

—— 'Popular Radicalism and the Socialist Revival in Britain', *Journal of British Studies*, 31: 2 (Apr. 1992).

—— 'Class and Gender in the Making of Urban Toryism, 1880–1914', *English Historical Review*, 108: 428 (July 1993).

—— 'The Dynamics of Urban Politics, 1867–1914', in Lawrence and Taylor (eds.), *Party, State and Society*.

—— and TAYLOR, M. (eds.), *Party, State and Society: Electoral Behaviour in Britain Since 1820* (Aldershot, 1997).

LAYBOURN, K., 'The Rise of Labour and the Decline of Liberalism: The State of the Debate', *History*, 80: 259 (June 1995).

—— and REYNOLDS, J., *Liberalism and the Rise of Labour 1890–1918* (1984).

LEES, L. H., *Exiles of Erin: Irish Migrants in Victorian London* (Manchester, 1979).

LEVIN, J. and ARLUKE, A., 'An Exploratory Analysis of Sex Differences in Gossip', *Sex Roles*, 12: 3/4 (1985).

LEWIS, J., 'The Working-Class Wife and Mother and State Intervention, 1870–1918', in J. Lewis (ed.), *Labour and Love: Women's Experience of Home and Family, 1850–1914* (Oxford, 1986).

LOVELL, J., *Stevedores and Dockers: A Study of Trade Unionism in the Port of London, 1870–1914* (1969).

LUMMIS, T., *The Labour Aristocracy 1851–1914* (Aldershot, 1994).

McCLELLAND, K., 'Time to Work, Time to Live: Some Aspects of Work and the Re-formation of Class in Britain, 1850–1880', in Joyce (ed.), *The Historical Meanings of Work*.

—— 'Some Thoughts on Masculinity and the "Representative Artisan" in Britain, 1850–1880', *Gender and History*, 1: 2 (Summer 1989).

McKENZIE, J. (ed.), *Imperialism and Popular Culture* (Manchester, 1986).

MCKENZIE, R. and SILVER, A., *Angels in Marble: Working Class Conservatives in Urban England* (Chicago, 1968).

McKIBBIN, R., *The Evolution of the Labour Party 1910–1924* (Oxford, 1974).

—— *The Ideologies of Class: Social Relations in Britain 1880–1950* (Oxford, 1991).

McLEOD, H., *Class and Religion in the Late Victorian City* (1974).

—— *Religion and Irreligion in Victorian England: How Secular Was the Working Class?* (Bangor, 1993).

—— 'Working-Class Religion in Late Victorian London: Booth's "Religious Influences" Revisited', in Englander and O'Day (eds.), *Retrieved Riches*.

MAYFIELD, D. and THORNE, S., 'Social History and its Discontents: Gareth Stedman Jones and the Politics of Language', *Social History*, 17: 2 (May 1992).

MORGAN, K. and J., *Portrait of a Progressive: The Political Career of Christopher, Viscount Addison* (Oxford, 1980).

O'DAY, A., 'Irish Influence on Parliamentary Elections in London, 1885–1914: A Simple Test', in R. Swift and S. Gilley (eds.), *The Irish in the Victorian City* (1985).

—— 'Katherine Buildings', in R. Finnegan and M. Drake (eds.), *From Family Tree to Family History* (Cambridge, 1994).

OFFER, A., *Property and Politics 1870–1914* (Cambridge, 1981).

PELLING, H., *Social Geography of British Elections 1885–1910* (1967).

—— *Popular Politics and Society in Late Victorian Britain* (1968).

PENNYBACKER, S., '"The Millennium by Return of Post": Reconsidering London Progressivism, 1889–1907', in Feldman and Stedman Jones (eds.), *Metropolis London*.

—— *A Vision for London 1887–1914: Labour, Everyday Life and the LCC Experiment* (1995).

PHILLIPS, G. and WHITESIDE, N., *Casual Labour: The Unemployment Question in the Port Transport Industry 1880–1970* (Oxford, 1985).

PRICE, R., *An Imperial War and the British Working Class: Working Class Attitudes and Reactions to the Boer War 1899–1902* (1972).

PUGH, M., *The Tories and the People 1880–1935* (Oxford, 1985).

RANDALL, A., 'The Industrial Moral Economy of the Gloucestershire Weavers in the Eighteenth Century', in J. Rule (ed.), *British Trade Unionism 1750–1850: The Formative Years* (1988).

READMAN, P., 'The Conservative Party, Patriotism, and British Politics: The Case of the General Election of 1900', *Journal of British Studies*, 40: 1 (Jan. 2001).

ROBERTS, E., *A Woman's Place: An Oral History of Working-Class Women 1890–1940* (Oxford, 1984).

ROSS, E., 'Survival Networks: Women's Neighbourhood Sharing in London Before World War One', *History Workshop*, 15 (Spring 1983).

—— '"Not the Sort that would Sit on the Doorstep": Respectability in Pre-World War I London Neighbourhoods', *International Labor and Working Class History*, 27 (Spring 1985).

—— 'Good and Bad Mothers: Lady Philanthropists and London Housewives Before the First World War', in K. D. McCarthy (ed.), *Lady Bountiful Revisited: Women, Philanthropy and Power* (New Brunswick, 1990).

RULE, J., 'The Property of Skill in the Period of Manufacture', in Joyce (ed.), *The Historical Meanings of Work*.

RYAN, P. A., 'Poplarism', in P. Thane (ed.), *The Origins of British Social Policy* (1978).

SAMUEL, R., 'Comers and Goers', in Dyos and Wolff (eds.), *The Victorian City*.

—— *East End Underworld: Chapters in the Life of Arthur Harding* (1981).

SAVAGE, M., *The Dynamics of Working-Class Politics: The Labour Movement in Preston, 1880–1940* (Cambridge, 1987).

SAVILLE, J., 'Trade Unions and Free Labour: The Background to the Taff Vale Decision', in A. Briggs and J. Saville (eds.), *Essays in Labour History* (1960).

SCHMIECHEN, J. A., *Sweated Industries and Sweated Labor: The London Clothing Trades, 1860–1914* (1984).

SCHNEER, J., *London 1900: The Imperial Metropolis* (New Haven, 1999).

SEYMOUR, C., *Electoral Reform in England and Wales: The Development and Operation of the Parliamentary Franchise, 1832–1885* (1915; repr. Newton Abbot, 1970).

SINDALL, R., *Street Violence in the Nineteenth Century: Media Panic or Real Danger* (Leicester, 1990).

STEDMAN JONES, G., *Outcast London: A Study in the Relationship between Classes in Victorian Society* (Harmondsworth, 1976).

—— 'The "Cockney" and the Nation, 1780–1988', in Feldman and Stedman Jones (eds.), *Metropolis London*.

—— *Languages of Class: Studies in English Working Class History 1832–1982* (Cambridge, 1983).

TANNER, D., *Political Change and the Labour Party, 1900–1918* (Cambridge, 1990).

—— 'Elections, Statistics and the Rise of the Labour Party, 1906–1931', *Historical Journal*, 34: 4 (1991).

—— 'Class Voting and Radical Politics: The Liberal and Labour Parties, 1910–31', in Lawrence and Taylor (eds.), *Party, State and Society*.

TEBBUTT, M., *Women's Talk?: A Social History of 'Gossip' in Working-Class Neighbourhoods* (Aldershot, 1995).

THANE, P., 'The Working Class and State "Welfare" in Britain, 1880–1914', *Historical Journal*, 27: 4 (1984).

—— 'Labour and Local Politics', in Biagini and Reid (eds.), *Currents of Radicalism*.

THOMPSON, E. P., 'The Moral Economy of the English Crowd in the Eighteenth Century', *Past and Present*, 50 (1971).

—— 'Eighteenth-Century English Society: Class Struggle Without Class?', *Social History*, 3: 2 (May 1978).

THOMPSON, P., *Socialists, Liberals and Labour: The Struggle for London 1885–1914* (1967).

VERNON, J., *Politics and the People: A Study in English Political Culture, c.1815–1867* (Cambridge, 1993).

VINCENT, D., *Literacy and Popular Culture: England 1750–1914* (Cambridge, 1989).

WALD, K. D., *Crosses on the Ballot: Patterns of British Voter Alignment Since 1885* (Princeton, 1983).

WHITE, J., *Rothschild Buildings: Life in an East End Tenement Block 1887–1920* (1980).

—— *The Worst Street in North London: Campbell Bunk, Islington, Between the Wars* (1986).

WILLIAMS, S. C., 'The Problem of Belief: The Place of Oral History in the Study of Popular Religion', *Oral History*, 24: 2 (Autumn 1996).

—— *Religious Belief and Popular Culture in Southwark, c.1880–1939* (Oxford, 1999).

WOHL, A. S., 'The Housing of the Working Classes in London, 1815–1914', in S. Chapman (ed.), *The History of Working-Class Housing* (Newton Abbot, 1971).

—— *The Eternal Slum: Housing and Social Policy in Victorian London* (Montreal, 1977).

(b) Theses Consulted

ADAMS, P., 'Tariff Reform and Popular Politics, 1903–06', University of Oxford, M.Litt., 1982.

BENNETT, J. J., 'East End Newspaper Opinion and Jewish Immigration, 1885–1905', University of Sheffield, M.Phil., 1979.

FELDMAN, D., 'Immigrants and Workers, Englishmen and Jews: Jewish Immigrants to the East End of London, 1880–1906', University of Cambridge, Ph.D., 1986.

FIELD, C. D., 'Methodism in Metropolitan London 1850–1920', University of Oxford, D.Phil., 1974.

GILLESPIE, J. A., 'Industrial and Political Change in the East End of London During the 1920s', University of Cambridge, Ph.D., 1984.

QUINNEY, N., 'Militarism and Edwardian Working Class Youth, 1902–1914', University of Oxford, D.Phil., 1987.

WILLIAMS, S. C., 'Religious Belief and Popular Culture: A Study of the South London Borough of Southwark c.1880–1939', University of Oxford, D.Phil., 1993.

INDEX

Printed in the United Kingdom
by Lightning Source UK Ltd.
117664UKS00001B/42